# SQL
## and Its Applications

Raymond A. Lorie
Jean-Jacques Daudenarde

PRENTICE HALL, Englewood Cliffs, New Jersey 07632

Library of Congress Cataloging-in-Publication Data

```
Lorie, Raymond A.
    SQL and its applications / Raymond A. Lorie, Jean-Jacques
Daudenarde.
        p.   cm.
    Includes bibliographical references and index.
    ISBN 0-13-837956-4
    1. SQL (Computer program language)  2. Data base management.
I. Daudenarde, Jean-Jacques.  II. Title.
QA76.73.S67L67  1991
005.75'6--dc20                                          90-39784
                                                            CIP
```

Editorial/production supervision: *Mary P. Rottino*
Cover design: *Lundgren Graphics, Inc*
Manufacturing buyers: *Kelly Behr and Susan Brunke*
Cover photo: *Larry Keenan/The Image Bank*

 © 1991 by Prentice-Hall, Inc.
A Division of Simon & Schuster
Englewood Cliffs, New Jersey 07632

The publisher offers discounts on this book when ordered
in bulk quantities. For more information, write:

> Special Sales/College Marketing
> College Technical and Reference Division
> Prentice Hall
> Englewood Cliffs, New Jersey 07632

Printed in the United States of America

10  9  8  7  6  5  4  3  2  1

ISBN 0-13-837956-4

Prentice-Hall International (UK) Limited, *London*
Prentice-Hall of Australia Pty. Limited, *Sydney*
Prentice-Hall Canada Inc., *Toronto*
Prentice-Hall Hispanoamericana, S.A., *Mexico*
Prentice-Hall of India Private Limited, *New Delhi*
Prentice-Hall of Japan, Inc., *Tokyo*
Simon & Schuster Asia Pte. Ltd., *Singapore*
Editora Prentice-Hall do Brasil, Ltda., *Rio de Janeiro*

*To*

*Ileana, Miguel, Ignacio, and Francisco*

*Hélène, Sophie, and Eric*

# Contents

# Preface

Many programs that run on data processing systems today rely heavily on data that are stored "permanently" on some medium such as magnetic disks. The collection of such preserved data is called a *database*. Any system that helps the user in managing a database is a *database management system* or *DBMS*. Some of the most important functions of such a system deal with the creation of a database, the insertion of information into the database, the retrieval of the stored information, its protection against unauthorized access, and its recovery from system malfunctioning.

The relational model for the management of data was introduced in 1970 in a paper by E. F. Codd, published in the *Communication of the ACM, 13:6* entitled "A Relational Model for Large Shared Data Banks." This original paper triggered an extensive research in the database field in the 1970's, both theoretical and practical. In the early 1980's, database management systems based on the relational model became available commercially. Starting modestly, it has now become a technology of major importance and several products are available from various companies such as IBM, Oracle, Ingres, and Teradata, to name a few. More and more data processing shops are installing these products, using them for developing applications, and/or querying their databases.

The data language used to interact with the database plays a fundamental role in a DBMS. Although several classes of languages have been proposed in the past, the *Structured Query Language*, or *SQL*, has emerged as the most commonly used relational language. Initially introduced in System R, a research prototype developed at IBM Research in San Jose, California, SQL is now used in a large number of products, and standardization efforts are under way.

Up to now, most users of relational systems were specialists, accustomed to learn new systems by reading long user's manuals or papers published in the technical literature, or by gaining hands-on experience on systems installed in large data processing accounts. But the situation is changing. First, more users are getting involved with relational systems because more applications are being developed based on the new technology. Second, relational systems are becoming available on much smaller processors, even personal computers, opening the field considerably. The new breed of users consists of application analysts and programmers or end users who are specialists in their fields, but not necessarily in data processing or database technology. These professionals know their information management problems and want to know if and how relational systems - and SQL in particular - can help. This book caters to their needs, as well as the needs of anybody who wants simply to learn about the relational approach to data management at a pragmatic level.

The book is divided into three parts. Part 1 is introductory in nature. Part 2 presents the different constructs of the language. Many short examples are given; they all refer to the same application, making it easy to remember the context and understand what each example is about. While Part 2 studies each SQL statement individually in a convenient order, Part 3 looks at various applications. Each chapter analyzes one of these applications, with emphasis on a certain generic problem. Each time, important questions are considered, such as how to organize the data, or can a certain logical operation be done with a single SQL statement? If not, can a sequence of statements do the job? When is it necessary to write some code in a host language? The same questions will eventually come up during the design of any application, and the case studies presented here should prepare the reader to recognize the multiple trade-offs, and make the right choices.

When developing Part 2 we realized that we had to face a certain dilemma. SQL is a language which is still young; and although a large portion of the syntax and semantics of the language is common to all implementations, there are differences. We could have chosen to cover one particular instance of SQL, or we could have chosen to discuss only what is common to all important implementations, or to concentrate on only those constructs that have practically been standardized. Instead, we chose to introduce all the concepts that exist in most SQL. When the syntax - or the semantics - differs, we say so and show one particular instance. This approach allows us to be complete in covering the concepts; we feel this is important. We do not claim to be exhaustive in giving all features of all implementations. Consider, for example, the functions that apply to data of type "character string": once the reader understands that there are such functions - for example to extract a substring - it is less important to give the exhaustive list of functions implemented in the various systems. Such a list is easily found in the reference manual specific to an implementation.

Again, the main goal of the book is to explain the concepts of SQL and show how these concepts can be helpful in solving a wide variety of information problems.

# Chapter organization

The first chapter provides an introduction to the relational way of organizing data. It describes a particular application and shows how its data can be couched in relational terms. Then, SQL is briefly introduced, showing examples of data definition, manipulation, and query capabilities. We believe it is important to know, from the start, how an SQL system handles the requests; for that reason, Chapter 1 covers the embedding of SQL in programs, as well as the issues of *dynamic* versus *static* SQL.

Chapter 2 considers another application and shows how the concept of *normalization* helps the designer to come up with an appropriate data organization.

Part 2 covers the language itself.

Chapter 3 introduces the basics of *data definition*. This is normally the first set of SQL facilities that a user would need when getting familiar with an SQL system in a hands-on session. It also discusses how data can be inserted into the database. At this point, the reader can create a table and populate it with data.

Chapter 4 discusses the basic *query* capabilities of SQL but only those that apply to a single table. Many examples are given; they are all based on the application introduced in Chapter 1.

Chapter 5 covers all other query features; in particular it introduces the notion of *join* and *subquery*.

Chapter 6 revisits the *data manipulation* facilities. They comprise all features that change the contents of the database, such as insertions, deletions, and updates. Since set-oriented data manipulation uses query capabilities to specify the set involved, we had to postpone their coverage until this point.

Chapter 7 studies some *performance* issues. At first, this chapter title may be somewhat surprising. After all, the scope of the book is the language, and many performance issues are very much linked to the implementation. But there are operations that are intrinsically complex and we want the user to be able to recognize them. Also, some techniques that are used by practically all implementations are somewhat visible at the language level (indexing, locking); they need to be covered here.

Chapter 8 deals with *views*. A view allows the user to see the data in a way that is different from the way the data are actually stored.

Chapter 9 studies the ***protection of data***. Data are an important asset and must be protected from any corruption or loss, as well as from unauthorized access. Although systems generally try to protect the data without putting any burden on the user, this cannot be done completely without some semantic knowledge that only the user has. This chapter discusses the SQL constructs used to communicate such knowledge to the system.

Part 3 of the book is dedicated to case studies.

Chapter 10 discusses a classical data processing example, with emphasis on simple *transactions* and *batch* processing. Chapter 11, on the contrary, focuses on *complex queries*. These two case studies, together with the examples of Part 2 should enable most users to develop straightforward applications.

The next chapters look at more advanced applications which all exhibit some kind of specific characteristics. Together, they enable the reader to build an arsenal of techniques that will be extremely useful in broad areas of application.

Chapters 12 and 13 look at problems which deal with interesting types of data. Chapter 12 is concerned with the management of ***textual information***; Chapter 13 addresses the management of ***object-oriented data***. Object data play a very important role in engineering applications, graphics, and office automation; the chapter looks at how to group the information into highly structured clusters. Although, in these chapters, the techniques are presented in specific application contexts, they are quite general in nature. The most likely situation is that some of these problems will come up when you design real-life applications, even if the context is apparently quite different.

Chapter 14 is concerned with a class of ***graph*** problems where a relationship is defined between instances of the same entity. Such a relationship can be represented by arcs between nodes in a graph. For example, a city A is connected to another city B, and B is connected to C, which is itself connected to D, or A, or B; or a part uses other parts in a ***bill of material*** application. The full exploitation of such relationships is not trivial; Chapter 14 discusses some interesting algorithms.

Finally, Chapter 15 goes through the design of an interactive, menu-driven application; it mainly illustrates the trade-offs between *static* and *dynamic* SQL and presents some details on how to use the dynamic approach. Chances are that you will never have to use dynamic SQL. But, just in case you have to, this chapter introduces the most important concepts.

Chapters 2 to 9 end with short series of exercises. All these refer to a common application context that is described in Chapter 2; the answers are given in Appendix.

### *Acknowledgments*

We would like to thank our colleagues at IBM Research for keeping up an environment in which relational databases and SQL in particular have been - and still are - the base for interesting research; we have learned a lot from them. We are grateful to Charles Bontempo, Horacio Terrizzano, and a third anonymous reviewer for their many comments and suggestions. Some of these suggestions resulted in significant changes. We also acknowledge the help of Ignacio Terrizzano and David Torney, who read an early manuscript and whose comments have been particularly valuable. Finally, we are indebted to the IBM Corporation, and the management of the Research Division in particular, for providing some of the computer resources needed for the production of this book; we also thank the editors and staff at Prentice Hall for their constant support.

Raymond A. Lorie
*IBM Corporation*
*Research Division*
*San Jose, California*

Jean-Jacques Daudenarde
*IBM Corporation*
*Storage Systems Products Division*
*San Jose, California*

# Part 1. Introduction

## Chapter 1

# Relational Data Management

Any human organization, from the simplest to the most complex, relies on information. In fact, any activity generates information about what happened, where, when, how, and so on. Any piece of information may be expressed as a sentence in a natural language. This representation may be satisfactory for some applications; for others it is not. In fact, for most applications, a better organization consists of representing the information as a collection of well-structured data. Additionally, since data generated today may be important for future activities and decisions, they must be recorded permanently, or at least until explicitly destroyed. The science - or art - of organizing permanent data is called **data management**.

It is fairly easy to save data on a permanent medium such as magnetic tape or disk. In general, the programming · languages such as Cobol, C, and Fortran provide commands to save the contents of program variables on permanent storage and to read them back into memory. However, these commands generally allow the user to save the data in a sequential manner, one data element after another or one record (a collection of data elements) after another. Sometimes, more sophisticated commands allow a program to store data in a way that supports direct access to a record, given the record number. Nevertheless, although such data organizations are extremely useful, they provide only low-level functions, leaving most of the data management problems to the user.

Fortunately, the state of the art in data management has improved tremendously in the last decade. Years of research and development in theoretical as well as practical aspects of data management have yielded impressive results: today, sophisticated languages and systems exist, which simplify the user's job by making it possible to think about data at a much more conceptual level without worrying about a myriad of details.

The most successful of these systems today are based on what is called the *relational model of data* and rely on SQL (Structured Query Language). Their success is in part due to the simplicity of the model and the power of the operations available to store, manipulate, retrieve, and control the data. Another reason for their success is the internal sophistication of the systems that support the relational model and SQL in particular; it is this sophistication that enables high-level functions to be executed very efficiently at an affordable cost.

This chapter will guide the reader unfamiliar with data management through four sections. The first section uses an example to illustrate the most important concepts of data management without referring to any computer implementation. The second section introduces the relational model and describes the data of an application in relational terms. The third section goes through some SQL scenarios for data manipulation and queries. Finally, the last section briefly discusses the facilities generally provided by a data management system and by most SQL systems in particular.

# 1.1  Introducing data management concepts

Let us consider an organization and analyze the data needed to ensure its functioning. The organization is a company which rents tools. The company purchases tools and rents them to customers.

Actions generate the data that need to be kept in order to do business. When a tool is purchased, its existence must be recorded. This is done by maintaining a file of cards, each card recording the information associated with a tool. Since it is important to be able to refer to a particular tool in an unambiguous way, each tool must have a unique name. A simple way of naming a new tool is to give it a sequential number; the first tool receives the number 1, the next tool, 2, and so on. Each tool card with its tool number is stored in the file - let us call it the TOOL file - in order of increasing tool number. (By the way, this makes it very easy to find the next available number since one can just add 1 to the number on the last card in the file.) In addition to the tool number, the tool card will also contain data associated with the tool, such as

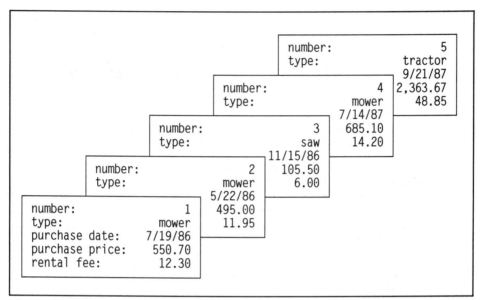

**Figure 1. The TOOL file**

the type of tool, the purchase date, the purchase price, and the rental fee. Figure 1 shows a very small TOOL file.

Note that data elements come in various types: the tool number is an integer, the type is a sequence of characters (often called a character string), the date is composed of three integer parts, while the purchase price and rental fee are decimal values. Values must be of the right type when they are inserted in the file: obviously ABC is not a valid tool number. But there may be other constraints on the values themselves. For example, a constraint may specify the valid range of values: obviously, 33/33/87 is an invalid date. This type of constraint is called *integrity constraint* because it ensures the integrity of the data when they are first created or later updated.

Let us now consider a different action: customer Adams wants to rent a tool. The company keeps a list of its customers. Here again a file is used with one card per customer. Each card contains the customer's name, the customer's address, and possibly other data elements which are irrelevant here. Figure 2 shows the CUSTOMER file.

Since the application needs to locate the customer's information when the customer shows up at the counter, it is appropriate to order the CUSTOMER file according to the alphabetical order of the names. Otherwise, finding the infor-

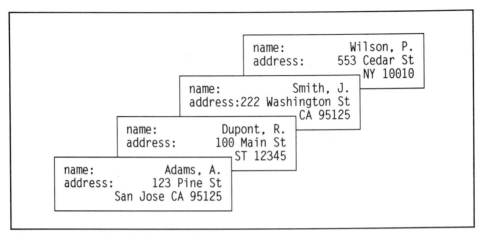

**Figure 2. The CUSTOMER file**

mation may require a sequential search of the entire CUSTOMER file until the right name is found.

The next action to consider is that Adams wants to rent a mower. Suppose at this point that we know that mower 2 is available and may therefore be rented to Adams. The rental data are recorded on a contract which specifies the name of the customer and the tool rented, together with the contract starting date and the presumed return date. The office will keep a copy of the contract and store it in a file containing all outstanding contracts (the CONTRACT file), ordered by increasing contract numbers (see Figure 3). When the customer returns the tool and the copy of the contract, the attendant can find the original and complete it with accounting information; he can then give a copy to the customer and file the original in a HISTORY file alphabetically ordered by customer name.

Let us come back to the problem of finding an available mower. We certainly have all the necessary information in the first three files described above. The attendant can look through all cards in the TOOL file and for each tool number corresponding to a mower look through all contracts to see if that tool has been rented or not. Obviously, this is a tedious way of finding an available tool of a given type. A much better method consists of keeping another file (the AVAILABLE file) which initially contains a card for each tool: each card contains the tool type and number, and the file is ordered according to the type. Then it becomes easy to locate a card corresponding to a mower; once found, the card can be removed from the file and kept with the contract. When the contract is terminated, the card is placed back in the AVAILABLE file at its right place (see Figure 4).

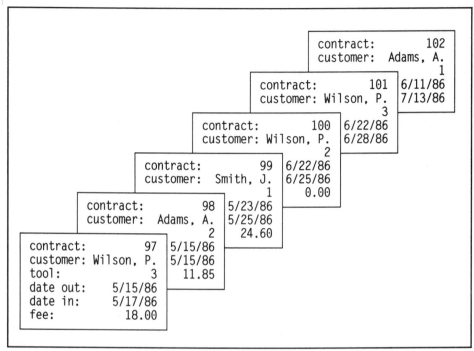

**Figure 3. The CONTRACT file**

To support the above scenarios, we introduced five files: TOOL, CUS-TOMER, CONTRACT, AVAILABLE, and HISTORY. Some information is duplicated (for example the tool number and type in TOOL and AVAIL-ABLE); several orderings are used (TOOL is ordered by tool number, CUS-TOMER by customer name, CONTRACT by contract number, HISTORY by customer name, and AVAILABLE by tool type). It is important to note that ordering, like duplication, does not actually carry any information per se.

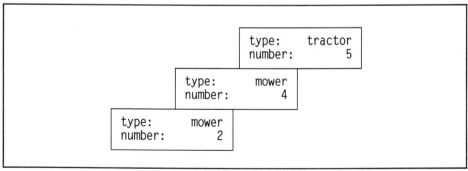

**Figure 4. The AVAILABLE file**

Both ordering and duplication are merely techniques used to facilitate access to the data.

# 1.2  The relational model

A data model is a formalism for organizing and manipulating data. A model specifies how data are organized into objects and which operations exist to manipulate these objects. In the relational model the objects are two-dimensional tables. A table has *rows* (also called *tuples*) and *columns*. At the intersection of any row with any column there is at most one value. Tables have unique names; columns have unique names inside a table. The order of the columns is irrelevant since the column name is used to identify a particular column in the table. The order of the rows is also irrelevant; no privileged order is specified when the table is defined. The set of tables needed to capture all data for the application environment is called the *schema*. The process of finding an appropriate schema is called the *database design*.

Obviously, operations are needed to create and destroy a table, to insert a row, delete a row, and update a row in a table. Finally, a powerful retrieval language is essential in order to retrieve the desired information. In the remainder of this section we consider the rental company example and show how a relational system may be used for managing its data.

First, we show that the data needed for the application can be couched in terms of tables. The TOOL and CUSTOMER files map quite naturally and directly onto two tables, TOOL and CUSTOMER. The information written on the cards is now entered into columns which have each a name and a type. Figures 5 and 6, respectively, show the format of these two tables; the data stored in the tables reflect the contents of the files shown in Figures 1 and 2.

It would be equally easy to specify tables for CONTRACT and HISTORY. Exactly as in manual bookkeeping, the initiation of a contract would cause the insertion of a row in CONTRACT, while termination of the contract would cause the row to be deleted from CONTRACT and another one to be inserted in HISTORY. However, the reason for having two files in the manual organization was to be able to order the entries in different ways, once by contract numbers and once by customer names. Since, in the relational model, a table is not defined with any inherent order, a single table can be used, called CONTRACT, with columns CONTRACT, CUSTOMER, TOOL, DATE_OUT, DATE_IN, and FEE, as shown in Figure 7. For contracts that are not terminated yet, DATE_IN is the presumed date of return. Since, in this case, FEE is not known, a special **null** value is stored (represented graphically by ?).

Both table designs (CONTRACT only or CONTRACT and HISTORY) capture the information needed for the application. This illustrates the fact that, generally, several schemas are possible, and the user has to decide which is the most suited to the application at hand. Chapter 2 will consider this issue in detail; Part 3 will show numerous examples of such alternative designs.

| TOOL | | | | |
|---|---|---|---|---|
| NUMBER | TYPE | PURCH_DATE | PURCH_PRICE | RENTAL_FEE |
| 1 | mower | 1986-07-19 | 550.70 | 12.30 |
| 2 | mower | 1986-05-22 | 495.00 | 11.95 |
| 3 | saw | 1986-11-15 | 105.50 | 6.00 |
| 4 | mower | 1987-07-14 | 685.10 | 14.20 |
| 5 | tractor | 1987-09-21 | 2363.67 | 48.85 |

**Figure 5. The TOOL table**

| CUSTOMER | | |
|---|---|---|
| NAME | ADDRESS | ZIP |
| Adams, A. | 123 Pine St, San Jose CA | 95125 |
| Dupont, R. | 100 Main St, Town ST | 12345 |
| Smith, J. | 222 Washington St, San Jose CA | 95125 |
| Wilson, P. | 553 Cedar St, New York, NY | 10010 |

**Figure 6. The CUSTOMER table**

| CONTRACT | | | | | |
|---|---|---|---|---|---|
| CONTRACT | CUSTOMER | TOOL | DATE_OUT | DATE_IN | FEE |
| 97 | Wilson, P. | 3 | 1986-05-15 | 1986-05-17 | 18.00 |
| 98 | Adams, A. | 2 | 1986-05-15 | 1986-05-15 | 11.95 |
| 99 | Smith, J. | 1 | 1986-05-23 | 1986-05-25 | 24.60 |
| 100 | Wilson, P. | 2 | 1986-06-22 | 1986-06-25 | 0.00 |
| 101 | Wilson, P. | 3 | 1986-06-22 | 1986-06-28 | ? |
| 102 | Adams, A. | 1 | 1986-06-11 | 1986-07-13 | ? |

**Figure 7. The CONTRACT table**

# 1.3   Introduction to SQL

In this section we give a brief overview of the SQL language by presenting a series of examples. Although the following chapters will cover the language in detail, the examples should help the reader to develop a general understanding of the nature and power of the SQL language.

We first present the command for defining a table, then the command to insert a row into a table, and, finally, various examples of queries.

## 1.3.1   Creating a table

You must issue a **create table** statement to define a new table to the system before any activity on the table can take place. The statement specifies the name of the new table and the name and data type of each of its columns. Some examples of data types are integer, character string (abbreviated as "char"), decimal, and date.  The following statement creates the table TOOL shown in Figure 5.

```
    create table TOOL                                         [1.1]
        (NUMBER integer,
        TYPE char(8),
        PURCH_DATE date,
        PURCH_PRICE decimal(8,2),
        RENTAL_FEE decimal(8,2))
```

All through the book, the SQL statements are shown on multiple lines and with some indentation; this is only for the sake of clarity.  Actually, a statement is a continuous string which can have an arbitrary number of blanks between the words.

## 1.3.2   Inserting a row

To **insert** a row in a table, you indicate the name of the table, the names of the columns in which values are to be inserted, and the values themselves. The values are specified in the same order as the column names.  The following statement inserts a row in table TOOL.

```
    insert into TOOL                                          [1.2]
    (NUMBER, TYPE, PURCH_DATE, PURCH_PRICE, RENTAL_FEE)
    values  (1, 'mower', '7/19/1986', 550.70, 12.30)
```

You may ask yourself what happens if you try to insert into TOOL a row for a tool 1 when tool 1 already exists. Actually, SQL will accept the insertion, whether the other attributes are identical or not. In other words, SQL does not know that, semantically, NUMBER is a *key* in table TOOL. A key is a column (or a set of columns) that uniquely identifies a row in the table. This "no knowledge of key" is the default. However, SQL does provide a facility for specifying the key of a table; it is covered in Chapter 9.

## 1.3.3  Exploiting relationships

With **create table** and **insert** you can build a database. But you could have as well used a file system, storing each table in a file. What makes a relational system quite unique is its ability to retrieve data, exploiting relationships between data elements (hence, the name "relational model"). A table relates data elements together: CUSTOMER relates ADDRESS to NAME. And relations are implemented among tables by the fact that a data element in one table has the same value than a data element in another table. For example, CONTRACT 97 is related to a rental fee of $6.00 a day, because the TOOL column for CONTRACT 97 contains 3 which also occurs in column NUMBER of TOOL. These particular matching values relate contract 97 to tool 3; but table TOOL relates RENTAL_FEE 6.00 to tool NUMBER 3; thus, the rental fee 6.00 is related to contract 97.

Relationships can also involve operators other than "equal": a value is also "related to" all values that are less or greater than itself. Finally, relationships may involve values that are not explicitly stored in the tables, but computed from stored values. For example, it is possible to find the values that are larger than the average of a set of values.

The following sections give a few examples of how SQL exploits these diverse types of relationships.

## 1.3.4  The select block

The simplest query construct in SQL is the **select** block. For example, the query below retrieves the purchase price, the rental fee, and the ratio between them, and this, for all mowers:

```
select PURCH_PRICE, RENTAL_FEE,                [1.3]
     PURCH_PRICE/RENTAL_FEE
from TOOL
where TYPE = 'mower'
```

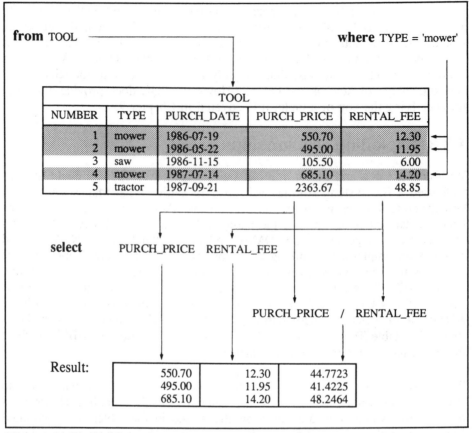

**Figure 8. Evaluation of a select block**

In general, the simplest **select** block comprises three clauses:

- The **from** clause specifies the table from which information is to be retrieved.

- The **where** clause specifies which rows should be selected.

- The **select** specifies the contents of the columns in the result table.

Figure 8 shows how the result table is constructed for statement [1.3]. The **where** clause selects the rows that have 'mower' in column TYPE. Then, for each of these rows, the value of PURCH_DATE is copied into the first column of the result, the value of RENTAL_FEE into the second column, and the result of the expression PURCH_PRICE/RENTAL_FEE into the third.

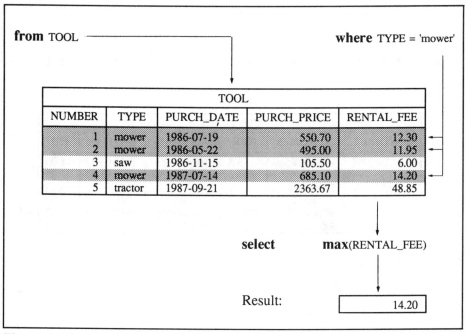

**Figure 9. Computation of an aggregate**

## 1.3.5 Aggregates

Instead of returning a series of rows, it is possible to return a single row containing one or more values of aggregates. For example, to find the mower which has the highest rental fee, you write

    select max(RENTAL_FEE)                                    [1.4]
    from TOOL
    where TYPE = 'mower'

Figure 9 illustrates the construction of the result (a single row).

## 1.3.6 Sets

In a **where** clause, a set can be used instead of a single value. For example, [1.5] retrieves the customers who rented tool 1 or 3.

    select CUSTOMER                                           [1.5]
    from CONTRACT
    where TOOL in (1, 3)

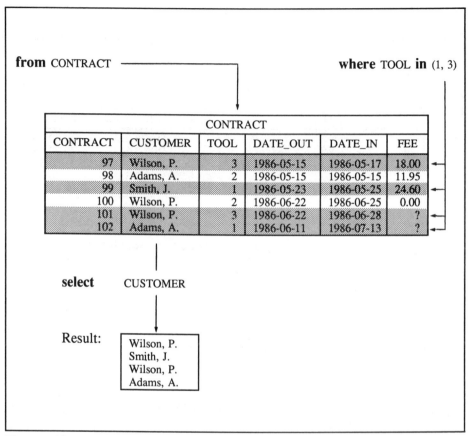

**from** CONTRACT ──────────── **where** TOOL **in** (1, 3)

**Figure 10. A query with an IN construct**

As shown in Figure 10, the **where** clause selects the rows that refer to one of these tools; then, according to the **select** clause, the values in column CUSTOMER are returned. Note that the **select** operation in itself does not eliminate the duplicates: "Wilson, P." appears twice in the result - once from contract 97, and once from contract 101.

## 1.3.7 Subqueries

In the **where** clause, a value or a set can be replaced by the result of an embedded query (also called a *subquery*). For example, the following query finds the customers who rented a mower:

```
select CUSTOMER                                              [1.6]
from CONTRACT
where TOOL in
    ( select NUMBER
    from TOOL
    where TYPE = 'mower' )
```

The syntax clearly shows two **select** blocks. The first one is

```
select CUSTOMER                                              [1.7]
from CONTRACT
where TOOL in ...
```

which is similar to [1.5], except that the argument of **in** (a set) is specified as the result of another **select** block:

```
select NUMBER                                                [1.8]
from TOOL
where TYPE = 'mower'
```

The latter block is a subquery; it returns a single column result containing the set (1,2,4). The complete query [1.6] is equivalent to

```
select CUSTOMER                                              [1.9]
from CONTRACT
where TOOL in (1, 2, 4)
```

which yields the following result:

```
Adams, A.
Smith, J.
Wilson, P.
Adams, A.
```

Note that Adams rented a mower twice and therefore his name appears twice in the answer.

## 1.3.8 Joins

The use of a subquery is only one way of exploiting relationships between tables. The *join* operation is another one. A join is indicated by the presence of more than one table in the **from** clause of a **select** statement. For example, the following query returns a table showing the name of the customers who rented a mower, together with the rental fee of the mower.

```
select CUSTOMER, RENTAL_FEE                          [1.10]
from CONTRACT, TOOL
where TYPE = 'mower'
    and TOOL = NUMBER
```

Figure 11 illustrates the computation of the query; it works as follows:

- Both tables CONTRACT and TOOL are involved. Therefore both names appear in the **from** clause.

- The first condition, TYPE = 'mower', refers only to a column of TOOL: it says that we are interested only in tools that are mowers (three rows qualify).

- Similarly, the **where** clause could contain a condition which refers only to columns of CONTRACT. There is none in the example, meaning that all rows in CONTRACT qualify. Note that the second condition (TOOL = NUMBER) does refer to both tables simultaneously; such a condition is called a *join predicate*.

- The join operation then considers each qualifying row in one table, and combines it with any qualifying row in the other table, keeping only the combinations that satisfy the join predicate(s). In the example, tool 1 is combined with all rows in CONTRACT. Of all these combinations, only two satisfy the join predicate TOOL = NUMBER (contracts 99 and 102).

- For each combination that qualifies, a result row is constructed, according to the **select** clause: the value of CUSTOMER is taken from CONTRACT, and the value of RENTAL_FEE from TOOL.

- The arrows in Figure 11 illustrate the computation for both combinations involving tool 1, producing two rows of the result. The third row in the result corresponds to the combination of tool 2 with contract 98, the fourth one, to the combination of tool 2 with contract 100. There is no combination involving tool 4 since there is no contract for that tool.

The join is an extremely powerful operation. Its full potential will become clearer in Chapter 5.

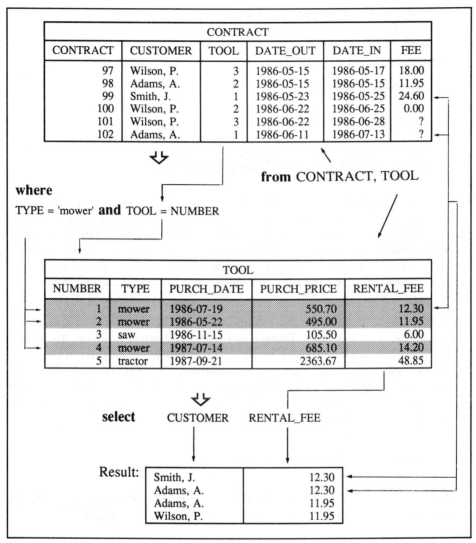

**Figure 11. Computation of a join**

## 1.3.9  Order

As mentioned before, no order is associated with a table. But a query can specify the order in which the resulting rows should be presented, by using an **order by** clause, as in

**select** NUMBER, RENTAL_FEE                                                                [1.11]
**from** TOOL
**where** TYPE = 'mower'
**order by** RENTAL_FEE

| | |
|---|---|
| 2 | 11.95 |
| 1 | 12.30 |
| 4 | 14.20 |

# 1.4  Overview of an SQL system

Although the above examples illustrate very important features of SQL, they only cover a portion of the language facilities. The next chapters will discuss many other features, such as **drop** a table, **alter** the definition of a table, **delete** or **update** one or several rows in a table, and eliminate duplicate rows in the result of a **select**, as well as mechanisms to control the access to the data (authorization) or define different views on a table or a set of tables.

The goal of SQL is to make the manipulation of the data and the queries as easy as possible for the user. Behind any SQL statement, however, there is a program which will be invoked in order to produce the desired result. The integrated collection of such programs constitutes the *SQL system*. How the system functions is clearly outside the scope of this book; however, we need to introduce a few concepts so that the reader may have a better perspective on how the language and the system interrelate.

Users of SQL may belong to any of two classes.

•    On one hand they may be programmers responsible for writing applications that invoke SQL to create and access information in a database.

•    Or they may be end users accessing the database without writing a specific program, relying instead on a general interactive SQL query product. Although such a product is usually provided by the manufacturer, SQL exposes the interface needed to allow a user to develop his own.

The form of the SQL statements shown in the above examples reflects the way the end user would specify the statements in an query product. We now turn our attention first to writing specific applications and then to developing a general query product.

## 1.4.1 Writing specific SQL applications

For illustration, let us assume you want to define a table T1 with two columns C1 and C2 and insert some rows into it. Using the syntax shown in [1.1] and [1.2], the SQL statements needed are as follows:

**create table** T1 (C1 **integer**, C2 **char**(8))                    [1.12]

and

**insert into** T1 (C1, C2) **values** (123,'abcdefgh')                    [1.13]

SQL statements can be embedded in a host program written in a general programming language such as C, PL/I, Cobol, Assembler, or others, depending upon the implementation. For the sake of generality, all programming examples in this book use a pseudocode which is largely language independent.

A program to create the table and insert three rows may look as follows:

```
exec sql include sqlca
exec sql create table T1 (C1 integer, C2 char(8))
exec sql insert into T1 (C1, C2) values (1,'aaaaaaaa')
exec sql insert into T1 (C1, C2) values (2,'bbbbbbbb')
exec sql insert into T1 (C1, C2) values (3,'cccccccc')
exec sql commit work
```

The words **exec sql** are used to identify the statements that are SQL and distinguish them from host language statements. The first statement is declarative. It is not actually executed when the program is run but only indicates to the compiler that the program uses SQL; it also defines a data structure used to interchange information with the system.

The execution of the **create table** statement creates the table T1, while the execution of each **insert** statement inserts a row into it. If, after the first **insert**, the program had interrogated the database to find the contents of T1, it would have found the row (1,'aaaaaaaa'). In other words, changes made by a statement are seen by the program as soon as the statement is executed. However, if a problem occurs and the program cannot proceed, then all changes are undone and the database is restored to the state that it had at the beginning of the program - or after the last **commit work** execution. In other words, a **commit work** statement permanently commits the changes to the database. For example, consider the following scenario:

```
... Insert 'A'
... Insert 'B'
... Commit Work
... Insert 'C'
... For some reason, the program is terminated.
```

After its execution, the database contains 'A' and 'B'. Insert 'C' has been undone.

## 1.4.2 Program variables

You are probably thinking that writing three **insert** statements is not very elegant - and you are right. Just imagine what would happen if the program had to insert 100 or 1000 rows! Obviously, an iterative mechanism should exist to avoid repeating the **insert** statement. But then again, since values appear explicitly in the statement, how can it be done? SQL solves the problem by introducing the notion of a *program variable*. In fact, the program in Figure 12 performs the task using a loop. Examine statement (4): rather than giving explicitly the values to be inserted, the statement specifies the names of program variables that will contain these values at each execution: the value for C1 is submitted in *V1*, and the value for C2, in *V2*.

The only thing that distinguishes these variables from any other variable in the program is the fact that they appear inside an SQL statement. Note the use of the semi-column. Many implementations use this semi-column to avoid confusion between variable names and columns names; others leave to the user the responsibility of avoiding conflicts. Similarly, some implementations insist on including in the program, an SQL **declare section**, delimited by a **begin declare section** and an **end declare section**. This section, which must precede any other SQL statement in the program, contains the declaration of all host language variables that are also referenced inside SQL statements (see program).

## 1.4.3 Using a program

Once the program is written it must be compiled. The compilation procedure varies from one implementation to another; here we just want to explain briefly what the compilation process accomplishes. If you submit the program in Figure 12 written in a particular language such as C to a C compiler, many errors will be signaled since any statement starting with **exec sql** is not a valid C statement. An SQL system provides a precompiler which converts this "bad" program into a "good" C program that can be compiled correctly. The precompiler in fact replaces each executable **exec sql** statement by a call to the

```
          exec sql include sqlca
(1)       exec sql begin declare section
              declare number V1
              declare string V2
(2)       exec sql end declare section

(3)       exec sql create table T1
              (C1 integer,
              C2 char(8))

          do until (no more values)
              read values to be inserted in V1 and V2
(4)           exec sql insert into T1 (C1, C2)
                  values (:V1, :V2)
              end
```

**Figure 12. A program to create and load a table**

database management system. The call includes parameters that tell the system what the statement actually is.

A possible form for such a call may be

*call dbms (* **'insert into** T1 (C1, C2)', *V1, V2)*

Every time the program executes this CALL, the invoked system looks at the three parameters. The first specifies the SQL statement to be executed, while the other two are program variables used to submit the actual values to be inserted. The system parses the SQL statement and interrogates the database catalogs to check if T1 is a valid table, if two values are all that is needed to create a row, and if the user is authorized to insert a row into that table. The above example is straightforward. However, as we shall see later, if the statement gets to be more involved, the system would have to perform a time-consuming analysis to determine the best strategy for executing it.

These various operations, performed at each call, impose quite a substantial overhead and degrade performance. For this reason, some systems do most of that work once at precompilation time, and produce an internal structure (we call it the *execution structure*) containing information used at execution time. The execution structure is stored in the database and its existence is recorded in a catalog. At execution time, the first parameter in the call statement is not

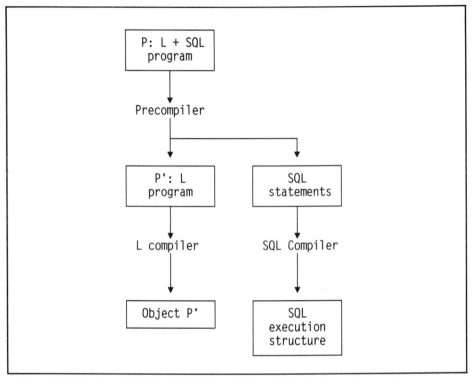

**Figure 13. The compilation process in a typical SQL system**

the SQL statement, as shown above in quotes, but the name of the execution structure. Then, the execution structure can be fetched from the database and interpreted.

To summarize the compilation process (see Figure 13), a program  P, written in language L (i.e. Fortran, C, and the like), with embedded SQL, is first pre-compiled by the SQL precompiler for language L.  That phase produces two outputs: the first is a file containing the program P' which can now be compiled with the L compiler; the second output is a series of SQL statements which is compiled into an execution structure (or collection of structures) that is stored in the database, ready to be fetched and interpreted at execution time.

Under certain conditions the contents of the execution structures may become invalid. This occurs, for example, when certain changes are made to the catalogs, affecting the table(s) involved in the statement. A good system takes care of such a situation by keeping track of the dependencies of an execution structure upon certain catalog data. If the catalog changes, affected structures are rebuilt automatically.

Examples of programs can be found in every chapter of Part 3.

## 1.4.4  Static SQL

In the example in Figure 12, although values can be computed at execution time and passed to SQL through program variables, the general form of each SQL statement is known at compilation time.  The **insert** statement is known to be an insert: it cannot be changed into, say, a **delete** at execution time. This explains why this form of utilization of SQL is called *static SQL*.

## 1.4.5  Dynamic SQL

The second way of getting access to information stored in an SQL database is by using an interactive program generally provided with the system.  Let us call it ISQL (Interactive SQL), although its name varies from system to system. Such a program provides some kind of user-friendly interface to specify a statement which is then submitted to the system. Once it obtains the answer back from the system, ISQL displays it on the screen.  This is by far the easiest way to access data since no specific program needs to be written.

In fact, ISQL is itself a program that reads a statement from the terminal and submits it to the system for execution. We suggest at this point that you take a minute or two to think about how to write such a program, relying only on the features previously explained in this chapter.  You will probably reach the conclusion that it is no easy task. In fact, the only way is to write a "generator" program which would read the statement and generate a short host program in which the statement could be embedded. Once generated, the program needs to be precompiled and compiled, an awkward procedure for a single statement indeed.  To avoid this, SQL systems provide a facility called *dynamic SQL*.

The technique consists of constructing in a program variable a character string representing a well-formed SQL statement and then invoking the **execute** function to execute it.

For example,

$$X = \text{'create table T1 (C1 integer, C2 char(8))'} \qquad [1.14]$$
**exec sql execute immediate** :X

has the same effect as the statement

**exec sql create table** T1 (C1 **integer**, C2 **char**(8))        [1.15]

The difference is that, in [1.14], the statement does not need to be known at compilation time. Dynamic SQL is an extremely powerful mechanism: the character string representing the statement can be read from the terminal or generated by program. For example, it is possible to design an application which is completely menu driven or controlled by a graphic interface. As a result of selecting some options, the program can generate an ad hoc SQL statement and then execute it. Such flexibility, however, comes with a cost. When the **execute** feature is used, the analysis of the statement, the catalog lookup and the choice of the best access strategy must be done at execution time, repeatedly, rather than once at compilation time. The level of performance cannot therefore be the same and the user should be careful to use the dynamic option only when absolutely necessary.

The application described in Chapter 15 makes intensive use of dynamic queries. It also discusses the respective merits of static and dynamic SQL, depending on the context.

## 1.4.6 Error handling

As in any program, errors may occur when using SQL. In static SQL, many errors can be detected at compilation time; in dynamic SQL this is not the case. Regardless, in both static and dynamic SQL, errors and special conditions can occur at execution time and the program must check for them. The SQL system informs the application program of runtime problems via a structure named **sqlca** (SQL Communication Area). Inside this structure, the integer **sqlcode** contains a return code which is generally zero if everything went right and nonzero otherwise. The program can check this variable after any executable SQL statement and take the appropriate action. Since this may be cumbersome to write, SQL provides a **whenever** facility which facilitates the specification of what to do when a special condition occurs.

The **whenever** statement indicates how the flow of the program is altered when an error or a special condition occurs at execution time. It has the general form

> **exec sql whenever** condition class **go to** label        [1.16]

where the condition class specifies the type of condition that this statement addresses. Conditions are classified into two classes: not found, and error.

- A not found condition occurs in conjunction with a **select** and will be covered in Chapter 4.

- An error condition is signaled to the user and does preclude normal completion of the operation. To alter the program flow in such a case, you simply write

    **exec sql whenever sqlerror go to** label.                              [1.17]

The portion "**go to** label" in a **whenever** statement may be replaced by "**continue**" or "**stop**". In the first case the condition is ignored; in the second case the program terminates. **Stop** is not supported by all implementations of SQL.

Since the **whenever** statement is not executable but declarative, its scope depends only on its position in the source file. It is active for all executable statements which appear after it in the source file, until another **whenever** statement is encountered for a condition of the same class (or until the end of program).

# 1.5  Summary

In this first chapter, we introduced the basic concepts of data management by showing the close relationship that exists between a manual organization and its corresponding representation in terms of tables in the relational model.

To create, manipulate, and retrieve data from the database, the user relies on the high-level language SQL. By now, the reader should have a general idea of the power and structure of the language and be prepared to go into the more detailed presentation given in the following chapters.

However, we believe it was important not to leave the reader wondering how SQL can be invoked and/or embedded in a program. For this reason we covered that subject in Chapter 1, introducing two complementary techniques.

- In a static SQL environment, the statement is known at compilation time. Some parameterization occurs through the use of program variables instead of explicit constants.

- In the dynamic SQL environment, the statement can be specified at execution time. This approach is much more flexible but also more costly.

In fact, it is important to use the right technique for the right situation. If static SQL can be used, by all means use it. If it cannot be used because the application requires the execution of queries specified only at execution time, then maybe a general query product provided by the manufacturer can do the job. If not, you will have to develop a program using dynamic SQL. This will be the case only if you need the power of a general programming language to process the result of the query or to compute the data to be inserted in the database, or because you want to provide the user with a more application-oriented interface. A classic example consists of using a menu to specify the elements of the query. Once all elements have been entered, they are assembled into a valid SQL statement which can be executed dynamically.

# Chapter 2

# Database Design

In the previous chapter, we chose a series of appropriate tables to contain all the information required for the management of the rental company. We started with an existing manual organization and found out that the mapping of manual files onto tables was quite straightforward. The fact that the mapping turned out to be so easy is a tribute to the designer of the manual organization; in a sense, he had already done the work for us.

In this chapter, we want to go through the exercise of designing a database from scratch. The starting point is a specific application; the end result, an appropriate schema. Finding such a schema is generally straightforward when the number of tables is small; but it gets much harder when the number of tables, and the complexity of the relationships between them, increase. Theoretical researchers in the field recognized the problem very early, and developed a useful theory called *normalization*. Although the work is quite mathematical, its results are intuitive. In fact, it provides hints on evaluating a possible schema, and also, on transforming an initial schema into another, better one. The remainder of this chapter shows how these results are immediately applicable to a practical database design problem.

For the sake of illustration, we have chosen an application environment familiar to everybody: the management of the student records in a college. Let us suppose you are in charge of the database design process. To understand the specific requirements, you convene a small study group including all interested parties: the Admission Administrator, the Dean of Studies, and the

Records Administrator.  Each of the participants describes the data that he or she wants to see.

- The Admission Administrator needs to store and retrieve data about all registered students.  He assigns each of them a student identification number (STUDENTNO) and wants to keep, associated with that number, attributes such as student name (NAME), initial registration year (FIRSTYEAR), and first day of class for that year (STARTDATE).  A straightforward possibility is to store the information in the following file (we show only one row):

| ADMISSION | | | |
|---|---|---|---|
| STUDENTNO | NAME | FIRSTYEAR | STARTDATE |
| 1467 | Alice | 1982 | 9/7 |

An entry in the file is related to a real world entity: a student. The entity is fully identified by a *key*.  Here, the key is the student number and STUDENTNO is a *key column*; by definition, the value 1467 appears only once in that column.

- Now, consider the data requirements of the Dean of Studies.  She deals with information about classes.  What she wants to see is a file - call it DEAN_FILE - which lists all classes, together with their subjects and prerequisites.

| DEAN_FILE | | | |
|---|---|---|---|
| CLASSNO | SUBJECT | REQUIRED | MINGRADE |
| 201 | Advanced Programming | 123<br>130 | 3.5<br>4.0 |
| 123 | Introduction to Programming | | |

The key column is CLASSNO; and each entry associates with CLASSNO, the simple attribute SUBJECT and two *multivalued* attributes: REQUIRED, and MINGRADE.  REQUIRED contains the prerequisite class number, while MINGRADE contains the minimum grade (on a 0 to 5 scale) that must be achieved in that class in order to qualify.  A multivalued attribute is a set of values, and it is the whole set that is associated with the class number.  For class 123 that set is empty.  Actually, in the example, the two sets REQUIRED and MINGRADE are not independent of one another: 123 is paired with 3.5, 130 is paired with 4.0.  We represent that fact by the brackets around the pair of columns.  We shall come back to sets that are independent, later in this chapter.

Finally, consider the data requirements of the Records Administrator. His most common task is to retrieve all information about a given student. This includes the name, the initial registration year, the start date, and the information on all classes that the student has taken. What he wants to see is a file - call it RECORDS_FILE - which shows the data about each student. Here also, STUDENTNO is the key column.

| RECORDS_FILE | | | | | | |
|---|---|---|---|---|---|---|
| STUDENTNO | NAME | FIRSTYEAR | STARTDATE | CLASSNO | YEAR | GRADE |
| 1467 | Alice | 1982 | 9/7 | 123 | 1982 | 3.8 |
| | | | | 148 | 1983 | 3.5 |
| | | | | 220 | 1986 | 4.5 |

The file associates with the key (STUDENTNO), the simple attributes NAME, FIRSTYEAR, and STARTDATE, plus three multivalued ones: CLASSNO, YEAR, and GRADE.

At this point, you understand the data needed by the community of users. The three files just described suffice to capture all the information. In that sense, they constitute a schema which we summarize as follows:

Schema A:
    ADMISSION (STUDENTNO, NAME, FIRSTYEAR, STARTDATE)
    DEAN_FILE (CLASSNO, SUBJECT, | REQUIRED, MINGRADE |)
    RECORDS_FILE (STUDENTNO, NAME, FIRSTYEAR, STARTDATE,
        | CLASSNO, YEAR, GRADE |)

However, schema A is not yet in a usable shape. The following sections will take this schema as a starting point and modify it in several steps; the first step is necessary in order to use SQL; the others are optional but generally recommended because they avoid some tricky problems.

# 2.1  First Normal Form

In Chapter 1, we illustrated briefly the main operations of SQL. As you recall, we never mentioned multivalued attributes. Actually, this was not an oversight: SQL only understands what is called a *flat table*: that is, a table that has only single value attributes. In other words, an SQL table has rows and columns, and there is a single value at each row/column intersection. ADMISSION satisfies that condition; it is a flat table and can therefore be used, as is, in SQL. On the other hand, the other two files do not satisfy the condition and need to be converted into flat tables.

First, we show a bad way of flattening a file. Consider DEAN_FILE and assume that the number of prerequisites is never larger than three. Then, it is sufficient to reserve 3 x 2 = 6 columns for storing a maximum of three pairs <required, mingrade>. If there are less than three prerequisites, the columns can be padded with **null** values. The table, with the information about classes 201 and 123, would look like this:

| DEAN_FILE1 | | | | | | | |
|---|---|---|---|---|---|---|---|
| CLASSNO | SUBJECT | RQ1 | GR1 | RQ2 | GR2 | RQ3 | GR3 |
| 201 | Advanced Programming | 123 | 3.5 | 130 | 4.0 | 0 | 0.0 |
| 123 | Introduction to Programming | 0 | 0.0 | 0 | 0.0 | 0 | 0.0 |

The objection against such an organization is that it gives different column names RQ1, RQ2 and RQ3 (or GR1, GR2 and GR3), to data elements that play the same role. This makes it difficult or even impossible to ask very reasonable queries. For example, to find the classes that have class 123 as prerequisite, the **where** clause needs to include three predicates:

$$\textbf{where } RQ1 = 123 \textbf{ or } RQ2 = 123 \textbf{ or } RQ3 = 123 \qquad [2.1]$$

In addition, if the number of elements in the set becomes large, the number of columns in the table increases, and queries become really awkward. We quickly reject this way of flattening a table.

Another approach consists of packing the six (or less) values in a single string stored in a single column, as in:

| DEAN_FILE2 | | |
|---|---|---|
| CLASSNO | SUBJECT | PREREQUISITES |
| 201 | Advanced Programming | 123, 3.5, 130, 4.0 |
| 123 | Introduction to Programming | ? |

But SQL handles an attribute such as PREREQUISITES as an atomic value and does not understand the structure inside the string. This means that SQL cannot be used to query its contents, which is generally a serious drawback (there are exceptions; the whole issue will be revisited in Chapter 13).

Now, let us look at a better approach. It consists of repeating the key and the single value attributes for each value in the multivalued set. Hence, we reorganized DEAN_FILE into the following table called CLASS1:

| CLASS1 | | | |
|---|---|---|---|
| CLASSNO | SUBJECT | REQUIRED | MINGRADE |
| 201 | Advanced Programming | 123 | 3.5 |
| 201 | Advanced Programming | 130 | 4.0 |
| 123 | Introduction to Programming | ? | ? |

The table CLASS1 is in *First Normal Form (1NF)*, according to the following definition:

*A table is in First Normal Form if there is a single data element at each row/column intersection.*

As you can imagine, the presence of "first" in this definition indicates that there are higher levels of normalization; they are the subject of the remainder of this chapter.

Although CLASS1 still contains all information about the classes and their subjects, each row in the table is actually about a particular prerequisite. What then is the key of the table? It is not CLASSNO since the same class number may appear in several rows; it is not REQUIRED since the same class may appear several times in that column (when a class is a prerequisite of more than one other class). But, the pair <CLASSNO, REQUIRED> is unique: it identifies a prerequisite unambiguously. So, <CLASSNO, REQUIRED> is the key of the table; it is called a *composite key* because it involves more than one column.

Let us turn our attention to RECORDS_FILE. Here, also, the file can be converted into a 1NF table by repeating the simple attributes as many times as needed. The process yields the following table RECORDS1:

| RECORDS1 | | | | | | |
|---|---|---|---|---|---|---|
| STUDENTNO | NAME | FIRSTYEAR | STARTDATE | CLASSNO | YEAR | GRADE |
| 1467 | Alice | 1982 | 9/7 | 123 | 1982 | 3.8 |
| 1467 | Alice | 1982 | 9/7 | 148 | 1983 | 3.5 |
| 1467 | Alice | 1982 | 9/7 | 220 | 1986 | 4.5 |

Here, a row describes a real world entity which is the enrollment of the student in a particular class. The key is also a composite key: <STUDENTNO, CLASSNO>. The three tables, ADMISSION, CLASS1, and RECORDS1, are all 1NF and our new schema is:

Schema B:
      ADMISSION (STUDENTNO, NAME, FIRSTYEAR, STARTDATE)
      CLASS1 (CLASSNO, SUBJECT, REQUIRED, MINGRADE)
      RECORDS1 (STUDENTNO, NAME, FIRSTYEAR, STARTDATE,
          CLASSNO, YEAR, GRADE)

We now proceed with a further refinement.

## 2.2  Looking at the data in multiple ways

Consider the information about students: STUDENTNO, NAME, FIRSTYEAR, and STARTDATE.    The same data appear in two tables: ADMISSION and RECORDS1.  This *redundancy* comes from the fact that the Admission Administrator and the Records Administrator wanted to see the data in different ways.  But redundancy has an obvious drawback: any change of the information about a student will have to be done in both tables. When a new student registers, an SQL insert is needed to add a row to ADMISSION. As soon as that student enrolls in a class, a row must be inserted into RECORDS1 and some of the data values in that row will have to be the same as the ones already stored at admission time (this may imply querying ADMISSION for each insert).  The same argument applies to delete or update.

The question is then how to get rid of the redundancy, without sacrificing the ability of a user to see the data according to his or her liking.  The answer is SQL itself. With SQL, the user - or the application program - can look at the data through tables that are structured differently from the ones that are defined in the schema.  The SELECT capability of SQL allows a user to build the table that he or she wants to see, from one or several schema tables.  This capability of SQL was already sketched in Chapter 1. As you recall, a select statement allows for building a result table that contains only a subset of the columns - and even a subset of the rows.  And a join allows for constructing a result table from information contained in two or more tables.

For example, to construct the contents of ADMISSION, starting with RECORDS1, you simply write:

      **select** STUDENTNO, NAME, FIRSTYEAR, STARTDATE      [2.2]
      **from** RECORDS1

Since ADMISSION can be so easily reconstructed from another table, it really does not need to be in the schema.  On the other hand, CLASS1 contains information that is not stored anywhere else; so CLASS1 must be kept.  In conclusion, after elimination of redundancy among different tables, the schema becomes:

Schema C:
      CLASS1 (CLASSNO, SUBJECT, REQUIRED, MINGRADE)
      RECORDS1 (STUDENTNO, NAME, FIRSTYEAR, STARTDATE,
           CLASSNO, YEAR, GRADE)

# 2.3 Functional dependencies

Look at table RECORDS1, particularly columns STUDENTNO and FIRSTYEAR. The semantics of FIRSTYEAR are such that there exists one FIRSTYEAR value per student; for example, student 1467 (Alice) was admitted in 1982. If that relationship appears several times in the database, it will always be the same. It would be incongruous to find, in one place, <1467, 1982>, and somewhere else, <1467, 1983>. This relationship property is called *functional dependency*, and FIRSTYEAR is *functionally dependent* on STUDENTNO. The notion is very important in evaluating the "goodness" of a schema.

In RECORDS1, the same student number does appear in several rows. There-fore, the FIRSTYEAR value, which is associated with a particular student, must also be repeated. This introduces a redundancy inside a single table, which is responsible for the following undesirable properties:

- Insert anomaly: every time a new row is inserted, one must ensure that the functionally dependent value agrees with the value that may already exist in another row. If Alice enrolls in a new class, the new corresponding row will have to contain 1982 as first year.

- Delete anomaly: to delete a <STUDENTNO, CLASSNO> association, a row is deleted from RECORDS1; but, if the row is the only (remaining) one for a particular student, all data about the student - such as name and first year - are lost. This is probably unintentional.

- Update anomaly: here also, one must be careful in updating a value that appears in several rows in a redundant way; again, all instances of that value must be updated.

# 2.4 Second Normal Form

The reason for the redundancy in the first year information is that FIRSTYEAR is functionally dependent on a strict subset of the key rather than the whole key. FIRSTYEAR is functionally dependent on STUDENTNO, while the key is <STUDENTNO, CLASSNO>. The same argument applies to NAME and STARTDATE as well. To avoid the problem described in the previous section, columns such as FIRSTYEAR, NAME, and STARTDATE should be removed from RECORDS1 and the information they contain should be stored in a table that has STUDENTNO as a key. Thus, RECORDS1 is split into two tables. The first one is RECORDS:

| RECORDS | | | |
|---|---|---|---|
| STUDENTNO | CLASSNO | YEAR | GRADE |
| 1467 | 123 | 1982 | 3.8 |
| 1467 | 148 | 1983 | 3.5 |
| 1467 | 220 | 1986 | 4.5 |

The second table associates a STUDENTNO with the corresponding values of NAME, FIRSTYEAR, and STARTDATE: it happens to be exactly ADMISSION; so we may as well call it so. RECORDS and ADMISSION are in *Second Normal Form*, according to the following definition:

*A 1NF table is also in Second Normal Form if it does not contain any column that is functionally dependent on a strict subset of the key.*

In order to provide the Records Administrator with his preferred view of the data, RECORDS will need to be joined with ADMISSION, as in

> **select** RECORDS.STUDENTNO, NAME, FIRSTYEAR,
> STARTDATE, CLASSNO
> **from** RECORDS, ADMISSION
> **where** RECORDS.STUDENTNO = ADMISSION.STUDENTNO

The **where** clause indicates that the join is based on matching the STUDENTNO in RECORDS with the STUDENTNO in ADMISSION.

We need to go through a similar procedure for CLASS1. The key is <CLASSNO, REQUIRED>. MINGRADE is functionally dependent on the key. But SUBJECT is functionally dependent on CLASSNO only. Therefore, the column SUBJECT should be removed and included in a table that has CLASSNO as key. Hence, the new representation of the information about classes will be

| CLASS | |
|---|---|
| CLASSNO | SUBJECT |
| 201 | Advanced Programming |

| PREREQ | | |
|---|---|---|
| CLASSNO | REQUIRED | MINGRADE |
| 201 | 123 | 3.5 |
| 201 | 130 | 4.0 |

The new schema is composed of four tables that are all in 2NF:

Schema D:
>       ADMISSION (STUDENTNO, NAME, FIRSTYEAR, STARTDATE)
>       CLASS (CLASSNO, SUBJECT)
>       PREREQ (CLASSNO, REQUIRED, MINGRADE)
>       RECORDS (STUDENTNO, CLASS, YEAR, GRADE)

# 2.5  Third Normal Form

Let us now turn our attention to column STARTDATE in ADMISSION. As you recall, STARTDATE was initially stored in RECORDS1. Since it did violate the condition for 2NF, it was moved to ADMISSION. As a result, the date is stored only once per student. But ADMISSION still exhibits redundancy, which again causes update anomalies similar to those already discussed; for example, STARTDATE cannot be updated at will because the same STARTDATE value must appear in all rows of students who entered the college in the same year. Such an anomaly comes from the fact that STARTDATE is functionally dependent on another attribute of the table (FIRSTYEAR), rather than being dependent on the key (STUDENTNO). This functional dependency is not directly between STARTDATE and STUDENTNO, but rather, *transitively*, between STARTDATE and FIRSTYEAR, and between FIRSTYEAR and STUDENTNO.

We can now define the *Third Normal Form (3NF)*:

*A table that is in 2NF is also in Third Normal Form if all its (non-key) attributes depend directly on the key*.

(Ignore, for the moment, the "non-key" term in this definition.) Clearly, ADMISSION is not 3NF; but the situation can be remedied easily by removing the culprit column (STARTDATE) from the table and moving the information to a table which has YEAR as key. Then, in that new table,

STARTDATE is directly functionally dependent on the key.  This new normalization step replaces ADMISSION with the following two 3NF tables:

| ACADEMIC_YEAR | |
| --- | --- |
| YEAR | STARTDATE |
| 1982 | 9/7 |

| STUDENT | | |
| --- | --- | --- |
| STUDENTNO | NAME | FIRSTYEAR |
| 1467 | Alice | 1982 |

Thus we obtain the new schema:

Schema E:
       STUDENT (STUDENTNO, NAME, FIRSTYEAR)
       CLASS (CLASSNO, SUBJECT)
       PREREQ (CLASSNO, REQUIRED, MINGRADE)
       RECORDS (STUDENTNO, CLASS, YEAR, GRADE)
       ACADEMIC_YEAR (YEAR, STARTDATE)

Again, in order to recreate ADMISSION, a query will join STUDENT with ACADEMIC_YEAR, matching the value in FIRSTYEAR with the value in YEAR.  Similarly, recreating RECORDS1 will require a three-way join between STUDENT, ACADEMIC_YEAR, and RECORDS.

## 2.6 More than one key

Consider the table STUDENT. We never clarified if NAME was also a key. In other words, we never said if NAME was unique and, therefore, could be used to identify a student unambiguously. Suppose for a moment that it is.  The presence of NAME in table STUDENT does not pose any problem since it is functionally dependent on the key STUDENTNO (and vice versa).

But now, suppose you would, for reporting purposes, prefer to see the column NAME included in RECORDS. In other words, you would prefer to see RECORDS2:

| RECORDS2 | | | | |
|---|---|---|---|---|
| STUDENTNO | NAME | CLASSNO | YEAR | GRADE |
| 1467 | Alice | 123 | 1982 | 3.8 |
| 1467 | Alice | 148 | 1983 | 3.5 |
| 1467 | Alice | 220 | 1986 | 4.5 |

How normalized is RECORDS2? Something special happens here because the NAME column is part of <NAME, CLASSNO> which is also a key. In fact, for reasons that go beyond this brief introduction to normalization, the definition of the third normal form does not impose any condition on the columns that are part of a key (that is why "non-key" appeared in the above definition). According to the definition, RECORDS2 is 3NF. However, it is clear that column NAME is misplaced: it introduces redundancy which comes with the usual anomalies. For example, if we had misspelled a student's name, we would have to update the column in more than one row.

It appears that the third normal form definition is, in a sense, too weak. A stronger form, called the *Boyce-Codd Normal Form (BCNF)*, asks for removing such a column from the table. This means that we should keep RECORDS in the schema, rather than replacing it with RECORDS2. If the contents of RECORDS2 is needed in the application, it can always be expressed as a join between RECORDS and STUDENT.

Note that, theoretically, the difference between 3NF and BCNF is a subtle one. In practice, the procedure to avoid redundancy is identical.

## 2.7 Multivalued dependencies

Let us complicate the application slightly in order to illustrate another aspect of normalization. We already dealt with a set of enrollments (class, year, and grade) associated with a student. Now, let us consider another set of items, also related to students, for example, the set of majors that the student is pursuing.

Suppose that, in our example, Alice is pursuing a double major: computer science and mathematics. Someone who ignores normalization may think about designing the following file, called STUDENT1.

| STUDENT1 | | | | | |
|---|---|---|---|---|---|
| STUDENTNO | \| | CLASSNO  YEAR  GRADE \| | \| | MAJOR | \| |
| 1467 | 123<br>148<br>220 | 1982         3.8<br>1983         3.5<br>1986         4.5 | \| \| | Mathematics<br>Computer Science | \| |

Again, the brackets indicate that sets of classes, years, and grades are associated with a student. The fact that 123, 1982, and 3.8 are on the same line is relevant: as mentioned above, the three sets are dependent. It is really like one set with three columns. But the fact that the major 'Mathematics' happens to be on the same line as class 123 is irrelevant. The set of majors and the set of classes are independent.

As usual, the first thing to do is to normalize the file to obtain a 1NF table. We certainly know how to normalize the information about students and classes (with years and grades); we have done it already, in RECORDS. Because a set of classes is associated with a student, the student number is replicated. The information about the majors requires an additional column. Since the student number is replicated, the set of majors will have to be duplicated as many times, yielding the following 1NF table (which is also BCNF).

| RECORDS3 | | | | |
|---|---|---|---|---|
| STUDENTNO | CLASSNO | YEAR | GRADE | MAJOR |
| 1467 | 123 | 1982 | 3.8 | Mathematics |
| 1467 | 123 | 1982 | 3.8 | Computer Science |
| 1467 | 148 | 1983 | 3.5 | Mathematics |
| 1467 | 148 | 1983 | 3.5 | Computer Science |
| 1467 | 220 | 1986 | 4.5 | Mathematics |
| 1467 | 220 | 1986 | 4.5 | Computer Science |

In a sense, the normalization forced the set of classes and the set of majors to be "multiplied". If a student took n classes and is pursuing m majors, RECORDS3 contains n × m rows for that student. This multiplication is due to the fact that more than one multivalued attributes are stored in the same table. Note that converting the table to 1NF does not alter the fact that it contains two independent multivalued attributes; this is a property of the data, not of its representation. The solution to the problem is to split the table. In our last schema, RECORDS3 contains two independent multivalued attributes; therefore two tables should be used instead:

| MAJOR | |
|---|---|
| STUDENTNO | MAJOR |
| 1467 | Mathematics |
| 1467 | Computer Science |

| RECORDS | | | |
|---|---|---|---|
| STUDENTNO | CLASSNO | YEAR | GRADE |
| 1467 | 123 | 1982 | 3.8 |
| 1467 | 148 | 1983 | 3.5 |
| 1467 | 220 | 1986 | 4.5 |

Both tables are not only 3NF; they are also in *Fourth Normal Form (4NF)* , according to the following definition:

*A 3NF table which does not have two (or more) independent multivalued attributes is in Fourth Normal Form.*

In practice, multivalued dependent columns are easy to detect, and it is generally wise to get rid of them as soon as possible during the database design process.

# 2.8  Summary

In this chapter, we considered the problem of designing a database schema for a given application. By analyzing the diverse requirements we came up with a preliminary schema.  We then discussed the drawbacks of data redundancy and showed how the principles of normalization can be used to transform a schema into another one with a higher level of normalization, until a schema without redundancy is obtained. The various rules can be summarized as follows:

- Transform any file with multivalued attributes into a flat table (1NF).  If there are several multivalued attributes, use several tables (4NF) .

- Remove from a table any column that is directly functionally dependent on a strict subset of the key (2NF).

- Remove from a table any column that is functionally dependent on another column (or set of columns) (3NF - BCNF).

A final note: there is a clear distinction between the normalization into 1NF and the others. The first normal form is required in order to use SQL; the others are optional. They eliminate redundancy and, with it, the insert, delete, and update anomalies.  It is finally a matter of trade-off.  Normalization simplifies insertions, deletions, and updates, but generally makes retrieval more costly, since joins may be required to obtain the desired result. However, it is good practice to start with the highest level of normalization possible; then, only if experimentation shows that the retrieval is too slow, de-normalization may be envisaged. It is absolutely important to understand when a table is not fully normalized, so that updates, insertions, and deletions may be handled properly. This requires a thorough understanding of the semantics of the data.

# 2.9  Schema for the exercises

All chapters of Parts 1 and 2, starting with this one, end with a series of exercises. Just as all examples in the text refer to the same application, the rental company management, we wanted all the exercises also to refer to a single application, the college records application. We used as schema a subset of schema E and renamed some columns for the sake of conciseness. What follows is a self-contained description of the four tables that were retained, with their full contents.

STUDENT

The STUDENT table contains one row for each student enrolled in the College. Each student is identified by a unique identifier which is stored in column STUDENTNO. Two other columns are associated with the student number, the name of the student (NAME) and the year he or she entered the school (FIRSTYEAR). The student identifier is an integer between 1,000 and 100,000. The student name is at most 100 characters long; the average length is 15. The first year is represented as an integer, not as a date. No value is **null** in any of the three columns.

CLASS

The CLASS table contains one row for each class taught at the college. Each class is uniquely identified by a class number, an integer between 100 and 400. Associated with the class is a subject. A subject is a character string of average length 20 and maximum length 32. Again, no value can be missing.

RECORDS

The RECORDS table contains one row for each occurrence of a class attended by a student. A row establishes a relationship between the student, the class that he or she attended, the year of attendance, and the grade when available. A **null** value is used to indicate that the grade is not yet known. The student number is in column STUDENTNO (it must match one of the numbers in table STUDENT, column STUDENTNO). Column CLASS contains the class

| STUDENT | | |
|---|---|---|
| STUDENTNO | NAME | FIRSTYEAR |
| 1467 | Alice | 1982 |
| 1342 | John | 1985 |
| 4742 | Claudia | 1986 |
| 6842 | Louis | 1982 |

| CLASS | |
|---|---|
| CLASSNO | SUBJECT |
| 123 | Introduction to Programming |
| 148 | Introduction to Database |
| 130 | Programming in Pascal |
| 201 | Advanced Programming |
| 220 | Advanced Database |

| RECORDS | | | |
|---|---|---|---|
| STUDENT | CLASS | YEAR | GRADE |
| 1467 | 123 | 1982 | 3.8 |
| 1467 | 148 | 1983 | 3.5 |
| 1467 | 220 | 1986 | 4.5 |
| 1342 | 123 | 1985 | 3.9 |
| 1342 | 130 | 1986 | 4.5 |
| 1342 | 201 | 1987 | ? |
| 4742 | 123 | 1986 | 2.3 |
| 4742 | 130 | 1986 | 4.5 |
| 4742 | 148 | 1987 | ? |
| 6842 | 123 | 1985 | 3.7 |
| 6842 | 130 | 1985 | 4.2 |
| 6842 | 201 | 1987 | ? |

| PREREQ | | |
|---|---|---|
| CLASS | REQUIRED | MINGRADE |
| 148 | 123 | 2.0 |
| 220 | 148 | 3.0 |
| 201 | 123 | 3.5 |
| 201 | 130 | 4.0 |

**Figure 14. Schema used in the exercises**

number (it must match one of the numbers in table CLASS, column CLASSNO). The year in column YEAR is an integer. The grade in column GRADE varies between 0.0 and 5.0 with a single decimal digit.

PREREQ

In order to enroll in a given class there may be a requirement to have attended and successfully completed one or more other classes with a specified minimum grade. Each row in PREREQ specifies that the class in column CLASS can be enrolled in only if the student got at least a certain grade (MINGRADE) in the REQUIRED class. The values in both columns CLASS and REQUIRED must match a CLASSNO in table CLASS. No value can be left **null**.

The contents of the four tables are shown in Figure 14.

# 2.10  Exercises

The exercises use the database application described in this chapter.

**2.1.** What does the following statement do?

> **create table** STUDENT
> ( STUDENTNO **integer**,
> NAME **char**(7),
> FIRSTYEAR **integer**)

**2.2.** What is the effect of

> **insert into** PREREQ
> (CLASS, REQUIRED, MINGRADE)
> **values** ( 148, 123, 2.0)

**2.3.** What is the result of

> **select** CLASS, GRADE
> **from** RECORDS
> **where** STUDENT = 1342

**2.4.** What is the result of

> **select count**(*)
> **from** STUDENT

**2.5.** Is there any difference between

> **select** REQUIRED
> **from** PREREQ
> **where** CLASS **in** (148, 201)

and

> **select** REQUIRED
> **from** PREREQ
> **where** CLASS = 148
>     **or** CLASS = 201

**2.6.** Formulate the following query in English.

> **select** *
> **from** CLASS
> **where** CLASSNO **not in**
>     ( **select** CLASS
>     **from** PREREQ )

**2.7.** Evaluate

> **select** NAME, SUBJECT
> **from** STUDENT, RECORDS, CLASS
> **where** STUDENT.STUDENTNO = RECORDS.STUDENT
>     **and** RECORDS.CLASS = CLASS.CLASSNO
>     **and** RECORDS.YEAR = 1987

**2.8.** Evaluate

> **select** CLASS, NAME
> **from** RECORDS, STUDENT
> **where** STUDENT.STUDENTNO = RECORDS.STUDENT
>     **and** RECORDS.YEAR = 1987
> **order by** CLASS, NAME

# Part 2. The Language

## Chapter 3

## Constructing a Table

The construction of a table implies two operations. The table must first be created to inform the system of its existence; then it must be populated with rows. In Chapter 1, we considered an example dealing with the management of a rental company and we determined the set of tables needed to store all relevant data. Although the example used **create table** and **insert** statements, it did not, by any means, illustrate the variety of options possible. Chapter 3 remedies this situation. In fact, by the time you reach the end of this chapter you should be able to define and populate any table required by your application.

## 3.1 Table creation

A **create table** statement creates a table in the sense that it makes the table known to the system; it gives the new table a name and defines its columns. A column is defined by its name, its data type, and a flag which indicates whether or not the column can accommodate **null** values.

### 3.1.1 Table names

Since the name of a table will be used later to identify the table without ambiguity, it must be system-wide unique. In a simple environment, the naming of objects such as tables is straightforward: TOOL, CUSTOMER, and CONTRACT are unique names, short and easy to remember. But as soon as the environment supports many users and many applications, the system must be slightly clever. Clearly, the user should be able to choose a name of his liking, without having to worry about all other table names for potential conflict. Some SQL systems solve this problem by allowing a user to choose names that are unique only among the set of tables that he or she created. The system-wide unique name is then obtained by concatenating the name of the table with the name of the user who creates the table (the creator) and separating them with a dot. For example, suppose there are two users ERIC and SOPHIE; then ERIC may create a table called TOOL, while SOPHIE does the same. The respective system-wide names are then ERIC.TOOL and SOPHIE.TOOL. Of course, users have to "register" into the system and their names must themselves be unique.

Other systems opted for a qualification of names by directory rather than creator. A table T is created in a specific directory, say X. Then the full table name is /X/T.

Generally, the system knows which user is submitting a particular request to the system. Therefore the short name, without the qualifier, is often sufficient, since the system itself can add the qualifier when needed.

A table name may contain any character. But under certain circumstances, the name must be enclosed in double quotes. This happens when the name

- is a reserved SQL keyword (the list of keywords varies with SQL implementations, although **select**, **like**, **date**, and others, are always reserved);
- contains blanks or other special characters;
- does not start with a letter.

For example, TOOL is a valid table name; SELECT is not valid, although "SELECT" is. The string 123ABC is not a valid name; but A1234 and "123" are.

## 3.1.2  Column names

Column names must be unique within a table. Reserved keywords are enclosed in double quotes as for table names. In an SQL statement, when two tables are used which contain columns of the same name (as in a join), the ambiguity is removed by prefixing the column name with the table name, separated by a dot. For example, if NUMBER is a column in TOOL, you can refer to it as TOOL.NUMBER.

The order in which column names are entered in a **create table** statement is not important; it does, however, define a *canonical order* that will remain associated with the table forever. The canonical order will be useful in some shorthand notation discussed later in this chapter.

## 3.1.3 Data types

In a table, all data stored in a given column must be of the same type. The type is therefore an attribute of the column and must be specified in the **create table** statement. The most commonly supported data types are the following:

**Integer:** For integer numbers between -2,147,483,648 and 2,147,483,647.

**Smallint:** For integer numbers between -32,768 and 32,767.

**Decimal(n,p):** For decimal numbers with a maximum total length of n digits including p decimal digits. For example, **decimal**(6,2) stores decimal numbers between -9,999.99 and 9,999.99. The word **number** is used in some implementations, instead of **decimal**.

**Float:** For floating point numbers.

**Char(n):** For a character string of fixed length n. The maximum value of n is generally fixed by the implementation (255 in many implementations). The data stored in a **char** column can include any character or byte. In SQL, character constants are specified in simple quotes (for example, 'mower').

**Varchar(n):** For a character string of varying length. The character string itself is preceded by a 2-byte integer containing the number of characters in the string. The actual length can vary from 0 to n and is determined at the time the data element is stored in the database by an **insert** or **update** statement. As for data of type **char**, a **varchar** data element may contain any character, and a constant is enclosed in simple quotes; note that the maximum value of n is implementation dependent.

**Long Varchar:** For a character string of varying length, when the length is larger than the limit for **varchar(n)**. Long varchar strings have also an implementation dependent limit, but it can be as much as 4k or 32k bytes. The use of long varchar, and of unformatted data in general, is discussed in Part 3, Chapters 12 and 13.

**Date:** For storing dates and times. The data type for date varies from one SQL product to another. We can distinguish between two implementations:

1. Different data types are used for date and time. Operations are explicitly made on year, month, and day.

2. A single **date** data type is used for both date and time. The internal representation is a decimal number. Its integer part represents a number of days (from a certain origin), while its decimal part represents the time in the day.

The examples of this book are mostly independent of these implementation variations, although they may have to be changed slightly in order to actually be run.

Since the external format of dates can vary, functions may be provided to transform the external representations of dates and times into the internal ones, and vice versa.

*Remark:*

The data type associated with a particular column specifies implicitly a set of permissible values for that column. Some implementations and/or language proposals introduce the notion of *domain* to allow for a more precise definition of the set. A domain is given a name and attributes such as a data type, a list of conditions that restrict the values that the domain contains, and a default value to be used in the absence of an explicitly specified value. Then, instead of specifying that a column must be of a certain type, the **create table** statement specifies that the column is based on a certain domain. For example, the designer of the rental application may want to define a domain PRICE, with data type decimal(8,2), condition $\geq 0$, and default = 0. Then columns PURCH_PRICE and RENTAL_FEE in TOOL, and FEE in CON-TRACT can all be defined on domain PRICE.

## 3.1.4  Missing information

SQL supports missing information by storing a **null** value instead of a specific value for a data element in a table. For example, consider table CONTRACT in Chapter 1. The column FEE contains a **null** value for a contract that is still outstanding. The **null** value should not be confused with a value of zero. In Figure 7, the value 0 indicates a free rental, while **null** indicates a tool which has not been returned. A **null** value can be thought of as a value which, compared with any value, including **null**, yields a value false. The use of **null** values in queries is covered in detail in Chapter 4.

To provide better control on the use of **null** values, a column is flagged as allowing or disallowing them. By default, **null** values are allowed in a column, except if the column name specified in the **create table** is followed by the keywords **not null**.

## 3.1.5  Examples

At this point, you should be able to write the **create table** statements needed for the rental application.  For example, the following statement fully defines table TOOL:

    **create table** TOOL                                     [3.1]
        (NUMBER **integer not null**,
        TYPE **varchar**(8) **not null**,
        PURCH_DATE **date**,
        PURCH_PRICE **decimal**(8,2),
        RENTAL_FEE **decimal**(8,2) **not null**)

Note that we use NUMBER in the application as a way to refer unambiguously to a specific tool; thus a null value in that column is not acceptable and the **not null** option must be specified.  For the correctness of the application, the type and rental fee of a tool must be specified.  Thus we also choose the **not null** option for the corresponding columns. The other columns may be **null**.

**Null** is specified by default; it does not appear explicitly in the statement.

Similarly, the following statements create the CUSTOMER and CONTRACT tables:

    **create table** CUSTOMER                                  [3.2]
        (NAME **varchar**(16) **not null**,
        ADDRESS **varchar**(64),
        ZIP **char**(5) )

    **create table** CONTRACT                                  [3.3]
        (CONTRACT **integer not null**,
        CUSTOMER **varchar**(16) **not null**,
        TOOL **integer not null**,
        DATE_OUT **date not null**,
        DATE_IN **date not null**,
        FEE **decimal**(10,2) )

As mentioned above, **null** means an unknown value, not a zero value.  You may of course always choose to implement a null concept yourself by setting aside a special value. But this may not always be easy and the user needs to remember what particular value plays the role of a null in a particular column. Another advantage of system support is space saving.  A **null** value can be stored as a single flag; the flag is OFF when a value is present and ON when it is not; when the flag is ON, no space is reserved for data.

The following diagram shows the syntax of the **create table** statement:

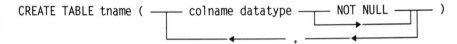

It reads as follows:

- **Create table** appears in uppercase; it is a keyword; it must be present.

- The keyword must be followed by a character string (called tname) and a parenthesis. Note that a word in lowercase, such as "tname", is just a placeholder in the syntax diagram. The names of the placeholders themselves are irrelevant; they were chosen to suggest the role that the actual values play in the statement.

- The horizontal line indicates that after the parenthesis a column name and a type must appear.

- The fork after the type represents an option. The presence of **not null** is one of the options; no **not null** is another option. In both cases, the paths join and a fork appears again, indicating another choice: either a parenthesis and end of statement, or a comma followed by column name, type, and so on. The loop clearly indicates an arbitrary number of pairs of column names and types separated by commas (with or without the **not null** attribute).

## 3.1.6  Table deletion

After having created a table, you may realize that it is not exactly what you wanted. If you reissue a **create table** statement with the same name, SQL will return an error code, telling you that the name already exists. You need to get rid of a table before re-creating it. SQL provides a statement to that effect; it is called **drop**. Its syntax is simply

```
DROP TABLE tname
```

The **drop table** statement generally causes the system to recover the space occupied by the table being dropped.

## 3.2 Data insertion

Now that you know how to create tables, you are ready to populate them with data. As mentioned earlier, rows are added to a table through execution of **insert** statements.

An **insert** statement specifies three sets of parameters: the name of the table, a sequence of column names, and a sequence of values. The sequence of values maps one to one onto the sequence of column names. Obviously, the submitted values must be compatible with the column types.

For example, statement [3.4] inserts a valid row in TOOL:

> **insert into** TOOL (NUMBER, TYPE, PURCH_DATE,                [3.4]
>     PURCH_PRICE, RENTAL_FEE)
> **values** (1, 'mower', **null**, 550.70, 12.30)

Note that we chose to write the column names in the canonical order defined when TOOL was created. But then the sequence of names becomes unnecessary and SQL allows for a short form:

> **insert into** TOOL                                          [3.5]
> **values**(1, 'mower', **null**, 550.70, 12.30)

Although the short form is attractive, it assumes that the user, programmer or program reader, remembers the canonical order exactly. With the longer form [3.4], the column names can be specified in any order, with data elements also in that order:

> **insert into** TOOL (NUMBER, TYPE, PURCH_PRICE,              [3.6]
>     RENTAL_FEE, PURCH_DATE)
> **values**(1, 'mower', 550.70, 12.30, **null**)

This form offers the additional advantage that **null** values do not need to be specified explicitly. If a column name is not specified, a **null** value is assumed by default, as in

> **insert into** TOOL                                          [3.7]
> (NUMBER, TYPE, PURCH_PRICE, RENTAL_FEE)
> **values**(1, 'mower', 550.70, 12.30)

```
exec sql include sqlca
exec sql begin declare section
        declare number N, Price, Fee
        declare string Date, Type
        declare small integer C1, C2
exec sql end declare section

exec sql create table TOOL
        (NUMBER integer not null,
        TYPE char(8) not null,
        PURCH_DATE date,
        PURCH_PRICE decimal(8,2),
        RENTAL_FEE decimal(8,2) not null)

do until end of input file
        read values to be inserted (from file)
        if Date is unknown then C1 = -1 else C1 = 0
        if Price is unknown then C2 = -1 else C2 = 0
        exec sql insert into TOOL (NUMBER, TYPE, PURCH_DATE,
                PURCH_PRICE, RENTAL_FEE)
        values(:N, :Type, :Date:C1,
                :Price:C2, :Fee)
        end
```

**Figure 15. Program inserting NULL values**

## 3.2.1 Inserting from a program

Although Chapter 1 illustrated the use of a program to insert a series of rows into a table, it did not discuss the issue of **null** values. Assume you want to write a program inserting many rows into a table as in Figure 12. If you know that all rows to be inserted will have **null** values in column PURCH_DATE, then form [3.7] can be used (obviously with program variables instead of actual values). But, if, for the same column, a null value may be specified for one row and an actual value for another row, then form [3.7] will not work. Any other form would work if we only had a way of specifying a **null** value in a program variable. To that effect, SQL uses an extra variable, called an *indicator variable*, associated with the variable that contains the value itself. The name of the indicator variable follows the name of the program variable with a colon in between. Figure 15 shows a complete creation and insertion program. The last statement specifies indicator variables

*C1* and *C2* for *Date* and *Price*, respectively. These variables must be declared as small integers in the **declare section**. An indicator variable is set to -1 to denote a **null** value and to 0 otherwise.

## 3.3  Summary

By now, you should be able to build any table required by your application. This chapter describes the two phases of the process: the creation of the table, using a **create table** statement, and the insertion of rows, using the **insert** statement.

The process looks very simple indeed. But, remember, the choice of the tables to be created is of paramount importance for the application and must be done very carefully, as discussed in Chapter 2. Part 3 will also be helpful in that respect since it discusses possible choices for various applications.

## 3.4  Exercises

The exercises use the database application described in Chapter 2.

**3.1.** Write the CREATE TABLE statement for table STUDENT.

**3.2.** Write the CREATE TABLE statement for table CLASS.

**3.3.** Write the CREATE TABLE statement for table RECORDS.

**3.4.** Write the CREATE TABLE statement for table PREREQ.

**3.5.** Write a program which reads information about a student from the terminal and inserts it into STUDENT.

**3.6.** Write a program which reads enrollment data from the terminal and inserts the corresponding rows in RECORDS. To indicate an unknown grade, the user enters -1 at the terminal.

# Chapter 4

# Elementary Queries

The previous chapter guided the reader through the creation of database tables and the insertion of rows into a table. In this chapter, we explain how the information stored in a table can be retrieved. In Chapter 1, we already alluded to the use of a **select** statement to retrieve data. In fact, **select** is the only SQL statement available to query the database. It is a rich and powerful statement. Because of its many options, we shall use two chapters to cover its capabilities in detail.

Before explaining the capabilities of **select**, we need to draw the reader's attention again to how statements can be embedded in a program. We saw how a program can prepare the data in program variables and then use **insert** to store the contents of these variables in the database. Only trust at this point that there exists a similar mechanism by which a **select** statement can fetch data from the database, returning the results in program variables. We shall come back to this point later (in Section 4.3). For the time being, we choose to use an interactive query program to concentrate on the **select** itself.

The general form of the **select** statement is shown in Figure 16. Note that the syntax diagram uses several lines; they should be read as a single continuous string (→▶  ▶▶– indicates continuation). This chapter covers statements that have only a single table name after the **from** keyword; it covers **group by**, **having**, and **order by** toward the end. Consider the example in [4.1] and interpret its syntax using the syntax diagram. The projection list is composed of two column names to retrieve the tool number (the value stored in column

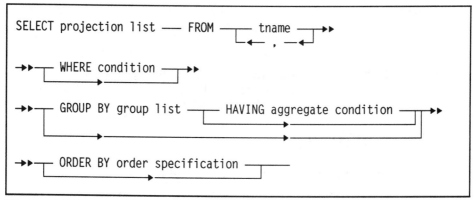

**Figure 16. Syntax diagram of the SELECT statement**

NUMBER) and the purchase price (the value stored in column PURCH_PRICE), for all tools (table TOOL) that satisfy the given condition. The condition says that the type of the tool (the value stored in column TYPE) must be equal to 'mower'.

> **select** NUMBER, PURCH_PRICE                                          [4.1]
> **from** TOOL
> **where** TYPE = 'mower'

The result consists of three rows with two columns:

| NUMBER | PURCH_PRICE |
|--------|-------------|
| 1      | 550.70      |
| 2      | 495.00      |
| 4      | 685.10      |

Although it is not stored in the database, the result of a query is always a two-dimensional table, often called the *query result table*. The types of the columns are fully determined by the projection list. A result table does not have a name, nor do its columns. This does not contradict the fact that result tables in this book are generally displayed with columns names. This is only for the sake of clarity. In fact, many interactive programs that invoke SQL generate such column headings from the query.

Unless it deals with aggregation (in Section 4.4), a **select** statement fetches from the source table the rows that satisfy the specified condition and for each row produces a row in the result table. The *projection list* determines the contents of the columns in the result table; it is sometimes called the *select list* for that reason.  The condition is often called a *filter* or a **where condition**.  If no filter is specified, a row will appear in the result table for each row in the source table.

The power of the **select** statement stems from the generality of both the projection list and the filter. The remainder of this chapter describes the various options available; all examples refer to the rental application.

# 4.1  Projection list

The syntax diagram for the projection list is as follows:

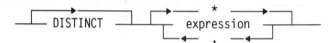

## 4.1.1  Selecting columns

An '*' is a particular projection list; it is a shorthand for selecting the values stored in all columns in their canonical order.

    **select** *                                                                [4.2]
    **from** TOOL

Example [4.2] produces a result table identical to TOOL.  When an '*' is used as projection list, nothing else can be added to the list.

If you want only a subset of the columns and/or if you want the columns to appear in an order which is not the canonical one, you need an explicit projection list.  In example [4.1] the projection list contains two expressions; each of these expressions is simply a column value.

## 4.1.2  Selecting computed values

Columns in the result table do not necessarily exist in the source table, but can be defined as the result of the computation of an expression on columns and/or constants.  An expression is built like a classical well-formed expression in algebra, using operators and parentheses.  The following expressions are valid for a **select** on TOOL:

    $(3 + 5) * 12$                                                          [4.3]

    $(3 + 5) * PURCH\_PRICE - (6 * RENTAL\_FEE)$                           [4.4]

RENTAL_FEE * 365 - PURCH_PRICE                                    [4.5]

As a more meaningful example, statement [4.6] finds, for each tool, the percentage of the purchase price that is paid for by a single day of rental.

**select** NUMBER, 100*RENTAL_FEE/PURCH_PRICE                    [4.6]
**from** TOOL

It produces the result

| NUMBER | 100*RENTAL_FEE/PURCH_PRICE |
|--------|----------------------------|
| 1 | 2.2335 |
| 2 | 2.4141 |
| 3 | 5.6872 |
| 4 | 2.0726 |
| 5 | 2.0667 |

Additionally, a constant is a (very simple) expression; it can be used as such:

**select** NAME, 'Zip code:', ZIP                                [4.7]
**from** CUSTOMER

produces the following result table:

| NAME | 'Zip code:' | ZIP |
|------|-------------|-----|
| Adams, A. | Zip code: | 95125 |
| Dupont, R. | Zip code: | 12345 |
| Smith, J. | Zip code: | 95125 |
| Wilson, P. | Zip code: | 10010 |

## 4.1.3 Operators

The operators that can be used in expressions depend on the type of the arguments.

The arithmetic operators +, -, *, and / apply to numerical values (most implementations automatically convert values from one type of numerical value to another - for example between **smallint** and **integer** or between **integer** and **float**).

The arithmetic operator '-' is applicable to dates as well. It computes the difference of two dates, yielding a duration.

The concatenation operator 'll' applies to character strings only. It makes a longer string from two shorter ones. For example, statement [4.8] retrieves the addresses of customers, including the zip code.

> **select** NAME, ADDRESS ll ' , ' ll ZIP                                [4.8]
> **from** CUSTOMER

| NAME | ADDRESS ll ' , ' ll ZIP |
|------|------------------------|
| Adams, A. | 123 Pine St, San Jose CA , 95125 |
| Dupont, R. | 100 Main St, Town ST , 12345 |
| Smith, J. | 222 Washington St, San Jose CA , 95125 |
| Wilson, P. | 553 Cedar St, New York, NY , 10010 |

"**select** NAME, ADDRESS, ZIP **from** CUSTOMER" would return three columns instead of the two retrieved by example [4.8]. Note that the concatenation operator is not available in all SQL products.

SQL also provides functions. A function is actually an operator that operates on a single operand; **value** is such a function. It specifies that **null** values that appear in the data should, for this particular query evaluation, be returned as having a user-specified default value. For example, if a FEE in CONTRACT is null, you may choose to return 999.99 instead:

> **select** CUSTOMER, **value**(FEE, 999.99)                                [4.9]
> **from** CONTRACT
> **where** TOOL = 1

| CUSTOMER | VALUE(FEE, 999.99) |
|----------|--------------------|
| Smith, J. | 24.60 |
| Adams, A. | 999.99 |

While the availability of functions varies among SQL products, many implementations support the following:

**value** or **nvl:** to give a default value to a **null** element,
**date** or **to_date:** to convert a character string into a date,
**char** or **to_char:** to convert a date into a character string,
**substr:** to extract a substring from a character string,
**translate:** to replace certain characters in a string,
**instr** or **index:** to find the first occurrence of a given substring in a character string,
**length:** to obtain the length of a character string,
**upper:** to translate a character string into uppercase.

**lower:** to translate a character string into lowercase.

## 4.1.4 Duplicate or distinct rows

Examine the result produced by statement [4.10]:

> **select** TYPE                                          [4.10]
> **from** TOOL

| TYPE |
| --- |
| mower |
| mower |
| saw |
| mower |
| tractor |

It contains duplicate values because several rows from the source table are selected, containing identical values. Often you may be interested in knowing only which types of tools are available for rent, independently of how many tools of the same type there are. What is needed then is a way to specify that duplicate values should be eliminated in the answer. SQL provides a construct to that effect: the word **distinct** at the beginning of the projection list. For example,

> **select distinct** TYPE                                 [4.11]
> **from** TOOL

returns the result

| TYPE |
| --- |
| mower |
| saw |
| tractor |

The word **distinct** applies to the whole projection list. For example, the statement below selects from CONTRACT the names of the customers and the days on which they rented at least one tool.

> **select distinct** CUSTOMER, DATE_OUT                    [4.12]
> **from** CONTRACT

| CUSTOMER | DATE_OUT |
|----------|----------|
| Adams, A. | 1986-05-15 |
| Adams, A. | 1986-06-11 |
| Smith, J. | 1986-05-23 |
| Wilson, P. | 1986-05-15 |
| Wilson, P. | 1986-06-22 |

Without **distinct** the last row would appear twice.

# 4.2  Filters

A filter is any expression that evaluates to true or false.  The **where** clause of a **select** statement specifies the filter that is applied to all rows of the table specified in the **from** clause.  When the filter evaluates to true, the row is considered (and a result row is computed according to the select list); otherwise it is discarded.

## 4.2.1  Simple comparison expression

The simplest form of a filter is a comparison between either the value of a column and a constant or between two columns.  For example, the following statement retrieves all information about tool 2:

**select** *                                                                    [4.13]
**from** TOOL
**where** NUMBER = 2

| NUMBER | TYPE | PURCH_DATE | PURCH_PRICE | RENTAL_FEE |
|--------|------|------------|-------------|------------|
| 2 | mower | 1986-05-22 | 495.00 | 11.95 |

Similarly, the following statement retrieves all "same day" contracts:

**select** *                                                                    [4.14]
**from** CONTRACT
**where** DATE_IN = DATE_OUT

| CONTRACT | CUSTOMER | TOOL | DATE_OUT | DATE_IN | FEE |
|----------|----------|------|----------|---------|-----|
| 98 | Adams, A. | 2 | 1986-05-15 | 1986-05-15 | 11.95 |

Inequalities can also be used. For example, find information on tools with a purchase price greater than 250:

**select** *                                                                                    [4.15]
**from** TOOL
**where** PURCH_PRICE > 250

| NUMBER | TYPE | PURCH_DATE | PURCH_PRICE | RENTAL_FEE |
|---|---|---|---|---|
| 1 | mower | 1986-07-19 | 550.70 | 12.30 |
| 2 | mower | 1986-05-22 | 495.00 | 11.95 |
| 4 | mower | 1987-07-14 | 685.10 | 14.20 |
| 5 | tractor | 1987-09-21 | 2363.67 | 48.85 |

The valid inequality operators are >, <, >=, and <=; the <, >, and = operators can be negated by preceding them with ¬ or ! (read 'not') depending upon the implementation. If A = B is true, then A != B is false. The operator <> is also used in some implementations instead of ¬=. Note that all comparison operators apply to all data types. Some additional operators are provided for character strings and dates.

## 4.2.2 Operators on character strings

All comparison operators apply to character strings. In addition, SQL introduces some operators that apply exclusively to character strings.

It is often useful to search for a character string that approximately matches a given constant. For example, one may hesitate on the spelling of a customer name. Is it Adam or Adams? SQL provides a **like** operator to that effect. The following query selects the customers who have names starting with Adam:

**select** *                                                                                    [4.16]
**from** CUSTOMER
**where** NAME **like** 'Adam%'

| NAME | ADDRESS | ZIP |
|---|---|---|
| Adams, A. | 123 Pine St, San Jose CA | 95125 |

The character '%' matches any character string. In contrast, the character '_' matches any single character.

A%B matches AX$ZB and AB
%A  matches M2A and A
A_B matches AXB
A_B does not match AXYB nor AB
A_ matches AX but not A

For example, if you need to retrieve information for customer Wilson or Wilsen, you simply write

**select** *                                                             [4.17]
**from** CUSTOMER
**where** NAME **like** 'Wils_n,%'

| NAME | ADDRESS | ZIP |
|------|---------|-----|
| Wilson, P. | 553 Cedar St, NEW YORK, NY | 10010 |

In addition to **like**, some SQL products provide other powerful operators to transform character string values: conversion to uppercase, shortening, and even operators that support a phonetic representation.

## 4.2.3 Operators on dates

All comparison operators work also on dates. SQL provides additional functions, however, that are specific to dates. For example, to search for rentals of duration greater than 2 days, you can write

**select** CUSTOMER, DATE_OUT, DATE_IN                                   [4.18]
**from** CONTRACT
**where** DATE_IN - DATE_OUT > 2

| CUSTOMER | DATE_OUT | DATE_IN |
|----------|----------|---------|
| Wilson, P. | 1986-06-22 | 1986-06-25 |
| Wilson, P. | 1986-06-22 | 1986-06-28 |
| Adams, A. | 1986-06-11 | 1986-07-13 |

A duration can be added or subtracted from a date. The support for operations on dates varies greatly from one implementation to another. In some implementations, a duration can be expressed in days, months, or years, using the corresponding SQL keyword. Example [4.18] can then be rephrased as

**select** CUSTOMER, DATE_OUT, DATE_IN                                   [4.19]
**from** CONTRACT
**where** DATE_IN > DATE_OUT + 2 DAYS

## 4.2.4 Expressions

All previous examples of filters are of the form

```
operand     comparison_operator     operand
```

where operands are column values or constants. But operands can also be expressions which, when evaluated, yield values of appropriate types. As in the projection list these expressions are constructed like algebraic expressions, using +, -, *, and / on numerical values or character operators on character strings. The statement below retrieves the identification number of the tools that are amortized in less than 4 weeks of rental (we used 4*7 instead of 28 for illustration).

**select** *                                                                                    [4.20]
**from** TOOL
**where** PURCH_PRICE/RENTAL_FEE <= 4 * 7

| NUMBER | TYPE | PURCH_DATE | PURCH_PRICE | RENTAL_FEE |
|--------|------|------------|-------------|------------|
| 3 | saw | 1986-11-15 | 105.50 | 6.00 |

This completes the analysis of simple comparison filters of the form

```
expression     comparison_operator     expression
```

SQL also supports two other forms of filters:

```
expression BETWEEN expression_1 AND expression_2
```

and

```
expression IN (  ──┬── value ──┬──  )
                   └─◄─ , ─◄─┘
```

## 4.2.5  Using between

**Between** is used to check if a value falls inside a given range. The **between** operator yields true if the value of the left operand falls inside the range determined by the two right operands. For example, the statement

**select** *                                                                                    [4.21]
**from** TOOL
**where** PURCH_PRICE **between** 250 **and** 500

asks for tools with a purchase price $\geq 250$ but $\leq 500$; it yields the result

| NUMBER | TYPE | PURCH_DATE | PURCH_PRICE | RENTAL_FEE |
|--------|------|------------|-------------|------------|
| 2 | mower | 1986-05-22 | 495.00 | 11.95 |

The three operands can also be general expressions.

## 4.2.6 The in operator

A data element in a column can also be matched against a list of values. The following expression finds the tools that are either 'mower' or 'saw':

**select** *                                                                [4.22]
**from** TOOL
**where** TYPE **in** ('mower','saw')

| NUMBER | TYPE | PURCH_DATE | PURCH_PRICE | RENTAL_FEE |
|---|---|---|---|---|
| 1 | mower | 1986-07-19 | 550.70 | 12.30 |
| 2 | mower | 1986-05-22 | 495.00 | 11.95 |
| 3 | saw | 1986-11-15 | 105.50 | 6.00 |
| 4 | mower | 1987-07-14 | 685.10 | 14.20 |

## 4.2.7 Complex filters

In all the above examples, the filters contain only a single comparison operator; this is hardly enough to express complex conditions. In fact, you can use the logical operators **and**, **or**, and **not**, together with parentheses, to develop complex filters, exactly as you would in classical algebra. Just take a minute to understand the following example:

**select** NUMBER, TYPE                                                      [4.23]
**from** TOOL
**where** TYPE = 'mower'
    **and** PURCH_DATE > '1/1/1987'
    **and not** (PURCH_PRICE < 500 **or** RENTAL_FEE < 11)

| NUMBER | TYPE |
|---|---|
| 4 | mower |

## 4.2.8 Effect of null

You may have asked yourself the question, what happens to a comparison involving a **null** as operand? To be able to select rows based on null values, SQL provides a predicate called **is null**. To retrieve all outstanding contracts (that is, with a **null** FEE), you write

**select** *                                                    [4.24]
**from** CONTRACT
**where** FEE **is null**

| CONTRACT | CUSTOMER | TOOL | DATE_OUT | DATE_IN | FEE |
|---|---|---|---|---|---|
| 101 | Wilson, P. | 3 | 1986-06-22 | 1986-06-28 | ? |
| 102 | Adams, A. | 1 | 1986-06-11 | 1986-07-13 | ? |

Another interesting question is, how does a **null** value compare to any other value? Assume there is one single comparison in the filter. Its evaluation will yield one of three answers: true, false, or unknown. When the comparison involves only values which are not null, the answer is clearly true or false. When at least one of the operands is null, the answer is unknown. Only rows for which the predicate evaluates to true are included in the result.

Things become more complex when logical operators are used in a complex filter. First, the negation operator (**not**) can be used to refer to the negation of a logical value; if the value is true (false), its negation is false (true). If the result of a comparison is unknown, the negation of that result is also unknown. When **or** and **and** conjunctions are used to combine logically the results of simple (or complex) predicates, the answer is determined according to a "three-value" algebra, as shown in Figure 17.

The implication of **null** values will be studied later for each specific SQL operation.

| One operand is: | Other operand is: | **and** | **or** |
|---|---|---|---|
| false | false | false | false |
| false | true | false | true |
| true | true | true | true |
| unknown | unknown | unknown | unknown |
| unknown | false | false | unknown |
| unknown | true | unknown | true |

**Figure 17. Conjunctions with NULL values**

# 4.3 Program interface

We now go back to the problem of embedding **select** statements in a program. Embedding means not only being able to insert an SQL statement in a program; it also implies the possibility of using program variables inside the

```
exec sql include sqlca
exec sql begin declare section
        declare number Tool_no
        declare string Tool_type
        declare number Tool_fee
exec sql end declare section

read Tool_no  /* specify the tool to be retrieved */

exec sql select TYPE, RENTAL_FEE
        into :Tool_type, :Tool_fee
        from TOOL
        where NUMBER = :Tool_no

/* process the result of the query */
display Tool_type, Tool_fee
```

**Figure 18. Getting information on one specific tool**

statement.   The use of such variables to parameterize the statement was covered in Chapter 3. But variables are also used to return the result of a query to the program so that it may be further processed or simply output. The mechanism has two flavors depending upon the fact that the statement is known to return exactly one row or not.  Of course, if there is a single row in the answer, you will get one, whichever flavor you use.

## 4.3.1 One-row query

The result of a query returning a single row can be obtained by executing a single **select** statement.  For example, the program in Figure 18 prints the type and rental fee for a given tool.  The declaration section defines three program variables; *Tool_no* is used to store the tool number for which the **select** statement will be executed.  *Tool_type* and *Tool_fee* are program variables used to return the results.  The **select** statement is actually executed at the place in which it occurs in the program, and its execution fills the variables specified in the **into** clause with the values in the result row.  The sequence of variables in the **into** clause is in a one-to-one correspondence with the sequence in the projection list.

Assume you execute the program for tool number 3. The execution of the **select** statement will put 'saw' in *Tool_type* and 6.00 in *Tool_fee*. If for any reason there are no rows or more than one row in the result, an error occurs.

## 4.3.2 Multiple-row query

When the result of a query contains more than one row, a *cursor* is used to access one row after another, in a mechanism very similar to the reading of a file in many data processing systems.

Consider the program in Figure 19, which retrieves the number and type of each tool.

Statement (1) gives a name to the result (the cursor) of a **select** statement. This name is only used to bind the declaration of the statement with the **exec sql fetch** used to retrieve the result rows. Statement (1) is not executed; it is only declarative. Statement (2) is also declarative; it specifies where the program should branch to when all rows of the result have been obtained. Statement (3) starts the evaluation of the result. At this point the system gathers the parameters submitted in program variables; the query is fully known, and its evaluation begins. The **exec sql open**, however, does not return any row. Instead, the **exec sql fetch** statement in (4) is the only one that returns result rows. Each time the **exec sql fetch** is executed, it refreshes the variables specified in the **into** clause with the values of the next row in the result table. (Remember: the order of the rows is arbitrary.)

In the example, the first invocation of **exec sql fetch** may return 1, 'mower'; the second invocation of **exec sql fetch**, 2, 'mower', the third, 3, 'saw', and so on. Since there are only five rows in the result the sixth **exec sql fetch** invocation will raise the **not found** condition and control will be transferred to *cursor_end* (5) where the cursor can be closed. The only actions generally supported in a **whenever not found** statement are **go to** and **continue**. In some implementations, a test for the **not found** return code is generated after every SQL statement, if a **whenever not found go to** is active. Statement (5) deactivates the **whenever** condition set by statement (2). It is always good practice to deactivate a **whenever** condition when it is not needed anymore. Statement (6) closes the cursor.

## 4.3.3 Retrieving null values

If a **null** value is expected in a selected column, an *indicator variable* must be provided for that column. For example, if the type of a tool could be **null**, statement (4) of Figure 19 should be changed into

```
            exec sql include sqlca
            exec sql begin declare section
                declare number Tool_no
                declare string Tool_type
            exec sql end declare section

(1)         exec sql declare C1 cursor for
                select NUMBER, TYPE
                from TOOL

(2)         exec sql whenever not found go to cursor_end

(3)         exec sql open C1

            do forever
(4)             exec sql fetch C1 into :Tool_no, :Tool_type
                process result
                end

            cursor_end:
(5)         exec sql whenever not found continue
(6)         exec sql close C1
```

**Figure 19. A program to read the table TOOL**

$$\text{exec sql fetch } C1 \text{ into } :Tool\_no, :Tool\_type:T \qquad\qquad [4.25]$$

where an additional program variable $T$ is used as an indicator variable associated with *Tool_type*. The indicator variable $T$ must be declared in the SQL **declare section** as a small integer. Note that the indicator variable is written immediately after the main variable with only a colon (:). If the execution of **exec sql fetch** returns a row with an actual value for the tool type, the variable *Tool_type* will contain it and the indicator variable $T$ will be set to 0. If the tool type is null, the value of *Tool_type* will be irrelevant, but the indicator variable $T$ will be set to -1.

The same indicator variable is also used to indicate truncation. If the program variable is too short to contain the full length of the data element, the extra characters are not returned; but the indicator variable will be set to a positive integer showing how many characters have been truncated.

# 4.4 Aggregates

In the **select** statements described up to now in this chapter, there is a one-to-one correspondence between the rows of the source table (that satisfy the conditions) and the rows of the result table. But this is not always the case. In fact, very often, SQL is used to extract aggregate values out of the database, rather than detailed information. For example, it may be more interesting to retrieve the average of some quantities rather than the set of all quantities.

If SQL did not provide such a facility, the only way to extract, say, the average PURCH_PRICE in table TOOL would be to execute a program similar to the one in Figure 19. It would fetch PURCH_PRICE for each row and compute the average. Instead, you can simply write

> **select avg**(PURCH_PRICE)                                      [4.26]
> **from** TOOL

| AVG(PURCH_PRICE) |
|---|
| 839.9940 |

The aggregation facility allows you to compute aggregate functions without explicitly reading all rows; the result comprises a single row. Internally, the system will most probably have to scan all rows, but it generally does it more efficiently since it does not have to return each to the program. In addition, you save yourself the effort of writing a program involving a cursor.

## 4.4.1 General aggregation

Example [4.26] illustrates the selection of an aggregate value computed on a column of a table.

The available aggregate functions vary from one system to another, but the basic set of **count**, **sum**, **avg**, **max**, and **min** is always available (**avg** is an abbreviation of average). The syntax for **count** is slightly different: the "expression" can be only an asterisk. The statement below simply counts the number of TOOL rows that satisfy the condition:

> **select count**(*)                                               [4.27]
> **from** TOOL
> **where** TYPE = 'mower'

| COUNT(*) |
|----------|
| 3 |

Computing an aggregate value on a single column is very common; but, in its general form, aggregation also works on expressions. Moreover, since the result of an aggregation is a value, it can itself be used inside an expression in a projection list. In fact, the general syntax of a projection list containing aggregate functions is as follows:

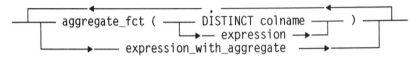

Both examples below illustrate respectively aggregation on expressions and expressions on aggregation (on a single column or on expression). The first computes the number of tools and the average rental fee of all tools; the second computes the difference between two quantities: the maximum and the minimum ratio of the rental fee over the purchase price.

**select count(*), avg(RENTAL_FEE)**                            [4.28]
**from** TOOL

| COUNT(*) | AVG(RENTAL_FEE) |
|----------|-----------------|
| 5 | 18.6600 |

**select max(PURCH_PRICE/RENTAL_FEE)**                          [4.29]
    **- min(PURCH_PRICE/RENTAL_FEE)**
**from** TOOL

| MAX(PURCH_PRICE/RENTAL_FEE)-MIN(PURCH_PRICE/RENTAL_FEE) |
|--------------------------------------------------------|
| 30.8030 |

The aggregate functions **max** and **min** return the value of some element. When both are used in the same **select** statement, they generally return values from different rows. The following statement finds the maximum and the minimum rental fee of tools.

**select max(RENTAL_FEE), min(RENTAL_FEE)**                     [4.30]
**from** TOOL

| MAX(RENTAL_FEE) | MIN(RENTAL_FEE) |
|---|---|
| 48.85 | 6.00 |

Statement [4.27] counts the number of rows in TOOL; no column name is specified. But you may, instead, be interested in counting the number of distinct types of tools only. This is where the keyword **distinct** comes into play, as illustrated in example [4.31]:

> **select count(distinct** TYPE)　　　　　　　　　　　　　　[4.31]
> **from** TOOL

| COUNT(DISTINCT TYPE) |
|---|
| 3 |

## 4.4.2 Aggregation with null values

The presence of null values in a column over which aggregate functions are computed may affect the result. You need to be careful and make sure you know what the SQL conventions are in that respect:

- **Count(\*)** does not look at a particular column. Its result is therefore not influenced by the presence of null values. The statement

> **select count(\*)**　　　　　　　　　　　　　　　　　　　[4.32]
> **from** CONTRACT

 returns 6.

- **Count(distinct** column_name) does not count the **null** values. Thus, the result is the number of distinct values, not including **null**. The statement

> **select count(distinct** FEE)　　　　　　　　　　　　　　[4.33]
> **from** CONTRACT

 returns 4.

- **Sum**(column_name) (and other aggregate functions which actually compute a number from the contents of a column) discard any **null** value. The answer to

> **select avg**(FEE)　　　　　　　　　　　　　　　　　　　[4.34]
> **from** CONTRACT

is (18 + 11.95 + 24.60 + 0) / 4 = 13.64.

If the aggregate function is computed on a set of values which are all **null**, the answer is itself **null**.

- The effect of **null** values can be altered by using the **value** function. For example, **avg**(**value**(column_name, default_value)) interprets all **null** values as having the same specified default value. The result of

    **select avg**(**value**(FEE,20))              [4.35]
    **from** CONTRACT

is (18 + 11.95 + 24.60 + 0 + 20 + 20) / 6 = 15.76.

## 4.5 Group by

In the previous section, aggregate functions were used to compute statistics on a single set of rows, either all rows in a table (if there is no **where** clause) or on the set of qualifying rows. It is often useful to compute the same statistics on different groups of records rather than on the whole set. For example, it may be interesting to compute the average rental fee of all tools, but it may be still more interesting to compute, for each type, the average rental fee of tools of that type. SQL provides a **group by** clause to obtain these group statistics in a single SQL query. The statement reads like

    **select** TYPE, **avg**(RENTAL_FEE)             [4.36]
    **from** TOOL
    **group by** TYPE

| TYPE | AVG(RENTAL_FEE) |
|---------|-----------------|
| mower | 12.8166 |
| saw | 6.0000 |
| tractor | 48.8500 |

The meaning is as follows: the operation groups the rows of the TOOL table by type and applies the aggregate function to each group of rows; the number of rows in the result is equal to the number of unique values of TYPE. Note that the projection list may only specify aggregate functions and/or the name of the column(s) on which grouping is done. The other columns probably have different values inside a group; therefore, there is no single value to be returned, but a set; and this is contradictory to the idea of aggregate. In the example, the group is on TYPE; so TYPE can appear in the projection list (but neither PURCH_PRICE nor RENTAL_FEE can).

Instead of grouping on the values of a single column, it is also possible to group on several columns. The statement below finds how many tools each customer checked out during a day.

> **select** CUSTOMER, **count(\*)**                              [4.37]
> **from** CONTRACT
> **group by** CUSTOMER, DATE_OUT

| CUSTOMER | COUNT(*) |
|----------|----------|
| Adams, A. | 1 |
| Adams, A. | 1 |
| Smith, J. | 1 |
| Wilson, P. | 1 |
| Wilson, P. | 2 |

Note that ADAMS and WILSON appear twice because of different values of DATE_OUT.

The result of an aggregate can be used to further restrict the result table. Suppose you are interested in the result of [4.36] but you want to restrict the result to those rows corresponding to groups that contain at least two rows. Just take a minute to convince yourself that such a restriction cannot be expressed with a **where** clause and, in fact, requires a new construct called **having**. You can write

> **select** CUSTOMER, **count(\*)**                              [4.38]
> **from** CONTRACT
> **group by** CUSTOMER, DATE_OUT
> **having count(\*)** > 1

| CUSTOMER | COUNT(*) |
|----------|----------|
| Wilson, P. | 2 |

The **having** clause is syntactically similar to the **where** clause. But instead of acting on the rows in the table, it acts on the aggregate rows. For that reason, **having** filters always contain aggregate functions.

In summary, the general syntax of the **group by** clause is

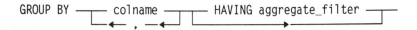

```
GROUP BY ──┬── colname ──┬─┬── HAVING aggregate_filter ──┬──
           └──◄── , ──◄──┘ └──────────────►──────────────┘
```

An aggregate filter is in general a logical expression on simple aggregate comparisons. A simple aggregate comparison involves aggregates on column or on expression of column values and constants. For example, the following is a valid statement:

> **select** TYPE, **avg**(RENTAL_FEE)                                    [4.39]
> **from** TOOL
> **group by** TYPE
> **having count**(*) > 2
>         **or** (**max**(PURCH_PRICE) > 1000 **and avg**(RENTAL_FEE) > 12.00)

| TYPE | AVG(RENTAL_FEE) |
|------|-----------------|
| mower | 12.8166 |
| tractor | 48.8500 |

For grouping purpose, all the **null** values in a grouping column are considered equal. In other words, the **null** value in a grouping column will appear once if there are one or more **null** in that column. For example,

> **select** FEE, **count**(*)                                    [4.40]
> **from** CONTRACT
> **group by** FEE

| FEE | COUNT(*) |
|-----|----------|
| 0.00 | 1 |
| 11.95 | 1 |
| 18.00 | 1 |
| 24.60 | 1 |
| ? | 2 |

# 4.6  Order by

Sometimes it is convenient to return the resulting rows of a **select** in a specified order. The **order by** feature provides sorting as part of the **select** statement itself. The syntax is as follows:

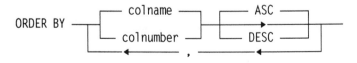

The result is sorted on the specified column values or on a sort key defined on several columns. For example,

**select** NUMBER, TYPE, RENTAL_FEE                                   [4.41]
**from** TOOL
**where** RENTAL_FEE < 30
**order by** TYPE, NUMBER

orders the resulting row first on the tool type and, under a same type, on the tool number. The answer is

| NUMBER | TYPE | RENTAL_FEE |
|---|---|---|
| 1 | mower | 12.30 |
| 2 | mower | 11.95 |
| 4 | mower | 14.20 |
| 3 | saw | 6.00 |

When an **order by** clause is applied to a column which is not a simple column (but rather a computed column or an aggregate), the column can be named by its position in the **select** list. The following example is similar to [4.36], but the result is ordered by decreasing values of the average rental fee.

**select** TYPE, **avg**(RENTAL_FEE)                                   [4.42]
**from** TOOL
**group by** TYPE
**order by** 2 **desc**

| TYPE | AVG(RENTAL_FEE) |
|---|---|
| tractor | 48.8500 |
| mower | 12.8166 |
| saw | 6.0000 |

If [4.42] is embedded in a program, the succession of **exec sql fetch** calls will return the rows in that order.

# 4.7 Summary

Chapter 4 covers the single table query facilities of SQL. The querying power of a **select** statement comes from its options for the select list, the multiple filtering capabilities, and the ordering and grouping features.

Given a particular need for information, which kind of **select** feature do you need? In fact, once there is only one table, the choice is rather straightforward.

If you need detailed information (information corresponding to individual rows of the source table), then you do not use any aggregate function or **group by**:

the number of rows in the result will be equal to the number of rows in the source table that satisfy the filtering expression. The filter can be any simple logical expression or complex logical expression that combines simple logical expressions. A simple logical expression is a comparison which returns true or false. Both operands of the comparison can be algebraic expressions computed on column values and/or constants.

The format of the answer and the type of its columns are entirely determined by the list of expressions which constitute the projection list. Each expression in the projection list, again, can be as simple as a constant or a column value; it can also be a complex algebraic expression on column values and/or constants.

If you want information that is the result of an aggregation on the whole table, you use the aggregate functions provided by SQL. You can compute aggregates simply on column values or on expressions. You can compute several aggregate functions or several expressions on the same or different aggregate function in a single **select**. For performance reasons, this is much better than using two different **select** statements since the system will have to look at all rows only once.

The **group by** feature works exactly as an aggregation, except that the aggregation is done on groups of rows rather than on the whole table. Therefore, the answer contains one row per group instead of simply one row.

In this chapter we also discussed the invocation of the **select** statement from a program. If you can perform your task by issuing one statement or a sequence of statements from the terminal, and if all you want to do with the answer is to display it on the screen or print it as a report, then you will most probably use a query product. But if you need the power of a program to compute the parameters of a query or to manipulate the answer, you will have to write your own program. All **select** features are available in both cases: although most examples show the SQL queries as you would type them in a query product, they could all be embedded in a program as well. You would use a one-row **select** for an aggregate; you would use a cursor for a **group by** since more than one row is generally returned.

Finally, it is important to note that some specific information can be retrieved from the database using different methods. We mention the fact that you could, in a program, easily compute an aggregate value by selecting all rows and computing the aggregate yourself. This is harder and also much less efficient. In general, if you find a way of expressing what you want in a single SQL statement, by all means use it: it is probably your best bet.

# 4.8 Exercises

The exercises use the database application described in Chapter 2.

**4.1.** List the student names.

**4.2.** Retrieve the student numbers and grades (on a scale of 0 to 100) for all rows in RECORDS.

**4.3.** Retrieve the class numbers of all the classes which have prerequisite(s).

**4.4.** Find the student identification of all students who had at least one grade lower than 4.0. Show only the student numbers.

**4.5.** Which classes have a subject starting with 'Introduction'? Which classes are programming classes?

**4.6.** Student 1342 wants to enroll in a class which requires successful completion of classes 123 and 130. Find the grades that he obtained in these classes.

**4.7.** Write a program which retrieves the grades of a given student. The student name is read from the terminal. Assume each student has a different name.

**4.8.** Using a single **select** statement, compute the average grade of student 4742 and count the number of classes she attended in the past or is attending this year. Do the same thing again, excluding from the answer the classes for which the grade is not known.

**4.9.** Compute the average grade of each student, and convert the result to a scale of 0 to 100. List the students in order of decreasing merit.

**4.10.** Find the students (student numbers) who have enrolled in more than one class in any year.

# Chapter 5

# Complex Queries

In Chapter 4, we showed the general form of a **select** statement containing a single **select** keyword and, possibly, several table names in the **from** clause. However, we mentioned that we would temporarily restrict our attention to queries with a single table name. We now remove that restriction and consider complex queries that refer to several tables.

There are actually three types of constructs that enable you to refer to multiple tables in a single query:

1. A reference to multiple table names in the **from** clause: the general syntax is shown in Chapter 4, and the operation expressed in such a way is called a *join*.

2. The use of the result of another query as a constant in a **where** clause. Consider the query

```
select ...                                                    [5.1]
from ...
where ...  = X
       ...
```

The value of $X$ can itself be computed as the result of a query, as in

```
select ...                                          [5.2]
from ...
where ...  =
       ( select ...
       from ...
       where ...)
              ...
```

The query in the **where** clause is called an *embedded* query, or *subquery*.

3. Finally, the use of a **union** keyword to specify that the result table is the union of the result tables of two or more queries, as in

```
select ...                                          [5.3]
union
select ...
```

In this chapter, we first study these three constructs separately, and then use them together to form queries of arbitrary complexity.

# 5.1 The concept of join

Let us first introduce the notion of *column matching*, which is the essence of a join.

Suppose that we are interested in the list of contracts and that we want to see, for each contract, the type of tool (instead of just its number). We clearly need to access the table CONTRACT; but, since only TOOL contains the tool type, it needs to be accessed too. In fact, we need to take the tool number in a CONTRACT row and find the row in TOOL that contains the same tool number. This row is said to *match* the contract row, according to equality between values in CONTRACT.TOOL and values in TOOL.NUMBER. These two columns are called *matching columns*.

If we were forced to solve this problem by relying only on elementary queries, we would have to write a program as shown in Figure 20. The program first uses a cursor to access the rows of CONTRACT and retrieve, among other data elements, the tool number (column TOOL) into a program variable called *Tool_no*. Then, it issues another **select** statement, this time on table TOOL, using the value of *Tool_no* in the **where** clause, in order to select the matching TOOL row. Note that, since a tool number uniquely identifies a single row in TOOL, there is no need for a cursor on table TOOL.

```
exec sql include sqlca
exec sql begin declare section
      declare number Tool_no
      declare string Tool_type
      declare number Contract_no
exec sql end declare section

exec sql declare CUR_CONTRACT cursor for
      select CONTRACT, TOOL
      from CONTRACT

exec sql whenever not found go to The_end

exec sql open CUR_CONTRACT
do forever
      exec sql fetch CUR_CONTRACT
            into  :Contract_no, :Tool_no

      exec sql select TYPE
            into :Tool_type
            from TOOL
            where NUMBER = :Tool_no

      process contract and tool information
      end
The_end:
exec sql whenever not found continue
exec sql close CUR_CONTRACT
```

**Figure 20. Exploiting matching columns (from CONTRACT to TOOL)**

Now, consider the program in Figure 21. How does it compare with the previous one? It opens a cursor on TOOL and, for each tool, scans the table CONTRACT to find the matching rows. Since more than one CONTRACT row may contain the same tool number, there will generally be several such rows that match a single TOOL row, forcing the use of a cursor to retrieve them all.

Clearly, both programs yield the same answer; and this answer is precisely the result of a join between the tables CONTRACT and TOOL, with a matching condition CONTRACT.TOOL = TOOL.NUMBER.   Theoretically, a join

```
        exec sql include sqlca
        exec sql begin declare section
            declare number Tool_no
            declare string Tool_type
            declare number Contract_no
        exec sql end declare section

        exec sql declare CUR_TOOL cursor for
            select NUMBER, TYPE
            from TOOL

        exec sql declare CUR_CONTRACT cursor for
            select CONTRACT
            from CONTRACT
            where TOOL = :Tool_no

        exec sql whenever not found go to The_end

        exec sql open CUR_TOOL

        do forever
            exec sql fetch CUR_TOOL
                into :Tool_no, :Tool_type

(1)        /**** here we have the tool data ****/
           process tool information

            exec sql whenever not found go to End_tool

            exec sql open CUR_CONTRACT
            do forever
                exec sql fetch CUR_CONTRACT
                    into :Contract_no

                process contract information
                end
        End_tool:
```

**Figure 21. Matching columns (from TOOL to CONTRACT) (Part 1)**

```
            exec sql whenever not found continue
            exec sql close CUR_CONTRACT

        end
The_end:

    exec sql close CUR_TOOL
```

**Figure 21. Matching columns (from TOOL to CONTRACT) (Part 2)**

between table A and table B is a subset of the Cartesian product of A and B
(A × B); the Cartesian product is the set of composite rows obtained by taking
any row of A and concatenating it with any row of B; and the subset is
obtained by keeping only the composite rows that satisfy the join predicate. A
detailed example was given in Chapter 1, Figure 11; the operation is summarized in Figure 22. For example, consider the program in Figure 21 again.
Two embedded *do* loops produce all combinations of CONTRACT and TOOL
rows, but only the composite rows that satisfy the join predicate
CONTRACT.TOOL = TOOL.NUMBER are kept.

Computing the result of a join by program has drawbacks. First, you have to
write a program; second, it is not clear which of both possible programs would
perform better. In fact, deciding which program is more efficient is hard if you

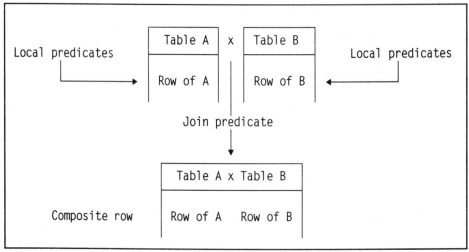

**Figure 22. Concatenation of rows in a join**

are not familiar with the internal details. Moreover, the best choice may vary as the database changes with time. It is to avoid these problems that SQL provides an explicit construct for specifying a join at a higher, less procedural level. The construct simply uses the normal **select** operation, allowing for multiple table names, as in

> **select** CONTRACT, CUSTOMER, TOOL, DATE_OUT,                [5.4]
>         NUMBER, TYPE
> **from** CONTRACT, TOOL
> **where** CONTRACT.TOOL = TOOL.NUMBER

| CONTRACT | CUSTOMER | TOOL | DATE_OUT | NUMBER | TYPE |
|---|---|---|---|---|---|
| 99 | Smith, J. | 1 | 1986-05-23 | 1 | mower |
| 102 | Adams, A. | 1 | 1986-06-11 | 1 | mower |
| 98 | Adams, A. | 2 | 1986-05-15 | 2 | mower |
| 100 | Wilson, P. | 2 | 1986-06-22 | 2 | mower |
| 101 | Wilson, P. | 3 | 1986-06-22 | 3 | saw |
| 97 | Wilson, P. | 3 | 1986-05-15 | 3 | saw |

The **from** clause specifies the tables to be joined; the **where** clause specifies the join predicate, while the **select** list specifies which fields need to be retrieved from CONTRACT and from TOOL.

The only predicate that appears in the **where** clause of statement [5.4] is a join predicate. In all generality, a **where** clause may contain more than one join predicate in addition to an arbitrary number of predicates that involve a single table (also called *local* predicates). The example of join given in Chapter 1 already illustrated that fact. Also, the following statement shows a where clause with one join predicate and two local predicates. In fact, we make the difference between these two types of predicates only for the sake of explanation. Actually, they are all predicates that apply to the Cartesian product of the various tables named in the **from** clause.

> **select** NUMBER, CONTRACT                                         [5.5]
> **from** TOOL, CONTRACT
> **where** TOOL.NUMBER = CONTRACT.TOOL
>         **and** CONTRACT.FEE > 20
>         **and** TOOL.TYPE = 'mower'

| NUMBER | CONTRACT |
|---|---|
| 1 | 99 |

## 5.1.1 Remarks

- The high-level join construct hides all asymmetry of the implementation. A join is commutative; that is,

      A join B = B join A

  Therefore, the order in which the names appear in the **from** clause is irrelevant.

- The notion of join generalizes in a straightforward manner to more than two tables. To perform a join between A, B and C, two tables are first joined; then the result is joined with the third table. The join operation is also associative. Therefore,

      (A join B) join C = A join (B join C) = B join (A join C)...

  and, again, the order in which the names appear in the **from** clause is irrelevant.

- In [5.4], all column names specified in the **select** list are unambiguous. Therefore, it is not necessary to qualify the column name with the table name. If the names were not unique across the various tables involved in the join, qualified column names should be used as in

      **select** CONTRACT.CONTRACT,... TOOL.NUMBER,...

- Instead of [5.4], consider

      **select** *                                                    [5.6]
      **from** CONTRACT, TOOL
      **where** CONTRACT.TOOL = TOOL.NUMBER

  Here an asterisk is used in the **select** list. Since the table specified in the **from** clause is the product of two tables, the asterisk specifies that we are interested in all columns of this product, which itself means that we are interested in all columns of both tables. Exactly as an asterisk in a single table query returns all columns in the canonical order, here all columns from the first table (CONTRACT) are returned in their canonical order, followed by all columns from the second table (TOOL), also in their canonical order. This is the only case where the order of the tables in the **from** clause is significant.

## 5.1.2 Null values in join

As mentioned in the previous chapter, **null** never successfully compares to anything. Thus, the rows containing **null** in the join column do not appear in the result of the join. The following query retrieves the contracts with a fee greater than twice the rental fee of the corresponding tool.

> **select** CONTRACT.CONTRACT [5.7]
> **from** CONTRACT, TOOL
> **where** CONTRACT.TOOL = TOOL.NUMBER
> **and** CONTRACT.FEE > 2 * TOOL.RENTAL_FEE

The first **where** condition is clearly a join predicate; the second condition is also a join predicate although it uses an inequality operator. Contracts 101 and 102 are not considered because FEE is null.

# 5.2 Uses of joins

Since SQL combines the selection of rows and the join operation in the same **select** statement, it provides a single, very concise notation for a broad range of queries. Although it is a single construct, it has various effects depending upon the conditions in which it is used. The following sections classify some of these uses in five categories:

- Cartesian product
- Decoding join
- Multiplicative join
- Selective join
- Inequality join

## 5.2.1 Cartesian product

We defined the join as a subset of the ***Cartesian product*** of two tables where the subset is obtained by applying a join predicate. It is possible, however, to omit the predicate. In this case, the result will contain all possible combinations of rows. If A contains $N_a$ rows, B, $N_b$ rows, and C, $N_c$ rows, then the Cartesian product is obtained by writing

> **select** *                                                              [5.8]
> **from** A, B, C

and the number of rows in the results is $N_a \times N_b \times N_c$ (generally a very large number). This form of join is very rarely used; but it is important to understand its meaning since it is the base for all joins. Also, predicates may be omitted by mistake, and the system will not complain. The following is a valid statement:

> **select** *                                                              [5.9]
> **from** CONTRACT, TOOL

The result of this statement is shown in Figure 23.

## 5.2.2  Decoding join

Refer to [5.4] and recall that we arrived at that query because we wanted to list the contracts. But, instead of just printing the tool numbers, we wanted to show the tool type, an information that is stored in the TOOL table. The semantics of the data are such that any tool number that appears in the column CONTRACT.TOOL must exist in TOOL.NUMBER in one and only one row (TOOL.NUMBER is a key column in TOOL). In other words, there will always be one and only one row in TOOL that matches any row in CONTRACT. Therefore, the result contains a row for each CONTRACT row, with each of these result rows containing information about a contract and about its tool. It is as if we had decoded the tool number and replaced it with the tool information; hence the name of *decoding join*. A decoding join introduces redundancy in the result by repeating the tool information for each row related to that tool.

It may be worthwhile to give another example. Assume you want to write a report which contains for each contract the tool type and daily fee, as well as the name and address of the customer, in addition to the contract attributes. The following SQL statement provides the answer:

> **select** CONTRACT.CONTRACT, CONTRACT.FEE,                              [5.10]
>           TOOL.TYPE, TOOL.RENTAL_FEE,
>           CUSTOMER.NAME, CUSTOMER.ADDRESS
> **from** CONTRACT, TOOL, CUSTOMER
> **where** CONTRACT.CUSTOMER = CUSTOMER.NAME
>      **and** CONTRACT.TOOL = TOOL.NUMBER

| CON-TRACT | FEE | TYPE | RENTAL FEE | NAME | ADDRESS |
|---|---|---|---|---|---|
| 102 | ? | mower | 12.30 | Adams, A. | 123 Pine St, San Jose CA |
| 99 | 24.60 | mower | 12.30 | Smith, J. | 222 Washington St, San Jose CA |
| 98 | 11.95 | mower | 11.95 | Adams, A. | 123 Pine St, San Jose CA |
| 100 | 0.00 | mower | 11.95 | Wilson, P. | 553 Cedar St, New York, NY |
| 101 | ? | saw | 6.00 | Wilson, P. | 553 Cedar St, New York, NY |
| 97 | 18.00 | saw | 6.00 | Wilson, P. | 553 Cedar St, New York, NY |

The **from** clause contains the names of the tables involved in the query; the **select** clause indicates which columns of the three tables are present in the result; and the **where** clause specifies how the tool is related to the contract

| CONTRACT | CUSTOMER | ... | FEE | NUMBER | TYPE | ... | RENTAL FEE |
|---|---|---|---|---|---|---|---|
| 97 | Wilson, P. | ... | 18.00 | 1 | mower | ... | 12.30 |
| 98 | Adams, A. | ... | 11.95 | 1 | mower | ... | 12.30 |
| 99 | Smith, J. | ... | 24.60 | 1 | mower | ... | 12.30 |
| 100 | Wilson, P. | ... | 0.00 | 1 | mower | ... | 12.30 |
| 101 | Wilson, P. | ... | ? | 1 | mower | ... | 12.30 |
| 102 | Adams, A. | ... | ? | 1 | mower | ... | 12.30 |
| 97 | Wilson, P. | ... | 18.00 | 2 | mower | ... | 11.95 |
| 98 | Adams, A. | ... | 11.95 | 2 | mower | ... | 11.95 |
| 99 | Smith, J. | ... | 24.60 | 2 | mower | ... | 11.95 |
| 100 | Wilson, P. | ... | 0.00 | 2 | mower | ... | 11.95 |
| 101 | Wilson, P. | ... | ? | 2 | mower | ... | 11.95 |
| 102 | Adams, A. | ... | ? | 2 | mower | ... | 11.95 |
| 97 | Wilson, P. | ... | 18.00 | 3 | saw | ... | 6.00 |
| 98 | Adams, A. | ... | 11.95 | 3 | saw | ... | 6.00 |
| 99 | Smith, J. | ... | 24.60 | 3 | saw | ... | 6.00 |
| 100 | Wilson, P. | ... | 0.00 | 3 | saw | ... | 6.00 |
| 101 | Wilson, P. | ... | ? | 3 | saw | ... | 6.00 |
| 102 | Adams, A. | ... | ? | 3 | saw | ... | 6.00 |
| 97 | Wilson, P. | ... | 18.00 | 4 | mower | ... | 14.20 |
| 98 | Adams, A. | ... | 11.95 | 4 | mower | ... | 14.20 |
| 99 | Smith, J. | ... | 24.60 | 4 | mower | ... | 14.20 |
| 100 | Wilson, P. | ... | 0.00 | 4 | mower | ... | 14.20 |
| 101 | Wilson, P. | ... | ? | 4 | mower | ... | 14.20 |
| 102 | Adams, A. | ... | ? | 4 | mower | ... | 14.20 |
| 97 | Wilson, P. | ... | 18.00 | 5 | tractor | ... | 48.85 |
| 98 | Adams, A. | ... | 11.95 | 5 | tractor | ... | 48.85 |
| 99 | Smith, J. | ... | 24.60 | 5 | tractor | ... | 48.85 |
| 100 | Wilson, P. | ... | 0.00 | 5 | tractor | ... | 48.85 |
| 101 | Wilson, P. | ... | ? | 5 | tractor | ... | 48.85 |
| 102 | Adams, A. | ... | ? | 5 | tractor | ... | 48.85 |

**Figure 23. Result of Cartesian product**

(by tool number) and how the customer is related to the contract (by customer name).

Again, since all columns have unique names, there is no need to qualify the column names by the table names. We could have written more concisely:

> **select** CONTRACT, FEE,                                          [5.11]
>         TYPE, RENTAL_FEE,
>         NAME, ADDRESS
> **from** CONTRACT, TOOL, CUSTOMER
> **where** CUSTOMER = NAME
>         **and** TOOL = NUMBER

## 5.2.3  Multiplicative join

Now, assume that you see the problem slightly differently: in fact, you want to list all tools and, for each tool, all contracts that refer to it. Again, query [5.4] provides the right answer. Note that it does not necessarily give you the answer in such an order that all contracts for a certain tool appear consecutively in the result. If you want such an order, you should write

> **select** CONTRACT, TOOL, DATE_OUT, NUMBER, TYPE       [5.12]
> **from** CONTRACT, TOOL
> **where** CONTRACT.TOOL = TOOL.NUMBER
> **order by** CONTRACT.TOOL

| CONTRACT | TOOL | DATE_OUT | NUMBER | TYPE |
|---------:|:----:|----------|-------:|------|
| 99 | 1 | 1986-05-23 | 1 | mower |
| 102 | 1 | 1986-06-11 | 1 | mower |
| 100 | 2 | 1986-06-22 | 2 | mower |
| 98 | 2 | 1986-05-15 | 2 | mower |
| 101 | 3 | 1986-06-22 | 3 | saw |
| 97 | 3 | 1986-05-15 | 3 | saw |

The difference between this join and a decoding join is that, although you thought about listing tools (exactly as you thought about listing contracts in the decoding join example), the answer may not contain all tools. This is because some tools may not have any matching contracts and therefore, will not appear in the result. More precisely, a particular tool will appear in the result as many times as there are matching contracts (hence the name of multiplicative join). In particular, if there is one matching contract, a particular tool will appear once in the result; if there are n matching contracts for a particular tool, this tool will appear n times; and if there is no matching contract, the tool will not appear in the result at all.

An interesting question is, therefore, what if we wanted to see all tools including those for which there is no matching contract? This problem is worth considering because it is often useful in generating reports.

A first option is to write a program. In fact, we have done it already. Consider Figure 21 again, and locate the comment (1)

> /**** *here we have the tool data* ****/

At that point in the program, you can simply output the data of the tool, even if the following **open** and **fetch** CUR_CONTRACT returns no row. Another method consists of using two **select** statements: a join to find the information about the tools which have matching contracts, and a subquery with a **not exists** clause (as discussed in Section 5.3.4) to find the tools which have never been rented.

Even if these options are always available, there exists, however, in the relational database community a tendency to favor the introduction in SQL of a special kind of join that would return a tool even if it did not have a matching contract and would simply concatenate with it as many null values as needed to complete the result row. Such a special join is called *outer join*.

The outer join is an asymmetric join; its syntax generalizes the **from** clause of the normal (symmetric) join,

> TOOL, CONTRACT

to a **left**, **right**, or **full** join. For example, a **from** clause

> **from** TOOL **left** CONTRACT

computes a join result which includes all rows of the symmetric join, plus one instance of each TOOL row for which there is not matching contract, concatenated with null values instead of values coming from CONTRACT columns. If **left** is replaced by **right**, the result will contain the rows of the symmetric join plus a row for each unmatched contract, with null values instead of values from TOOL. A **full** join returns the union of the results of the **left** and **right** joins. Figure 24 summarizes these definitions graphically.

Since few SQL systems support the outer join at this time, all further references to a join will always refer to the normal, symmetric one.

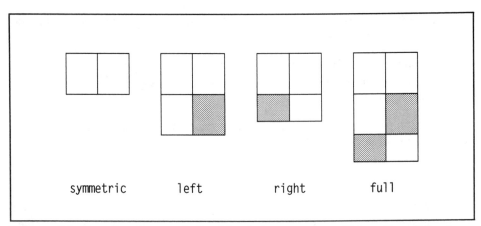

**Figure 24. Results of outer joins (shaded areas show the null padding)**

## 5.2.4 Selective join

Consider the problem of listing the contracts involving mowers. Suppose first that there is a stored table S with a single column N that contains all mower numbers:

| N |
|---|
| 1 |
| 2 |
| 4 |

Then the statement

**select** CONTRACT, CUSTOMER, TOOL                 [5.13]
**from** CONTRACT, S
**where** CONTRACT.TOOL = S.N

| CONTRACT | CUSTOMER | TOOL |
|---|---|---|
| 99 | Smith, J. | 1 |
| 102 | Adams, A. | 1 |
| 98 | Adams, A. | 2 |
| 100 | Wilson, P. | 2 |

yields precisely the desired result. The query uses the property that a contract will not appear if there is no matching row in S or, in other words, if the tool is not a mower.

But S can be obtained by doing a selection on TOOL. Since, in SQL, the selection and join can be done in a single statement, we can avoid building S and simply write

**select** CONTRACT, CUSTOMER, TOOL, TYPE                    [5.14]
**from** CONTRACT, TOOL
**where** CONTRACT.TOOL = TOOL.NUMBER
    **and** TOOL.TYPE = 'mower'

| CONTRACT | CUSTOMER | TOOL | TYPE |
|---|---|---|---|
| 99 | Smith, J. | 1 | mower |
| 102 | Adams, A. | 1 | mower |
| 98 | Adams, A. | 2 | mower |
| 100 | Wilson, P. | 2 | mower |

Earlier in this chapter we did use * as projection list. Such a projection list will return the columns from both tables. If you are only interested in the columns of CONTRACT, replace **select** * by **select** CONTRACT.*:

**select** CONTRACT.*                                        [5.15]
**from** CONTRACT, TOOL
**where** CONTRACT.TOOL = TOOL.NUMBER
    **and** TOOL.TYPE = 'mower'

| CONTRACT | CUSTOMER | TOOL | DATE_OUT | DATE_IN | FEE |
|---|---|---|---|---|---|
| 99 | Smith, J. | 1 | 1986-05-23 | 1986-05-25 | 24.60 |
| 102 | Adams, A. | 1 | 1986-06-11 | 1986-07-13 | ? |
| 98 | Adams, A. | 2 | 1986-05-15 | 1986-05-15 | 11.95 |
| 100 | Wilson, P. | 2 | 1986-06-22 | 1986-06-25 | 0.00 |

## 5.2.5 Joins: a summary

We have seen in Chapter 2 that a good database design calls for no replication of data. For that reason, the data are distributed into several individual tables such as CONTRACT, TOOL, and CUSTOMER. But this is often not the way the user wants to see the data; on the contrary, it is often useful to see redundant data in the result of a query. The join operation is then used to combine rows from various tables to form a set of composite rows. Such a set of composite rows can then be used in any **select** statement, as if it were a regular stored table. In particular, aggregates, **group by**, and **order by**, apply to the result of a join. For example, let us find the number of contracts for each type of tool:

**select** TOOL.TYPE, **count**(*)                                    [5.16]
**from** TOOL, CONTRACT
**where** TOOL.NUMBER = CONTRACT.TOOL
**group by** TOOL.TYPE

| TYPE | COUNT(*) |
|------|----------|
| mower | 4 |
| saw | 2 |

In this query, we first form a table with tools and contracts as we did in [5.4]. Then, we group the rows on their type of tools and count them. Remember that in the answer to [5.4] only the tools which have been rented at least once appear. Thus, the tools for which the count is zero do not appear in the result of [5.16].

Many interesting applications of joins are demonstrated in Chapters 13 and 14. Chapter 11 and 14 show examples of joining a table with itself.

# 5.3  Subqueries

We now study the second type of complex queries, where a **select** statement is embedded in the **where** clause of another statement. Wherever a constant can appear in the **where** clause it can be substituted by a query that produces, as its result, a constant of the appropriate type. The constant may be a scalar or a set. Every time the **where** clause is evaluated, the embedded **select** is evaluated (logically at least); its value may or may not change with each evaluation.

## 5.3.1  Subquery returning a single row

We first look at a query where the evaluation of the subquery yields always the same constant. For example, let us find the tools that were purchased for a price greater than the average purchase price of all tools. To solve this problem using only elementary queries, we could first find the average tool purchase price, writing

**select avg**(PURCH_PRICE)                                    [5.17]
**from** TOOL

| AVG(PURCH_PRICE) |
|------------------|
| 839.9940 |

Second, given this value, we would use it in the query

**select** *                                                    [5.18]
**from** TOOL
**where** PURCH_PRICE > 839.994

| NUMBER | TYPE | PURCH_DATE | PURCH_PRICE | RENTAL_FEE |
|--------|------|------------|-------------|------------|
| 5 | tractor | 1987-09-21 | 2363.67 | 48.85 |

Such a technique has an obvious drawback: it forces the user to transfer the result of one query into another. This is easy within a program, but becomes cumbersome when using an interactive query system.

Writing a **select** statement with a subquery solves the problem since statements [5.17] and [5.18] can simply be rewritten together as

**select** *                                                    [5.19]
**from** TOOL
**where** PURCH_PRICE >
    ( **select** avg(PURCH_PRICE)
    **from** TOOL)

where the subquery replaces the constant 839.994. Conceptually, the subquery is evaluated each time the **where** clause is evaluated. Generally, the optimizer of a relational system is smart enough to recognize that the subquery yields the same value for each row of TOOL and that it is therefore unnecessary to re-evaluate it each time.

The syntax of a subquery is similar to the syntax of any **select** statement. The subquery is enclosed in parentheses and can be as complex as needed. In particular, it can itself contain subqueries in its where clause; these subqueries also may invoke other subqueries, and so on, on an arbitrary number of levels. The query in which a subquery is embedded is called the *parent query* of the subquery. The query without parent is the *main query*.

## 5.3.2  Correlated subquery returning a single row

The subquery in [5.19] returns the same value for each TOOL row. But this is not always the case; often the value of the subquery does vary with the row of the parent query. Consider the following question: what are the tools that cost more than the average purchase price of tools of the same type? For example, which mowers cost more than the average purchase price of mowers? If a particular tool is a mower, we want the **where** clause to compare its purchase price to the result of

**select** avg(PURCH_PRICE)                                    [5.20]
**from** TOOL
**where** TYPE = 'mower'

| AVG(PURCH_PRICE) |
|---|
| 576.9333 |

But if the tool is a saw, then the **where** clause should actually be

**where** TYPE = 'saw'

and so on for all tools. The values 'mower', 'saw', and the like, are constants that vary with the type of the tool. In other words, the subquery is *correlated* with the parent row. SQL supports such a correlation by having the subquery refer to a value in the parent query:

**select** *                                                   [5.21]
**from** TOOL A
**where** A.PURCH_PRICE >=
     ( **select** avg(B.PURCH_PRICE)
     **from** TOOL B
     **where** B.TYPE = A.TYPE)

| NUMBER | TYPE | PURCH_DATE | PURCH_PRICE | RENTAL_FEE |
|---|---|---|---|---|
| 3 | saw | 1986-11-15 | 105.50 | 6.00 |
| 4 | mower | 1987-07-14 | 685.10 | 14.20 |
| 5 | tractor | 1987-09-21 | 2363.67 | 48.85 |

In example [5.21] the main query is on table TOOL; the subquery is also on table TOOL. To clearly indicate which column is involved in a particular predicate, names (A and B) are locally assigned to the two instances of TOOL. A similar naming technique is used when the same table is used twice in a join. An example of such a use is given in Exercise 5.4.

## 5.3.3 Subquery returning a set

In the cases above, the constant returned by a subquery is a scalar. We now turn our attention to cases where a subquery returns a set of values.

Let us ask ourselves which tools have ever been rented. Clearly, a join between TOOL and CONTRACT will eliminate the tools that were never rented since there will be no matching rows in CONTRACT. But, in the answer, we want only one row for a tool that has been rented, not as many rows as there are contracts involving that tool. One solution is to count the number of entries as in [5.16]. Another solution is to select only columns from TOOL and use the **distinct** keyword to eliminate the duplicate entries:

> **select distinct** TOOL.NUMBER                                  [5.22]
> **from** TOOL, CONTRACT
> **where** TOOL.NUMBER = CONTRACT.TOOL

| NUMBER |
|--------|
| 1 |
| 2 |
| 3 |

The subquery facility of SQL provides several other ways to get the same information.

A first solution uses the **in** clause already described in the previous chapter. It is used now to verify that an element of a row belongs to a list resulting from a **select** statement. Let us rephrase the query as follows: find the tools with a number that is in the list of tool numbers extracted from CONTRACT:

> **select** *                                                              [5.23]
> **from** TOOL
> **where** TOOL.NUMBER **in**
>    ( **select** CONTRACT.TOOL
>    **from** CONTRACT)

| NUMBER | TYPE | PURCH_DATE | PURCH_PRICE | RENTAL_FEE |
|--------|------|------------|-------------|------------|
| 1 | mower | 1986-07-19 | 550.70 | 12.30 |
| 2 | mower | 1986-05-22 | 495.00 | 11.95 |
| 3 | saw | 1986-11-15 | 105.50 | 6.00 |

A second solution exploits the **exists** facility by rephrasing the query as finding the tools for which a contract exists:

> **select** *                                                              [5.24]
> **from** TOOL
> **where exists**
>    ( **select** *
>    **from** CONTRACT
>    **where** CONTRACT.TOOL = TOOL.NUMBER )

The **exists** clause is true if the number of rows returned by the subquery is greater than zero.  Example [5.24] is equivalent to

> **select** *                                                        [5.25]
> **from** TOOL
> **where** 0 <
>    ( **select count(*)**
>    **from** CONTRACT
>    **where** CONTRACT.TOOL = TOOL.NUMBER)

The third solution uses the **any** quantifier.  Again, rephrase the query as follows:  find the tools with a number that is equal to any of the TOOL numbers extracted from CONTRACT. This can be expressed as

> **select** *                                                        [5.26]
> **from** TOOL
> **where** TOOL.NUMBER = **any**
>    ( **select** CONTRACT.TOOL
>    **from** CONTRACT)

Let us now consider another problem. Assume you want to know which tool is the most expensive to buy.  We can use a formulation similar to [5.19], with a **max** in the subquery:

> **select** *                                                        [5.27]
> **from** TOOL
> **where** PURCH_PRICE =
>    ( **select max**(PURCH_PRICE)
>    **from** TOOL)

| NUMBER | TYPE | PURCH_DATE | PURCH_PRICE | RENTAL_FEE |
|-------:|------|------------|------------:|-----------:|
| 5 | tractor | 1987-09-21 | 2363.67 | 48.85 |

But, here also, another solution is possible using the **all** quantifier.  The query is rephrased as follows: find the tools with a purchase price larger than or equal to **all** purchase prices.  This is coded in SQL as

> **select** *                                                        [5.28]
> **from** TOOL
> **where** PURCH_PRICE >= **all**
>    ( **select** PURCH_PRICE
>    **from** TOOL)

which gives the same answer as [5.27]. Note what happens if there is a tie and several tools have the same maximum price. If the operator >= is used as in [5.28], all tools with the maximum price will be returned. If we replace >= by >, then none of the tools will be returned, since no price can be larger than the maximum.

The same question can also be correlated to obtain the most expensive tool in each category, as in

> **select** *                                                                    [5.29]
> **from** TOOL A
> **where** A.PURCH_PRICE >= **all**
>     ( **select** B.PURCH_PRICE
>     **from** TOOL B
>     **where** B.TYPE = A.TYPE)

| NUMBER | TYPE | PURCH_DATE | PURCH_PRICE | RENTAL_FEE |
|--------|------|------------|-------------|------------|
| 3 | saw | 1986-11-15 | 105.50 | 6.00 |
| 4 | mower | 1987-07-14 | 685.10 | 14.20 |
| 5 | tractor | 1987-09-21 | 2363.67 | 48.85 |

## 5.3.4  Where the join does not help

On several occasions we looked for tools that had been rented at least once, and we saw in [5.4] how a join can help finding the answer. Now, we may also be interested in finding the tools which have never been rented. Surprisingly, the problem is quite different, at least if you think in terms of a join; this is not true, however, if you think in terms of a subquery. In this case, the query can be rephrased as: find the tools for which there exists no contract. The **not exists** predicate can be used to make this formulation very straightforward:

> **select** *                                                                    [5.30]
> **from** TOOL
> **where not exists**
>     ( **select** *
>     **from** CONTRACT
>     **where** CONTRACT.TOOL = TOOL.NUMBER )

| NUMBER | TYPE | PURCH_DATE | PURCH_PRICE | RENTAL_FEE |
|--------|------|------------|-------------|------------|
| 4 | mower | 1987-07-14 | 685.10 | 14.20 |
| 5 | tractor | 1987-09-21 | 2363.67 | 48.85 |

The **not exists** clause is true only if the subquery returns an empty result table.

Instead of negating the **exists** clause of [5.24], SQL also allows for the negation of the **in** clause. Statements [5.31] and [5.30] are equivalent:

            **select** *                                                   [5.31]
            **from** TOOL
            **where** TOOL.NUMBER **not in**
                ( **select** TOOL
                **from** CONTRACT)

Finally, you should be able to achieve the same result by negating the "equal **any**" predicate. But the negation of "equal **any**" is equivalent to "not equal **all**". The following form is valid and is equivalent to [5.31]:

            **select** *                                                   [5.32]
            **from** TOOL
            **where** TOOL.NUMBER <> **all**
                ( **select** TOOL
                **from** CONTRACT)

Chapter 11 looks at many interesting queries that rely on the **exists** and **not exists** predicates. They illustrate the actual power of the subquery facility.

## 5.3.5  More complex examples

A subquery can be embedded in another subquery and combined with joins as necessary. All features discussed in the chapter on elementary queries can also be used in conjunction with joins and subqueries. Consider, for example, finding the tools (numbers and types) which have been rented to customers who have been issued more than one contract and who live in zip code area 95125.

Since all the needed information is in TOOL the main query can select data from TOOL only. So, it will start with

            **select** NUMBER, TYPE                                        [5.33]
            **from** TOOL
            **where** ...

The condition refers to the fact that the TOOL has been rented. Thus, a subquery finding these tools will refer to the CONTRACT table, and the query becomes

```
select NUMBER, TYPE                          [5.34]
from TOOL
where NUMBER in
    ( select TOOL
    from CONTRACT
    where ... )
```

The new condition is that the customer for the current contract must have been issued more than one contract. Since the information is also in CONTRACT, the condition will use a second subquery on CONTRACT:

```
select NUMBER, TYPE                          [5.35]
from TOOL
where NUMBER in
    ( select TOOL
    from CONTRACT A
    where 1 <
        ( select count(*)
        from CONTRACT B
        where A.CUSTOMER=B.CUSTOMER ) )
```

Note that the second subquery is correlated with the parent row in CONTRACT (named A). The last condition is on the customer zip code. Since the zip code is in CUSTOMER, a join is used to access it. The complete query is

```
select NUMBER, TYPE                          [5.36]
from TOOL
where NUMBER in
    ( select TOOL
    from CONTRACT A, CUSTOMER
    where 1 <
        ( select count(*)
        from CONTRACT B
        where A.CUSTOMER=B.CUSTOMER )
    and CUSTOMER.NAME = A.CUSTOMER
    and CUSTOMER.ZIP = '95125' )
```

| NUMBER | TYPE |
|--------|------|
| 1 | mower |
| 2 | mower |

Several subqueries can also be used in the same **where** clause. Let us find the tools which have either never been rented or rented more than 5 times.

> **select** *                                                    [5.37]
> **from** TOOL
> **where not exists**
>     ( **select** *
>     **from** CONTRACT A
>     **where** A.TOOL = TOOL.NUMBER)
>     **or** 5 <
>     ( **select count**(*)
>     **from** CONTRACT B
>     **where** B.TOOL = TOOL.NUMBER)

| NUMBER | TYPE | PURCH_DATE | PURCH_PRICE | RENTAL_FEE |
|---|---|---|---|---|
| 4 | mower | 1987-07-14 | 685.10 | 14.20 |
| 5 | tractor | 1987-09-21 | 2363.67 | 48.85 |

Note that many SQL system implementations forbid the use of **group by** and **having** clauses in subqueries. Check your user's manual to find out if this is the case. If it is, you will have to materialize the result of the subquery in a temporary table and then refer to that table in the subquery. The view mechanism (see Chapter 8) may provide another way of solving the problem.

# 5.4  Union

The general syntax of the **union** feature is

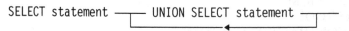

```
SELECT statement ──┬── UNION SELECT statement ──┬──
                   └──────────────◄──────────────┘
```

Its purpose is to bring together, in a single result, the result rows of all **select** statements that appear in the **union** statement. Duplicate rows (all values identical) are eliminated from the result of the union (**null** values are considered equal when determining if two rows are identical). Some SQL implementations support the **union all** operator, which ensures that all rows are kept, without elimination of duplicates.

Since the result rows have to fit in the same result table, their format must be compatible: the number of columns must be the same and the type of each column must be the same across all **select** results. Some conversions may be done automatically by the system. For example, short integer and integer values are considered of the same type for the purpose of **union**, and the result column will be of type integer. Depending upon the implementation, SQL systems are more or less strict on the definition of type compatibility. Some of them allow for conversion; others do not.

The remainder of this section discusses three uses of the **union** operation.

1. The **union** operator can be used to select rows that satisfy at least one of several conditions. It is just an alternate form of the OR conjunction between various predicates in the **where** clause. To find customers whose names start with a D or who live in zip code area 95125, you have a choice between using OR, as in

> **select** *                                                      [5.38]
> **from** CUSTOMER
> **where** NAME **like** 'D%'
> **or** ZIP = '95125'

| NAME | ADDRESS | ZIP |
|------|---------|-----|
| Adams, A. | 123 Pine St, San Jose CA | 95125 |
| Dupont, R. | 100 Main St, Town ST | 12345 |
| Smith, J. | 222 Washington St, San Jose CA | 95125 |

or using **union**, as in

> **select** *                                                      [5.39]
> **from** CUSTOMER
> **where** NAME **like** 'D%'
> **union**
> **select** *
> **from** CUSTOMER
> **where** ZIP = '95125'

In a good implementation, the way a query is expressed should not necessarily imply how it is evaluated internally. However, implementations are not perfect, and it is quite possible, even likely, that the fact that you use **union** in the statement will force the independent evaluation of the two sets followed by their **union**. This may be better or worse than looking at the customer rows once and evaluating the predicate expression with OR, depending on the circumstances.

2. The **union** operator can also be used to simulate an outer join. Let us consider again the outer join described in 5.2.3. Its result can be evaluated by taking the union of two sets: the set of tools which have been rented

and the set of tools which have not been associated with any contract. To obtain identical row formats, the rows from the second set must be padded with a default value for the (nonexisting) contract (we chose 0):

> **select** T1.NUMBER, C1.CONTRACT, T1.TYPE        [5.40]
> **from** CONTRACT C1, TOOL T1
> **where** C1.TOOL = T1.NUMBER
>
> **union**
>
> **select** T2.NUMBER, 0, T2.TYPE
> **from** TOOL T2
> **where not exists**
>     ( **select** *
>     **from** CONTRACT C2
>     **where** C2.TOOL = T2.NUMBER )

| NUMBER | CONTRACT | TYPE |
|--------|----------|------|
| 1 | 99 | mower |
| 1 | 102 | mower |
| 2 | 98 | mower |
| 2 | 100 | mower |
| 3 | 97 | saw |
| 3 | 101 | saw |
| 4 | 0 | mower |
| 5 | 0 | tractor |

3. In both previous uses of the **union** operator, the information always came from the same table. But this is not always necessary. For example, let us find the number of contracts issued for each tool, making sure that we get a zero result if the tool has never been rented. The first set of rows corresponding to tools which have been rented comes from CONTRACT, the second, corresponding to tools which have never been rented, comes from TOOL.

> **select** C1.TOOL, **count(*)**        [5.41]
> **from** CONTRACT C1
> **group by** C1.TOOL
>
> **union**
>
> **select** T1.NUMBER, 0
> **from** TOOL T1
> **where not exists**
>     ( **select** *
>     **from** CONTRACT C2
>     **where** C2.TOOL=T1.NUMBER)

| TOOL | COUNT(*) |
|------|----------|
| 1 | 2 |
| 2 | 2 |
| 3 | 2 |
| 4 | 0 |
| 5 | 0 |

Now, assume that you want to aggregate the tools by type as we did in [5.16], with the condition however, that all tools, even those that were never rented, are considered in the computation. Note that a tool of a certain type may have been rented while another tool of the same type might not; hence the relative complexity of the statement:

> **select** T1.TYPE, **count(*)**                    [5.42]
> **from** TOOL T1, CONTRACT C1
> **where** T1.NUMBER=C1.TOOL
> **group by** T1.TYPE
>
**union**
> **select** T2.TYPE, 0
> **from** TOOL T2
> **where not exists**
>     ( **select** *
>     **from** CONTRACT C2, TOOL T3
>     **where** C2.TOOL=T3.NUMBER
>         **and** T3.TYPE = T2.TYPE)

| TYPE | COUNT(*) |
|------|----------|
| mower | 4 |
| saw | 2 |
| tractor | 0 |

The result of a **union** is, as always in SQL, a table. Some implementations, however, limit the operations that can be applied to such a result table. In particular, some systems do not allow subqueries to include a **union**.

## 5.5 Summary

This chapter described three ways to build a result table based on more than one table.

If the result in which you are interested must contain data from two (or more) tables, then you have to use a join. If the result table must contain data from one table only, but the predicates refer to another table, then you may use a subquery (or a join). The **union** combines, in a single result table, the results from various **select** statements.

# 5.6 Exercises

The exercises use the database application described in Chapter 2.

**5.1.** For each student, in alphabetical order, list the classes that he or she attended; include the following information:

1. Student name
2. Class subject
3. Year attended
4. Grade

**5.2.** Find the subjects of the classes which had students enrolled in 1987. Find the subjects of the classes which had no enrollment in 1987.

**5.3.** What is the result of the following query:

> **select distinct** SUBJECT
> **from** CLASS, RECORDS
> **where** CLASSNO <> CLASS
>     **and** YEAR = 1987

Compare with the answer to the previous exercise.

**5.4.** Display all prerequisite information; make sure that subjects rather than class numbers appear in the result.

**5.5.** Show four different ways of finding the subjects of classes which have prerequisite(s).

**5.6.** List in alphabetical order the name of the students and their average grade.

**5.7.** Prepare a listing showing the subjects of all classes together with the number of students enrolled in these classes in 1987.

**5.8.** This exercise verifies the qualification or nonqualification of students for attending class 201:

1. Provide the names of the students who meet all requirements.
2. Provide the names of the students who have attended the prerequisite classes but achieved below the minimum grade.

3. Provide the names of the students who did not attend all the required classes.

**5.9.** Find the name of the student who had the lowest grade ever.

**5.10.** List, for each class subject with some enrollment, the names of the students who had the lowest grade in the subject.  Think about two slightly different ways of writing the query.

**5.11.** Find the classes attended by students in their first year of attendance, without using the column FIRSTYEAR in table STUDENT.

# Chapter 6

# Changing a Table

Very early in this book we covered the insertion of rows into a table. In doing so we were guided by our desire to follow the order of things as they happen in normal usage of an SQL system. Clearly, before data can be queried, they must be entered. We saw how to define tables and how to populate them, using the following form of the **insert** statement (which uses 4 constants and 1 program variable):

> **insert into** TOOL (NUMBER, TYPE, PURCH_DATE,          [6.1]
>     PURCH_PRICE, RENTAL_FEE)
> **values** (1, 'mower', '7/19/1986', 550.70, *:V1*)

In this chapter, we cover all SQL facilities that change the contents of an existing table, starting with the generalization of **insert**.

## 6.1  Set insert

The **insert** form used in [6.1] inserts a single row, and the values making up the row are specified as constants or program variables. SQL also supports a set-oriented form of **insert**. Suppose you want to save the current rental fees of all mowers in a table for further reference. First, a table must be created to receive that information. Since the table needs to contain the tool numbers and the rental fees, it needs two columns of appropriate types: integer and decimal. The following definition can be used:

> **create table** MOWERS (                                    [6.2]
>     NBR **integer**,
>     RENTAL_FEE **decimal**(8,2))

Once the table exists, it can be populated by inserting the information directly from TOOL. To specify what information needs to be inserted, a **select** is used; the result of the select is a set of rows that are inserted in the target table. The **select** and **insert** specifications are combined in a single statement:

> **insert into** MOWERS (NBR, RENTAL_FEE)                     [6.3]
>     **select** NUMBER, RENTAL_FEE
>     **from** TOOL
>     **where** TYPE = 'mower'

Referring to Figure 5 in Chapter 1, the contents of MOWERS after execution of this **insert** statement is

| MOWERS | |
| --- | --- |
| NBR | RENTAL_FEE |
| 1 | 12.30 |
| 2 | 11.95 |
| 4 | 14.20 |

Taking into accounts both forms of **insert**, the general syntax of the statement is

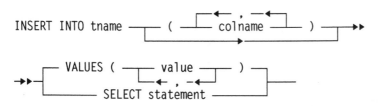

The table in which rows are inserted is called the **target table**; any table appearing in any **from** clause in the select statement is a **source table** (the select statement may have several **from** clauses if it contains one or several subqueries). The select statement can be as general as shown in Chapters 4 and 5, except for the fact that it cannot have an **order by** clause. This is appropriate since, when stored in the database, rows are not ordered. It is important to note that the number of columns in the result of the **select** and their types must match the number and types of columns in the table in which the rows are inserted. Some systems do not require the types to match literally; in some cases, a translation may happen automatically. For example, the selection may return integers to be inserted in a column of type decimal. Sometimes, functions are provided supporting conversions between character strings and numerical values.

Another restriction must be taken into account: the target table cannot also be a source table. The reason for such a restriction is that the content of a source table would otherwise change during the selection itself, producing unpredictable results. In fact, such a situation often causes the insert to loop indefinitely, selecting what has just been inserted and inserting it again. It would be possible to implement the function by first selecting the rows to be inserted and storing them in a temporary table before they can be inserted from the temporary table into the target. But most implementations do not do it that way and simply enforce the restriction. This means that the user or the application program may have to explicitly go through the extra step.

The set insert feature of SQL is exercised in Chapter 12.

## 6.2  Delete and set delete

The inverse operation of an **insert** is a **delete**. In SQL, the **delete** statement deletes one or more rows in a specified table. Which rows are to be deleted is determined by a **where** clause.

Suppose that, periodically, you want to get rid of all entries in CONTRACT that are older than a certain date, say end of 1986. You simply write

> **delete**                                                            [6.4]
> **from** CONTRACT
> **where** DATE_IN > '12/31/1986'

The general form is

```
DELETE FROM tname WHERE where_clause
```

Again, the **where** clause can have all the generality described in the context of **select** in Chapters 4 and 5. This form of delete makes no difference between deleting a single row or a set of rows. If the **where** clause specifies the value of a unique (and existing) key, a single row will be deleted. If no row qualifies, then none will be deleted. If a set of rows qualify, all rows in the set will be deleted. Note that

> **delete**                                                            [6.5]
> **from** CONTRACT

without any **where** clause, deletes all rows in the table. As a result, the table CONTRACT becomes empty. It is important to note that, even if it is empty, the table still exists. Therefore, an **insert** operation can be executed immediately to repopulate the table. If you really want to get rid of the table all together, you have to execute a **drop table**. The syntax of **drop table** is simply

```
DROP TABLE tname
```

The command **drop table** is the inverse of **create table**. After a drop, the table does not exist anymore. It must be created again before any row can be inserted. If a **drop table** is executed on a nonempty table, all rows are automatically deleted before the table definition is deleted from the system.

As mentioned above, the **where** clause can be as complex as needed for identifying the rows to be deleted. Since the **from** clause in the **delete** identifies a single table (the table from which rows are to be deleted), there is no way to use a join to identify the rows to be deleted. Subqueries can be used instead.

Consider the problem of deleting all CONTRACT rows that relate to mowers. For selecting these rows you could use a join as in

> **select** *                                                         [6.6]
> **from** CONTRACT, TOOL
> **where** CONTRACT.TOOL= TOOL.NUMBER
>     **and** TYPE = 'mower'

To delete the same rows, the following statement uses a subquery instead:

> **delete**                                                            [6.7]
> **from** CONTRACT
> **where** TOOL **in**
>     ( **select** NUMBER
>     **from** TOOL
>     **where** TYPE = 'mower')

# 6.3  Update and set update

A row can be changed by simply deleting it and inserting a new row containing the new values. But SQL provides a special **update** feature that can be used to change a row by specifying new values or computing new values from the old ones.

Assume you want to increase the rental fee of tool number 1 by $2.50. You can use the following **update** statement:

> **update** TOOL                                                          [6.8]
> **set** RENTAL_FEE = RENTAL_FEE + 2.50
> **where** NUMBER = 1

The **where** clause identifies the rows that are to be updated; the SET clause specifies the new values either explicitly or by giving an expression that computes them.

The general syntax of **update** is described by the following diagram:

```
UPDATE tname SET ──┬── colname = expression ──┬── WHERE condition
                   └──────────◄──────────┘
                              ,
```

The **where** clause in an **update** has the same syntax and power as in a **select**. The **set** clause specifies, for each column to be updated, the column name and an expression for computing the new values.  The expression syntax is the same as the one shown in Chapter 4 for the select list of a **select** statement. As in the **delete** statement, the **where** clause may identify zero, one, or more rows and, accordingly, zero, one, or more rows will be updated.  For example, to update the rental fees of all mowers to 5% of their purchase price, you would write

> **update** TOOL                                                          [6.9]
> **set** RENTAL_FEE = 0.05 * PURCH_PRICE
> **where** TYPE = 'mower'

Some systems accept that the expression of the **set** clause be replaced by a **select** statement returning a single row / single column value.  This **select** statement can be a correlated subquery, but the subquery cannot reference the table being updated.  In some implementations, more than one column can receive their new values from a multi-column row returned by a single subquery.

## 6.4  Delete based on a cursor

Let us ask ourselves the following question: is the power of the **delete** feature sufficient to support all possible needs?  This question can be rephrased as follows: is the power of the **where** clause sufficient to always be able to determine which rows need to be deleted? The example in [6.4] is very simple.  In more complex cases, the **where** clause may contain more than one predicate, connected by **and**'s. In still other cases, there may be disjunctive conditions as in "delete tools which are either old and cheap or new and expensive" (where old means bought before or in 86 and new after 86, and where cheap is less than $200 and expensive more than $400). The condition is more complex; but, again, the logical power available in the **where** clause is sufficient, as shown below:

> **delete** [6.10]
> **from** TOOL
> **where** ( PURCH_DATE <= '12/31/1986' **and** PURCH_PRICE < 200 )
>     **or** ( PURCH_DATE > '12/31/1986' **and** PURCH_PRICE > 400 )

Of course, you can also have more than two such cases; you can use subqueries, joins in subqueries, and so on. So, a very large portion of the cases that may come up in useful applications can indeed be expressed in the **where** clause; and, as a result, the delete can be done in a single statement.

But this is not always true. Imagine you would actually like to write

> **delete** [6.11]
> **from** TOOL
> **where** $F$(PURCH_DATE, PURCH_PRICE) > 0

where $F(X,Y)$ is a function that can only be computed by a subroutine. In real applications, this subroutine may perform a long series of computations and table lookups and even read data from a file that is not part of the database. Since there is no way to define $F(X,Y)$ to SQL, you cannot write [6.11]. What happens is that SQL, although very powerful, is not as powerful as a full general-purpose programming language. And it is that full power that you need in this example.

Thus, you have no other choice than writing a program. Figure 25 shows such a program. It uses SQL to fetch successively the rows of TOOL and, for each row, performs the test to see if it needs to be deleted or not. If yes, it uses the primary key fetched in *:Vn* to specify which row must be deleted.

There are two drawbacks with such an approach. The first is a performance issue; the second is a logical one.

- The performance issue. The cursor is actually "pointing" at the row. In other words, the database system knows internally exactly where the row is located. But the program statement

```
exec sql include sqlca
exec sql begin declare section
        declare number Vn
        declare string Vd
        declare number Vp
exec sql end declare section
declare number X
exec sql declare C cursor for
        select NUMBER, PURCH_DATE, PURCH_PRICE
        from TOOL

exec sql open C

exec sql whenever not found go to The_End

do forever
        exec sql fetch C
        into :Vn, :Vd, :Vp

        X = F(Vd, Vp)
        /* test for the condition to be true */
        if X > 0 then do
                exec sql delete
                from TOOL
                where NUMBER = :Vn
                end

        end
The_End:
exec sql close C
```

**Figure 25. A program to delete rows**

$$\text{exec sql delete} \qquad\qquad\qquad\qquad\qquad [6.12]$$
$$\text{from TOOL}$$
$$\text{where NUMBER} = :Vn$$

does not exploit that fact. It simply gives the key, and the system will have to perform a selection to find the row again before it can be deleted. A natural solution to the problem consists of telling the system to delete the row "pointed to" by cursor C.

• The logical problem. As mentioned before, SQL does not prohibit several rows in the same table to be identical. Therefore, it is not always possible to use a predicate to identify uniquely the rows to be deleted. And, in this case, the only solution is to tell the system to delete the row "pointed to" by a cursor.

To avoid these drawbacks, SQL provides a special predicate called **where current of**. The program statement shown in [6.12] is simply replaced by

```
exec sql delete                                    [6.13]
from TOOL
where current of C
```

Of course, the tables names that appear respectively in the cursor declaration and in the **delete** statement must be identical. In addition, the **delete** statement contains a single table in its **from** clause.

Some implementations provide a mechanism that is functionally equivalent, but based on the notion of unique row identifiers (**rowid**). The **fetch** returns, together with the normal result row, the **rowid** of the corresponding row in the source table, say in variable $I$. Then, the delete statement uses a predicate **rowid** = $:I$ to identify the row to be deleted.

## 6.5  Update based on cursor

The analysis done for **delete** is also applicable to **update**. In fact, the need to write a program may be greater for updating rows than for deleting rows. The reason is that the computation of the new value in a **set** clause may also require the execution of a program written in a general-purpose language. Aside from this, the construct **where current of** is used in the same way, as illustrated by the program in Figure 26.

You may wonder why the updated columns are also listed in the **for update of** clause of the **declare cursor** statement. The reason is that most SQL compilers do not know at the time the cursor declaration is processed which columns are actually going to be updated. Then the compiler may choose an access path based on some order of the values in the columns being updated. Since the update may change that order, strange things may happen. To illustrate the point, just suppose that the access is along the following order:

   1    7    10    17

```
exec sql include sqlca
exec sql begin declare section
        declare number Vn
        declare string Vd
        declare number Vr
        declare number Y
exec sql end declare section
declare number X
exec sql declare C cursor for
        select NUMBER, PURCH_DATE, RENTAL_FEE
        from TOOL
        for update of RENTAL_FEE


exec sql open C
exec sql whenever not found go to The_End

do forever
        exec sql fetch C
        into :Vn, :Vd, :Vr
        X = F(Vd, Vr)
        Y = new value of rental_fee
        /* test for the condition to be true. */
        if X > 0 then
        exec sql update TOOL
                set RENTAL_FEE = :Y
                where current of C
        end
The_End:
exec sql close C
```

**Figure 26. A program to update rows**

Assuming that the **update** statement increases these values by 10, the first update will change 1 into 11; that value will end up, in the order, between 10 and 17. The remaining portion of the ordered list is therefore

$$7 \quad 10 \quad 11 \quad 17$$

The problem is that the access path will later fetch the value 11 corresponding to a row that has already been updated; that row will be updated again, move back in the order list, be updated again, and so on. The use of **for update of** will force the system to use an access path that will avoid the problem.

# 6.6  Adding a column to a table

All statements discussed in the previous sections deal with the data in a table. In no way do they change any of the parameters that are specified at the time the table is created. In other words, they do not change the structure of the table which is determined by the number of columns and their types. Most SQL implementations offer very limited support for changing a table structure. The only facility generally provided is **alter table**. The **alter table** statement adds a single column to a table. Recall that the canonical order of columns is initially the one specified in the **create table**. The new column added by **alter table** automatically gets to be the last in the canonical order. Initially, the new column is filled with **null** values for all rows already in the table (this operation is performed logically in many implementations; so if you add a column to an existing table with many rows, do not be surprised if the operation takes practically no time). These **null** values can later be changed using the **update** command described above. The syntax of the **alter table** statement is

```
ALTER TABLE  tname  ADD  colname  datatype
```

The other options, besides **add**, supported in the **alter** command are very specific to each implementation of SQL and are beyond the scope of this book.

# 6.7  Summary

In Chapter 3, we had already shown how the construct

> **insert into** TABLE_NAME (...)
> **values** (...)

could be used to insert rows in a table. In this chapter, we studied other ways of changing the contents of a table. We not only extended the statement to insert into one table, the result of an SQL **select** statement retrieving data from other tables, but we also showed how **delete** and **update** are used to suppress or update information in the database.

Except for the simplest form of **insert**, all three operations **insert, delete,** and **update** actually combine two suboperations. They first locate some rows and then operate on them. We have shown that cases exist where the power of a general purpose language is needed to locate the rows (in **delete** or **update**) or to compute new values (in **update**). In these cases, two SQL statements are used in a program: the first to locate the rows (**select**), the second to operate on them (**delete** or **update**). The construct **where current of** is introduced to relate both suboperations.

Just a warning: you probably noticed by now that you could always use the **where current of** for updates and deletes. However, you must realize that doing so decreases the performance. As we mentioned several times already, it is always advisable to reduce the number of times SQL is invoked. Thus, if the operation can be specified in one statement, by all means use that statement.

Besides **insert**, **delete** and **update**, two other functions can change the contents of a table. The first, **drop**, deletes all rows from a table and suppresses its definition. The second, **alter**, adds a column to a table. Note that there is no command to delete a column from a table.

# 6.8 Exercises

The exercises use the database application described in Chapter 2.

**6.1.** Write a program to fill in the grades at the end of the year. The program will scan RECORDS to find all rows with a **null** grade. For each of these rows, it will print the student name and the class, read the grade from the terminal, and store it in the database.

**6.2.** Create a table ARCHIVE to keep old records, and fill it with all RECORDS entries of 1983 and older. Be sure the old entries are deleted from RECORDS.

**6.3.** Delete all information about students who are no longer enrolled in any class (this will affect STUDENT and RECORDS).

**6.4.** Add a column AVERAGE to table STUDENT, and fill the column with the average grade of the students.

# Chapter 7

# Controlling the Performance

## 7.1 Introduction

In the previous chapters we saw quite a few examples of SQL queries: we discussed the syntax, the semantics of the operations, and the results; but we paid little attention to the fact that a particular query was easy or difficult to evaluate. Of course, in an idealized world, the user should not have to worry about the problem at all: all queries should be answered quickly enough. But, in practice, this cannot be achieved. The power of SQL is such that very complex operations can be expressed in a single statement, and it is quite reasonable to expect a delay in getting the result. What is important then is to understand what is intrinsically simple or complicated, what are the implementation techniques most commonly used, and how they perform in various cases. This is precisely the purpose of this chapter.

Consider the statement

> **select** RENTAL_FEE                                                       [7.1]
> **from** CONTRACT
> **where** CONTRACT=155

It actually involves a single row; and you certainly expect a response time in the order of a second. Then consider

**select avg** (RENTAL_FEE)                                                    [7.2]
**from** CONTRACT

In [7.2], the answer involves values in all rows of the table CONTRACT. Therefore, you probably expect the response time to be much longer and to grow with the size of the table.

Actually, things are not so simple, mainly because performance depends very much on the implementation. In fact, if you expect [7.1] to be answered in a second, independently of the size of the table, it is because you assume intuitively that there exists some mechanism - often called *associative access* - that allows the system to locate very quickly the single row of interest. If such a mechanism is not used, [7.1] can only be evaluated by examining successively all rows in CONTRACT to find those (one in this case) with value '155' in the column CONTRACT. By contrast, in [7.2], all rows are relevant to the computation of the average, and therefore no associative access can be used to reduce the number of rows to be examined.

Examples [7.1] and [7.2] illustrate two important points: 1) some SQL queries are intrinsically more complex than others and will require a longer evaluation time, and 2) an associative access can, in certain cases, reduce the evaluation time dramatically.

In this chapter we want to accomplish two things:

• Discuss the relative cost of basic relational operations (this is important because a user should be able to understand why a query can be answered in a second... or an hour).

• Show how the performance of a database system can be controlled by the optional use of associative accesses (this is important because it is finally the user who decides which access paths should be maintained by the system).

This is no easy task, however, since the performance of a relational system depends so much on the implementation, and the implementations are numerous and diverse. Fortunately, there is a basic technology which is common to most systems, and it is this technology that we are going to describe and use as basis for our analysis.

# 7.2  Storage of rows

SQL deals with rows in tables. These rows must be stored on a permanent medium such as a magnetic disk. A row, which is a collection of values stored in a certain order (generally the canonical order defined in the **create table** statement), is stored as a record in which each field corresponds to a column in the row. The question then is how to store such records on disk?

## 7.2.1  Files

Records are stored in files. A *file* is a logical sequence of physical blocks called *pages* (see Figure 27). We use the adjective logical because pages that are logically contiguous in the sequence may not necessarily be stored contiguously on disk. If pages are stored contiguously, it is easy to compute from the logical page number the physical address where the page is stored on disk. If pages are not stored contiguously, a structure of pointers must be used to indicate where each logical page is physically stored. In other words, the pointers establish a mapping from logical pages to disk locations.

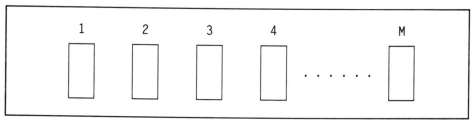

**Figure 27.  A file as a logical sequence of pages**

For the sake of explanation, let us assume contiguity and neglect the fact that pointers will be needed at some point when new pages need to be added in the middle of the file.

In any case, the system contains a component (let us call it the *Page Manager*) that supports the following operations:

- Scan pages: reading all pages, one after the other, in logical page number sequence.

- Reading a specified page (identified by its logical page number).

- Writing a specified page.

## 7.2.2  Storing records in a file

We assume that all records corresponding to rows of a given table are stored in the same file, and that a given file contains only records corresponding to rows of a single table.  In other words, there is a one-to-one relationship between a table and a file.

A record is stored on any page which happens to have enough room to receive it.  As a result, records are stored in any order.  Figure 28 shows a page of the file containing the CONTRACT table.  Note that each page contains a vector of displacements indicating where the jth record on the page is.  The concatenation <logical page number : record number> uniquely identifies a record in a file and is often called *rid* (short for *record identifier*).  The pair can be easily stored in a 4-byte word, using 3 bytes for the page number and 1 byte for the record number inside the page.  As we shall see later, rid's play an important role in indexing.

The above organization is extremely simple; it easily supports the reading of all records: the Page Manager is invoked to read all pages, one after the other, and, in each page, the vector of pointers is used to locate the individual records.  We shall refer to this access method as a *table scan*.

We now analyze the performance of a table scan.  We refer to the rental company example. However, to make the analysis meaningful, we consider a database of reasonable size, with the following number of records in each table:

TOOL            $nr = 5,000$ rows
CUSTOMER        $nr = 10,000$ rows
CONTRACT        $nr = 100,000$ rows

All row's lengths   $rl = 50$ bytes

Before embarking on the analysis, we have to make some assumptions on the characteristics of the system and the performance of some elementary operations:

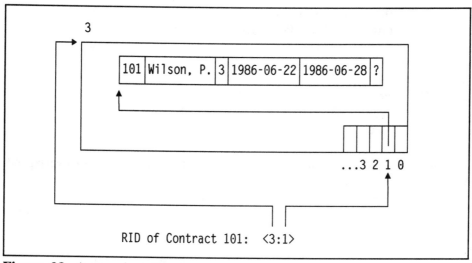

**Figure 28. A page in a file**

| | |
|---|---|
| page length | pl = 4,000 bytes |
| average occupancy of a page<br>(that is, a page is typically 80% full) | oc = 0.8 |

| | |
|---|---|
| Number of rows per page | $pr = pl \times oc/rl$<br>$= 4000 \times 0.8/50$<br>$= 64$ |

| | |
|---|---|
| CPU time to read a page | cp = 0.005 sec. |
| CPU time to extract a record from a page | ce = 0.001 sec. |
| CPU time to prepare a result record | cr = 0.001 sec. |

| | |
|---|---|
| IO time to read or write a page | io = 0.030 sec. |

The timings are just reasonable values for a machine that would perform 1 million instructions per second; they do not correspond to any particular implementation or machine.

Consider the use of a table scan to evaluate query [7.2]. The following analysis is straightforward (neglecting second-order effects):

$$CPU = (nr/pr) \times cp + nr \times ce$$
$$= (100,000/64) \times 0.005 + 100,000 \times 0.001$$
$$= 8 \text{ sec} + 100 \text{ sec.}$$
$$= 108 \text{ sec.}$$

$$IO = (nr/pr) \times io$$
$$= (100,000/64) \times 0.030$$
$$= 47 \text{ sec.}$$

In a simple implementation where CPU and disk activities are not overlapped, the response time will be

$$Total = 108 \text{ sec.} + 47 \text{ sec.} \tag{7.3}$$
$$= 155 \text{ sec.}$$

Now consider [7.1]. Since a CONTRACT number is unique, there is only one row in the answer set.

If a table scan is used as access method, rows are accessed exactly as for [7.2] above, and for each row the CONTRACT value is compared to 155. The table scan can be terminated once the record corresponding to 155 has been found; since this may happen at the beginning of the scan, at the end, or anywhere between, the average response time for the query will be about one half of [7.3] or 77 seconds. If the system does not know a priori that the value is unique, it will scan the whole table and the cost will be the same as in [7.3]: 155 seconds. This is far from the 1-second response time that a user normally expects; it shows that an associative access mechanism is absolutely essential.

Both [7.1] and [7.2] return only a single row in the result set. For this reason, constructing the result rows from the information stored in the table has been neglected. If many rows are returned in the result, the time to construct the result rows is not negligible anymore. In fact, the execution time for

**select** *                                                            [7.4]
**from** CONTRACT

can be estimated by adding to the 155 seconds estimated in [7.3], the time needed to construct the result rows, or $nr \times cr$. Therefore,

$$Total = \text{time in [7.3]} + nr \times cr \tag{7.5}$$
$$= 155 \text{ sec.} + 100,000 \times 0.001$$
$$= 255 \text{ sec.}$$

Depending on how many rows are returned, the response time will vary between 155 and 255 seconds. This may be quite acceptable if many rows are returned, but unacceptable if the answer set is very small. Here, also, associative access is necessary. In fact, the following two sections will describe the two associative access mechanisms that are most commonly used in relational database systems: *indexes* and *hashing*.

# 7.3 Indexes

An index is an access path enabling rows to be retrieved by values in an efficient way. For example, suppose you want to perform [7.1] very efficiently. If an index exists on column NUMBER in CONTRACT, then it should enable the system to go very directly to the correct row in CONTRACT. The column NUMBER is called the *key column* for that index; and the values in the key column are simply called *keys*. Note that index keys should not be confused with the key of a table. In an index, the key is not necessarily unique. As we shall see in Section 7.11, an index can be specified as being "unique". Then it will be used by the system to ensure uniqueness of a key in the table.

The index structure most commonly used in relational systems is known as a B-tree. Figure 29 shows a portion of a B-tree index built on the column CONTRACT of table CONTRACT (we added a few contracts for the sake of explanation). The index is a collection of pages organized as a hierarchy. The *root* page contains a series of pairs <key value, k> ordered by key value. The k's identify a series of pages at the next level down; each of these pages also contains pairs with k's identifying pages at the next level down, and so on. For the pairs <key value, k> stored in pages at the last level (also called *leaf* pages), the meaning of k is different: k is then the record identifier of the record which contains that key value in the key column. At all levels, pairs are stored in sequence of key values.

Note that, in our example, we assume there are only 4 entries in a page. In practice, page lengths are such that one single page contains dozens or hundreds of entries. We simply use a very small number for convenience.

Consider the pair <103, 1> in the root page. Since it is the first entry in the root page, its meaning is that all detailed information on keys smaller or equal to 103 can be found by looking at page 1. The second entry, <208, 2>, indicates that, for information about keys greater than 103 but not greater than 208, page 2 should be accessed. Suppose we want to find the record for contract 155; the index can be used as follows:

1. Read the root page and determine the entry corresponding to the key interval which contains 155. The value 155 is greater than 103 but less than

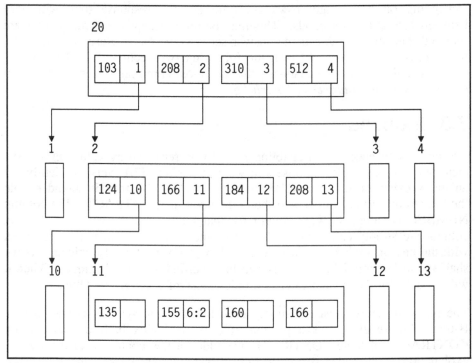

**Figure 29. A B-tree index**

208; therefore the entry of interest is <208, 2>, and the next page to be addressed is 2.

2. Read that page 2; look again for the entry corresponding to 155. The second interval is relevant since 155 is greater than 124 but less than 166. The next page to be accessed is thus 11. Repeat this process until a leaf page is reached: the leaf page will have an entry for 155 if such a key value exists.

3. The entry found in the leaf page 11 contains the record identifier that indicates which data page must be accessed and which record in that page corresponds to the specified key. Here, the entry <155, 6:2> indicates that page 6 must be fetched and that record 2 in that page contains the row corresponding to contract 155.

## 7.3.1 Index performance

The power of the B-tree organization comes from the fact that very few pages need to be accessed in order to find a record, knowing its key. Let us do a little arithmetic, considering again the index on CONTRACT.CONTRACT. In Figure 29, we only stored a few entries on each page; in reality, many more entries fit in a single page. Again, let us assume some characteristics for the database systems:

| | |
|---|---|
| Index page length: | ipl = 4000 bytes |
| CPU time to search a page: | cs = 0.010 sec. |
| Length of an rid: | 4 bytes |

and, for the particular database that we are considering, key size = 6 bytes. With these assumptions, an entry in the CONTRACT index page is 6 bytes + 4 bytes = 10 bytes, and the number of entries per (full) index page is ipl/10 = 400. So, if the file has not more than 400 records, the root page can contain the 400 entries <key, rid>. In such an index, the root page is also a leaf page, and the tree has a height of 1. If a tree has two levels, it supports 400 leaf pages, each with 400 entries, for a total of 160,000 records. This limit, however, will not be reached in practice because pages are rarely full: deletions happen, leaving unused space in pages, or additions force splits of pages that may leave a page half-empty. Thus, the actual number of records supported by a tree of height 2 may be closer to $300 \times 300$, rather than $400 \times 400$. This means that a height of 3 is needed to support the 100,000 entries for CONTRACT; the tree will then have 334 leaf pages, 2 second level pages, and 1 root, in total, 337 pages.

To evaluate [7.1], the number of pages to be accessed is 3 to get to the identifier of the data page, plus 1 for the data page itself. The time required can be evaluated as follows:

$$
\begin{aligned}
\text{CPU} &= 4 \times \text{cp} + 3 \times \text{cs} + \text{ce} + \text{cr} \qquad\qquad [7.6]\\
&= 4 \times 0.005 + 3 \times 0.01 + 0.001 + 0.001\\
&= 0.052 \text{ sec.}
\end{aligned}
$$

$$
\begin{aligned}
\text{IO} &= 4 \times 0.030\\
&= 0.120 \text{ sec.}
\end{aligned}
$$

$$
\text{Total} = 0.172 \text{ sec.}
$$

This response time is to be compared to the average 155 seconds required to do the same operation without an index.

Such an advantage does not come for free, however. You pay for it at the time rows are inserted. Each time a row is added, an entry needs to be made in the index. This implies looking up the index to see where the entry must be added and then adding it. The index operation may be roughly 3 times more expensive than just adding a new row. Also, the index does require extra space in the database. On the other hand, remember, a single retrieval will now be done in a fraction of a second instead of minutes.

## 7.3.2 Index maintenance

The efficiency of the B-tree for accessing a record, given its key, is based on the small height of the tree. An important characteristic is that the tree is always balanced, meaning that the height - and therefore the number of page accesses needed to locate a key - is constant for all key values. To ensure this property, insertions are handled as follows.

Assume we need to add an entry in a file. We first look up the tree as explained above to find the leaf page p in which the new entry should be made. If there is room on page p, the entry is inserted. If there is no room on page p, a *page split* occurs. A new page p' is used; one-half of the entries on p remain on p; the second half is moved onto p'; there is then room on both p and p', and the new entry can be made on the appropriate page, p or p', depending upon its key value. When such a split occurs, an additional entry needs to be added in the parent page. This addition itself may cause a page split and an additional insertion at the next level up.

In some cases an entry needs to be added in the root page. If the root page does not have room for a new entry, it needs to be split: it becomes two pages; a new root page is then used which will contain two entries. This operation increases the height of the tree by 1. Figure 30 shows the contents after addition of a contract (163), assuming all pages in Figure 29 were full. Page 11 is split into 26 and 27; page 2 is split into 24 and 25; page 20 is split into 22 and 23; and 21 becomes the new root of the tree which now has a height of 4.

# 7.4 Hashing

Hashing is a very simple and efficient associative access, although functionally poorer than indexing. It works as follows.

When a record with a key K is inserted into the database, the system will store the record in a page R. But here, rather than picking up R more or less randomly, it is computed as a function of the key value. There are many methods for computing R. Just as an example, consider adding the ASCII values of each character in the key and dividing the sum by an integer N.

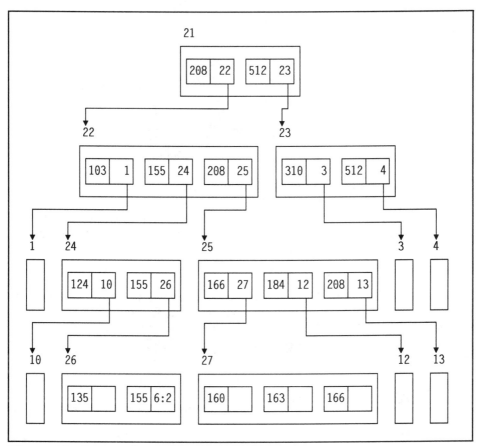

**Figure 30.  Result of update of a B-tree**

Then, R is always in the range 0 to (N-1), and, statistically, the values of R obtained for a large set of keys are distributed uniformly in that range.

When hashing is chosen as a storage method for the records of a table T, the system will put aside a set of N pages. Then it will always attempt to store a record which yields a hash value R into the page R of that set.  When the page is full, an overflow page outside the page set will be allocated and chained to page R (see Figure 31).

The way the associative access works with hashing should be clear by now. When asked to find the record corresponding to a certain key K, the system hashes the key to compute R, fetches the page R, and compares K with the keys in that page. If it exists, the record is fetched; if not, the process looks up the next pointer; if it is zero, the key is not found; otherwise the overflow

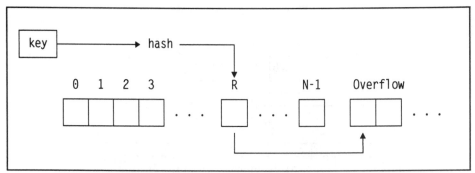

**Figure 31. Implementation of a hashing scheme**

page is fetched and searched, then the next one, and so on.  If the number N is chosen carefully, overflow should be rare, and the record corresponding to a unique key is located in a single page access.

This, in fact, may be slightly more efficient than an index, since an index search may require more than one page access, depending on the height of the B-tree. On the other hand, the associative access to a record, given a key, is the only operation that hashing supports efficiently.  Since an index supports the same operation with good performance, but in addition, retrieves the rows in key order, we only use indexing in the remainder of this chapter.

# 7.5  Support of order by

Consider the SQL query

> **select** *                                              [7.7]
> **from** CONTRACT
> **order by** CONTRACT

Here, also, the presence of an index may be of great value.  Most relational systems use one of two common techniques to evaluate a query such as [7.7]. The first is to do the selection exactly as if there were no **order by** clause and then sort the result table on the column CONTRACT. The second method uses the appropriate index if it exists. Let us evaluate each of these strategies.

## 7.5.1  Using a sort

The method consists of simply scanning the table and then sorting the result table before returning the rows to the caller. For evaluating the efficiency of this method, we need to understand the performance of a sort.  The performance of a sort depends very much on the algorithm used. However, all reasonable algorithms provide sort times that grow slightly more than proportionally to the number of items sorted. In fact, the time needed to sort a file of N records is

$$Tsort = k \times N \log_{10}(N)$$

where the value of k depends upon the length of the records to be sorted and the length of the ordering key. For rows of 50 bytes and keys of 6 bytes, a possible value of k is 0.001 for a 1-Mips processor, using a single disk. For [7.3] the sorting time would thus be

$$Tsort = 0.001 \times 100,000 \log_{10}(100,000) \qquad [7.8]$$
$$= 100 \times 5$$
$$= 500 \text{ sec.}$$

We can evaluate the total time by adding [7.5] and [7.8]:

$$Total = \text{time to scan and return all rows} + Tsort \qquad [7.9]$$
$$= 255 \text{ sec.} + 500 \text{ sec.}$$
$$= 755 \text{ sec.}$$

## 7.5.2 Using an index

If an index on CONTRACT.CONTRACT exists, it can be used to retrieve the records in key order with the following algorithm. Read the root page, then access the first page at the second level, and from there the first page at the third level, and so on, until a leaf page is encountered. On that leaf page, take the first entry <key, i> and read the record identified by i. Then consider the second entry, the third one, and so on, until the first leaf page has been exhausted. Go back to the page at the previous level to find the identifier of the second leaf page. When the first page at the second level has been completely used, go back to the first level to find the identifier of the next page at the second level, and so on. This operation traverses the tree completely from left to right, returning all records in key order.

To facilitate the traversing, some implementations put in each leaf page the identifier of the next leaf page. Then, only one page at each nonleaf level needs to be accessed to find the first leaf page; afterward the chaining can be used to retrieve the leaf pages in order.

At this point, we note that using the index for sequentially retrieving records in key order may be very efficient or less efficient, depending on whether the index is *clustered* or *nonclustered*.

An index is said to be clustered if the records are physically stored in the order implemented by the index. Suppose that, reading sequentially the entries in the leaf pages of the index, we obtain a list of rid's 1:1, 1:2, 1:3,... 2:1, 2:2,... 3:1, 3:2, 3:3,.... Then, to get the records themselves, we have to access page 1 for the first record; this operation probably implies reading the page from disk. Then the second record can be read again from page 1, the same for the third one, and so on. When page 1 is exhausted, page 2 is read to get records 2:1, 2:2...; finally, each page is read once. When all records on a page have been accessed, the page never needs to be fetched again, at least for this scan.

Suppose now that the list of rid's is 1:3, 3:2, 2:1, 1:2, 5:1, 2:3.... Then page 1 needs to be read to find 1:3; then page 3, then page 2, and then page 1 again. For a small table, this may not be too important since several pages can generally fit in memory. But, for a large table, each page access may imply the physical read of the page from disk, and, in the worst case, this could happen for each record. Figure 32 illustrates graphically a) a clustered index, and b) a nonclustered one.

We now compare access paths using indexes with those relying on sort. In our analysis, we need to make the difference between the clustered and nonclustered index cases.

- Clustered index

$$\begin{aligned}
CPU &= CPU \text{ for index pages} + CPU \text{ for data pages} &\quad [7.10]\\
&= \text{Nbr index pages} \times (cp + cs) + (nr/pr) \times cp + nr \times (ce + cr)\\
&= 337 \times (0.005 + 0.01) + (100,000/64) \times 0.005\\
&\quad + 100,000 \times (0.001 + 0.001)\\
&= 213 \text{ sec.}
\end{aligned}$$

$$\begin{aligned}
IO &= (\text{Nbr index pages} + \text{Nbr data pages}) \times io\\
&= (337 + (100,000/64)) \times 0.030\\
&= 57 \text{ sec.}
\end{aligned}$$

Total = 270 sec.

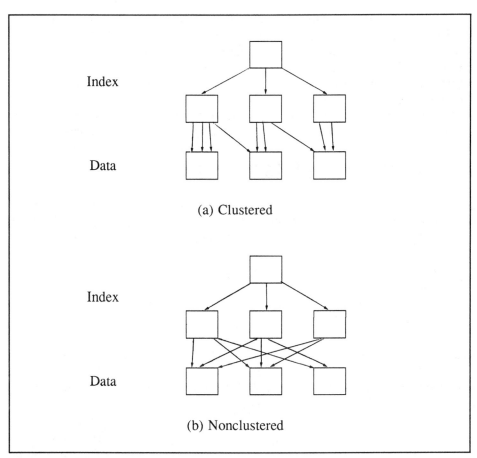

Index

Data

(a) Clustered

Index

Data

(b) Nonclustered

**Figure 32. Types of indexes**

- Nonclustered index

$$CPU = CPU \text{ for index pages} + CPU \text{ for data pages} \qquad [7.11]$$
$$= Nbr \text{ index pages} \times (cp + cs) + nr \times (cp + ce + cr)$$
$$= 337 \times (0.005 + 0.01) + 100,000 \times (0.005 + 0.001 + 0.001)$$
$$= 705 \text{ sec.}$$

$$IO = (Nbr \text{ index pages} + Nbr \text{ data pages}) \times io$$
$$= (337 + 100,000) \times 0.030$$
$$= 3,010 \text{ sec.}$$

$$Total = 3,715 \text{ sec.}$$

The total times are, respectively, 270 and 3,715 seconds. This is to be compared to the 755 seconds needed when no index exists. A clustered index is clearly an outstanding access path. If there is no clustered index, then a table scan is generally better than a nonclustered index. Thus, if only one index is defined on a table, it should be a clustered index, without doubt. But, since a clustered index determines in which order the records are physically stored in pages, there can only be a single clustered index for a table. If several indexes are defined on a single table, all indexes except one, are nonclustered.

# 7.6 Query with a filter

Queries [7.1] and [7.2] represent two extreme cases where only one row is relevant and where all rows are relevant, respectively. It is often interesting to find the set of rows that satisfies a given condition. Consider the query

> **select** ...                                                             [7.12]
> **from** CONTRACT
> **where** CONTRACT > 40000
>     **and** CONTRACT < 50000

If there is no index on the column CONTRACT, the time needed to answer [7.12] can be computed as in [7.5], taking into account, however, the fact that only a subset of the CONTRACT rows are involved in the answer set. Calling p the fraction of CONTRACT involved, we have

$$T = 155 \text{ sec.} + p \times nr \times cr \qquad\qquad [7.13]$$
$$= 155 \text{ sec.} + p \times 100$$

If $p = 1$, we clearly get the result computed in [7.5], 255 seconds.

If there is an index, the following alternate strategy may be more efficient. First, find the value 40,000 in the index. It may or may not exist; in fact, the index search will find the first value that is larger or equal to 40,000. From there, the entries will be accessed in order until 50,000 is reached. The evaluation goes as follows:

• Clustered index

$$CPU = \text{Nbr relevant index pages} \times (cp + cs)$$
$$+ \text{Nbr relevant data pages} \times cp$$
$$+ p \times nr \times (ce + cr)$$

$$\begin{aligned} CPU &= (3 + p \times 334) \times (0.005 + 0.01) \\ &\quad + (100{,}000/64) \times p \times 0.005 \\ &\quad + p \times 100{,}000 \times 0.002 \\ &= 0.045 + 213 \times p \text{ sec.} \end{aligned} \qquad [7.14]$$

$$\begin{aligned} IO &= (\text{Nbr of index pages} + \text{Nbr of data pages}) \times io \\ &= ((3 + p \times 334) + p \times 100{,}000/64) \times 0.03 \\ &= 0.090 + 57 \times p \text{ sec.} \end{aligned}$$

$$\text{Total} = 0.135 + 270 \times p \text{ sec.}$$

• Nonclustered index

$$\begin{aligned} CPU &= \text{Nbr relevant index pages} \times (cp + cs) \\ &\quad + p \times nr \times (cp + ce + cr) \\ &= (3 + p \times 334) \times (0.005 + 0.01) \\ &\quad + p \times 100{,}000 \times (0.005 + 0.001 + 0.001) \\ &= 0.045 + 705 \times p \text{ sec.} \end{aligned} \qquad [7.15]$$

$$\begin{aligned} IO &= (\text{Nbr relevant index pages} + \text{Nbr relevant data pages}) \times io \\ &= ((3 + p \times 334) + p \times 100{,}000) \times 0.03 \\ &= 0.090 + 3{,}010 \times p \text{ sec.} \end{aligned}$$

$$\text{Total} = 0.135 + 3{,}715 \times p \text{ sec.}$$

For p=1, we obtain the same values as those computed in [7.10] and [7.11]. For p=0.1, we obtain, respectively, 27 and 372. Again, the clustered index is good; and the scan is better than a nonclustered index. For p=0.01, we obtain, respectively, 2.7 and 37. At this level, even the nonclustered index is better than a scan. The fewest rows that qualify, the best the nonclustered index looks. Clearly, when a single row qualifies, clustered or nonclustered indexes are equally efficient.

The graph in Figure 33 summarizes the results.

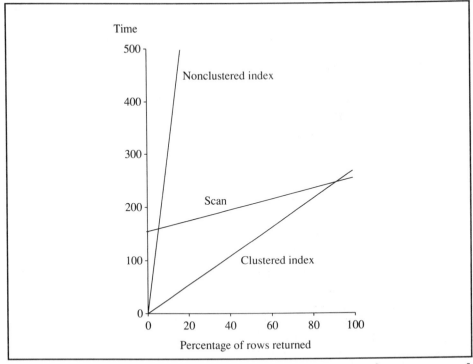

**Figure 33. Efficiency of indexes as a function of number of rows returned**

# 7.7  Support of group by

A previous section addressed the performance of sorting. The same analysis applies to the evaluation of queries that contain a **group by** clause, since the most common technique for evaluating a **group by** is to sort on the grouping column and then aggregate the rows by groups. Consider, for example,

      **select** TYPE, AVG(RENTAL_FEE)                          [7.16]
      **from** TOOL
      **group by** TYPE

which computes the average rental fee for each type of tool. Most implementations extract the type and rental_fee from each row in TOOL, making sure the result is ordered on type. This can be done either by accessing the TOOL rows via an index on TYPE or by sorting the rows <TYPE, RENTAL_FEE> on TYPE. In any case, the resulting rows corresponding to the same type are all together, making the aggregation straightforward.

# 7.8 Summary: indexes

The analysis given so far in this chapter yields several useful rules for deciding which indexes should be maintained:

- If most queries done on a table are for all or practically all rows, then no index is needed; a table scan is a very good strategy.

- If a table has a unique key, an index must exist on the key column; otherwise, the burden of checking if the key to be inserted already exists or not is on the application program. The unique index can be clustered or nonclustered.

- If a column contains duplicate values but the repetition factor is low, then a value in that column is selective, and an index on that column is very efficient. Here again, the index can be clustered or nonclustered.

- If the duplication factor becomes larger, the selectivity is low. A nonclustered index is of little value; but a clustered index is extremely useful for range queries or queries with **order by** or **group by** on that column. It should be noted that lots of insertions may destroy the physical sequencing of records following a clustered index. When this happens, it may be necessary to unload and reload the table (utilities are generally provided to that effect). Of course, some percentage of space on a page can be left unused so that new insertions will not destroy the clustering, at least for a while.

The information on clustering and other physical attributes of the data is kept in a catalog. Since the query optimizer uses that information to determine the best access path, it is important that it be up-to-date. SQL systems generally provide a command to update the information. It is a good practice to execute that command periodically, particularly if lots of changes have been made to the database.

To complete this section, let us choose the indexes for the rental application.

- For TOOL: An index on NUMBER is needed for direct access; it can be nonclustered since it is very selective (actually unique), and the order on NUMBER is not relevant. Type is not very selective, but it may be interesting to find all tools of a certain type. Therefore, a clustered index is appropriate.

- For CUSTOMER: a **unique index** on NAME is needed; if it is the only index, it may as well be clustered (this would help a **select ... order by** NAME). But, for mailing purposes, it may be good to be able to select or order customers by zip code; then a clustered index on ZIP (and nonclustered on NAME) may be preferable.

- For CONTRACT: a similar reasoning yields a choice of a clustered index on TOOL and nonclustered indexes on CONTRACT and CUSTOMER.

We mentioned that statistics are used by the SQL optimizer to decide which access path is the best. Some systems use a simpler technique to decide on the access path, like using an index every time one can be found. The degree of sophistication of the query optimizer should be a critical parameter in the choice of an SQL system supporting large amounts of data.

# 7.9  Joins

The more complex the SQL statement, the more difficult it is to estimate the performance. In particular, the time required to do a join varies very much with the implementation, and therefore we can only try to provide some insight. Several join methods are used in relational systems. Here we consider two of the most common ones.

## 7.9.1  Nested loops

The simplest algorithm for join evaluation is the **nested loops** algorithm. Consider the statement

**select** *                                                                                    [7.17]
**from** CONTRACT, TOOL
**where** CONTRACT.TOOL = TOOL.NUMBER

The nested loops algorithm works as follows: choose an **outer** table, for example CONTRACT, and scan it using any method. Each row returned by that scan contains a tool number. For each such row (and tool number), find, using any method, the rows of TOOL (the **inner** table) that contain a matching tool number (this is the method already used in Figure 21). Since the tool number is a key of TOOL, the number of matching TOOL rows will be one for each CONTRACT row; the result row is then obtained by concatenating the CONTRACT and TOOL rows together.

If we choose CONTRACT as the outer table and if there is no index on TOOL.NUMBER, the execution time for [7.17] will be extremely long since the inner table will have to be scanned as many times as there are rows in the outer table. Choosing TOOL as the outer table means scanning CONTRACT as often as there are rows in TOOL. Here, also, if there is no index on

CONTRACT.TOOL, performance is very poor. In fact, the method of nested loops is of little interest without indexes.

Assume now that CONTRACT is chosen as the outer table, but that there exists an index on TOOL.NUMBER. Then the time needed to evaluate [7.17] is equal to the sum of t1 and nr $\times$ t2, where nr is the number of outer rows, t1 the time needed to scan these nr rows, and t2 the time to find a matching row in TOOL (the index on TOOL.NUMBER is assumed to have a height of 2 only). Thus,

$$Total = t1 + nr \times t2 \qquad\qquad [7.18]$$

$$t1 = 255 \text{ sec.} \qquad\qquad See [7.5]$$

For t2:

$$CPU = 3 \times cp + 2 \times ci + ce + cr$$
$$= 3 \times 0.005 + 2 \times 0.01 + 0.001 + 0.001 \text{ sec.}$$
$$= 0.037 \text{ sec.}$$

$$IO = 3 \times io$$
$$= 3 \times 0.030$$
$$= 0.090 \text{ sec.}$$

$$t2 = 0.037 + 0.090 = 0.127 \text{ sec.}$$

$$Total = 255 + 100,000 \times 0.127$$
$$= 12,955 \text{ sec.}$$

We can also choose TOOL as the outer table. Then, for each row in TOOL, the inner loop must find all rows in CONTRACT that have a matching tool number. The time T can be computed in a similar way. The optimizer of a relational system generally carries out these computations and adopts the strategy that is most efficient. The computation above shows clearly that the cost is high, because T2, which is repeated 100,000 times, is relatively high. This, in turn, is due to the fact that each row in CONTRACT yields a value of TOOL.NUMBER that is arbitrary, and the system has to "jump" to an arbitrary location in TOOL.

There are, however, cases where the method performs quite well. Suppose that the inner table is small. Then it will tend to remain in the memory buffer during the duration of the join evaluation. As a result, the time to find a matching row is much reduced, and the method is quite appropriate. When this is not the case, another method is used, as described in the following section.

## 7.9.2 The merge-join algorithm

We now discuss a second join method. This method has the advantage of never being very poor. So, when the previous nested loops method is not appropriate, the optimizer will generally choose the merge-join. The method consists of two steps:

1. Make sure that there is a way to scan the rows of both tables in the order of the values in the join columns. In the example, it means that we need to be able to scan TOOL in the order of the tool numbers. If there existed a clustered index on NUMBER, it would be used to provide the rows in the appropriate order; otherwise a sort is needed. But we also need to be able to scan CONTRACT in the order of the tool numbers. If there is a clustered index on CONTRACT.TOOL, it can be used; if there is no such index, then table CONTRACT must be sorted on that column.

2. Once these two scans are available, merge them to find the rows that match. Let us show how this works on a simple example. Suppose the scan of the first table produces the following join keys in order:

    A   A   B   B   B   C   D   D   E   E   E   F

    while the scan on the second table yields

    B   B   C   D   F   F

    The first values in both scans are compared. Since A is less than B, it is clear that A does not exist in the second table, and the whole group of A's in the first scan can be discarded. The rest of the scans yield, respectively,

    B   B   B   C   D   D   E   E   E   F

    and

    B   B   C   D   F   F

    The same comparison is done again; this time the B values match, and each row with a B value in the first scan is concatenated with each row with a B value in the second scan (yielding 6 result rows). When finished, the groups are discarded, giving

```
C   D   D   E   E   E   F
```

and

```
C   D   F   F
```

The next steps produce one result row for the value C and two for the value D.  Value E is discarded because there is no matching group in the second table. Finally, the matching group on F produces two other rows in the result.

Referring to results obtained earlier, we can easily compute the cost associated with the merge-join method:

For CONTRACT:

| | | |
|---|---|---|
| Scan | 155 sec. | see [7.3] |
| Sort | 500 sec. | see [7.8] |
| Read result of sort | 155 sec. | see [7.3] |
| | | |
| Total | 810 sec. | |

A similar computation for TOOL yields:

| | |
|---|---|
| Scan | 6 sec. |
| Sort | 19 sec. |
| Read result of sort | 6 sec. |
| | |
| Total | 31 sec. |

Then, the rows obtained by reading the sort results are merged (we can neglect the time of the comparison, compared to the time needed to fetch the rows themselves).  Finally, 100,000 rows need to be returned, taking another 50 seconds.  The total join time is less than 800 seconds, clearly demonstrating the efficiency of the algorithm, compared to the use of nested loops (12,955 seconds).  Note that, if there should exist a clustered index on CONTRACT.TOOL, the sort would be unnecessary and the time much shorter.

# 7.10  Subqueries

To evaluate the performance of SQL queries containing subqueries, we need to make the distinction between correlated and uncorrelated subqueries.  Consider

```
select *                                              [7.19]
from CONTRACT A
where FEE >
  ( select avg(FEE)
    from CONTRACT)
```

The result of the subquery does not depend on any value in row A (A is not necessary here; it is added for the sake of explanation). Therefore, the subquery can be evaluated only once, at the beginning of the query evaluation, exactly as if we had told the system

*put in X the result of*                                              [7.20]

```
select avg(FEE)
from CONTRACT
```

*and compute*

```
select *
from CONTRACT
where FEE > X
```

The total time will be the sum of the times for the first and second queries.

Assume now that you are interested in

```
select ..., CUSTOMER                                              [7.21]
from CONTRACT A
where FEE >
  ( select avg(FEE)
    from CONTRACT B
    where B.CUSTOMER = A.CUSTOMER )
```

Here the value of the subquery depends on the value of A.CUSTOMER. It must therefore be computed for each row returned by the evaluation of the parent query. Thus, the time to evaluate the query is equal to the time to evaluate

```
select ..., CUSTOMER                                              [7.22]
from CONTRACT
where FEE > X              (and get answer in Y)
```

plus n times the time to evaluate

**select** avg(FEE) [7.23]
**from** CONTRACT
**where** B.CUSTOMER = *Y*

where n is the number of CUSTOMER rows found, and *X* and *Y* are values.[1]
If there is an index on the column CONTRACT.CUSTOMER, then the
embedded subquery can be computed very quickly. If there is no index, a full
scan of CONTRACT is required for each row in CONTRACT, yielding very
poor performance.

# 7.11 Index creation

It should be clear by now that the performance of a relational system for the
evaluation of most queries is influenced drastically by the availability or non-
availability of the appropriate indexes. But, as we have seen, indexes do not
come for free, and a system cannot automatically decide to build an index on
each column of all tables, much less on all combinations of columns. This is
why most system implementations leave to the user the choice of indexes. To
exercise that choice, SQL provides two statements that can be used to *create*
or *drop* an index.

The syntax for the **create index** statement is:

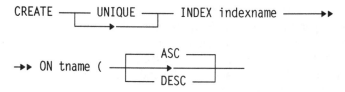

**Note:** When neither **asc** nor **desc** is specified, **asc** is assumed.

For the **drop index** statement, the syntax is:

```
DROP INDEX indexname
```

Note that the indexes created on a table are automatically dropped when the
table is dropped. So use **drop index** only when you want to destroy an index
without dropping the table.

---

1 There are ways to improve the performance of this type of subquery, but they are beyond the
scope of our analysis, and of many system implementations as well. For example, the system
may choose to order the CONTRACT rows by customer numbers so that the subquery may be
evaluated only once for each customer, and then reused for all contracts for the same customer.

The **create index** statement creates an index on the specified table name and gives it a name. The index is built on one or more columns specified by their names, either in ascending (**asc**) or descending (**desc**) order. If you want the system to ensure the uniqueness of a key, an index must be created on the key column(s) with the attribute **unique**. When such an index exists, any update of the index, when a row is added to or updated in the table, will determine if the key value already exists in some row. If it does, the insert or update is rejected.

For example, to create an index on TOOL.NUMBER and to ensure that no two rows can be inserted with the same NUMBER, you would write

      **create unique index** IND1                              [7.24]
      **on** TOOL (NUMBER **asc**)

The fact that ascending was specified means that the index may be used to retrieve tools, ordered on ascending tool number, without invoking a sort. To create an index on TOOL.RENTAL_FEE, you would simply write

      **create index** IND2                                  [7.25]
      **on** TOOL (RENTAL_FEE **desc**)

Here, **unique** is not specified since it is quite normal to have various tools with the same fee; and **desc** was chosen because we felt that it was more likely for lists of tools to be requested in descending order, showing the expensive tools first. Therefore the fact that the index is in descending order may save sorts and improve performance.

Both previous examples create indexes on a single column. This is certainly the most frequent case. But it may be appropriate, or even necessary, to create an index which covers several columns. For example, the availability of the index created by

      **create index** IND3                                  [7.26]
      **on** CONTRACT (DATE_OUT **asc**, DATE_IN **desc**)

may be useful for certain queries; and

      **create unique index** IND4                              [7.27]
      **on** TOOL (NUMBER, TYPE)

could have been used to ensure the uniqueness of a tool, if we had decided to assign tool numbers that were unique among the tools of the same type, instead of among all tools.

## 7.12  Summary

In the first part of this chapter, we discussed the importance of indexes to evaluate queries on a single table. We then discussed the join problem. Although the two methods most frequently used complement themselves rather well, indexes, again, are extremely useful. For these reasons, SQL provides the user with explicit control over the creation and destruction of indexes, with **create index** and **drop index** statements. It should be noted that the existence of indexes is generally stable: one does not create an index and drop it soon after, except maybe for trying out what the effect of an index is on the performance of a certain query.

Creating an index is, by the way, a complex operation in itself as soon as the size of the relation is not trivially small. But a good system implementation uses sorting to speed it up. In fact, the sorting time is the main component in the total time needed to create an index. The performance of dropping an index may vary from one system to another; but the operation is essentially very fast if the system only marks as free the pages that were occupied by the index.

## 7.13  Exercises

The exercises use the database application described in Chapter 2.

**Note:** For the exercises of this chapter, we assume the following characteristics of the tables:

**STUDENT:** There are 20,000 students, who entered the college between 1982 and 1986. The same number of new students enroll each year (4,000 per year).

**CLASS:** There are 500 classes open to students.

**RECORDS:** While the number of entries per student varies, the average is 5 rows per student, for a total of 100,000 rows.

**PREREQ:** Half the classes have no prerequisite. Each of the other 250 has an average of 2 prerequisite classes. Thus, the table contains 500 rows.

For the sake of simplification, we also assume that all rows are 25 bytes long and stored in pages of 4,000 bytes, with an occupancy factor of 80%.

**7.1.** How many rows of each table fit in a page? How many pages are used for each table?

**7.2.** If there is no index at all, how much longer is the evaluation of

    **select** *
    **from** RECORDS

compared to the evaluation of

    **select** *
    **from** STUDENT

**7.3.** Consider the following query:

    **select avg**(GRADE)
    **from** RECORDS
    **where** YEAR = 1985

1. If there is no index, how many rows are touched internally to evaluate the query?
2. What if there is an index on column YEAR of table RECORDS?
3. How many page I/Os will be performed if there is no index?
4. How many page I/Os will be performed if the index on YEAR is clustered?
5. How many page I/Os will be performed if the index on YEAR is not clustered?

**7.4.** Repeat exercise 7.3 for the query

    **select avg**(GRADE)
    **from** RECORDS
    **where** STUDENT = 5257

(When it exists, the index is on column STUDENT instead of YEAR.)

**7.5.** Repeat exercise 7.3 for the query

    **select count**(*)
    **from** RECORDS
    **where** YEAR = 1985

**7.6.** If there is no index, how many rows (on average) are going to be touched internally in order to find all courses taken by John?

**7.7.** Write the statements needed to create the index or indexes that would ensure optimal performance for the query in the previous exercise. How many rows will be touched internally?

**7.8.** Which indexes should be created on each of the tables in the college database? Justify your decisions. Write the corresponding **create index** statements.

# Chapter 8

# Views

## 8.1 Introduction

Suppose you work for the rental company and are in charge of keeping track of customers who have outstanding contracts. You watch for specific conditions that require some action. For example, you may be interested in all contracts that are outstanding and older than a certain number of days so that you can send an appropriate note to the customer. More precisely, assume you want to notify the customers who have had an outstanding contract for more than ten days. The following SQL statement will provide you with all needed information.

[8.1]

```
select NAME, ADDRESS, DATE_OUT, DATE_IN
from CUSTOMER, CONTRACT
where CUSTOMER.NAME = CONTRACT.CUSTOMER
    and FEE is null
    and DATE_OUT + 10 days < current date
```

| NAME | ADDRESS | DATE_OUT | DATE_IN |
|------|---------|----------|---------|
| Adams, A. | 123 Pine St, San Jose CA | 1986-06-11 | 1986-07-13 |

A join is used to get not only the contracts themselves, but the customer addresses as well. The predicate on FEE assures that only outstanding contracts are considered (for these rows, FEE is null).

Later, you may want to check for another condition on outstanding contracts. You may want to send another kind of note to customers who have five-day-old contracts for tools that have a fee greater than a certain threshold. Again, you need the join and the predicate "FEE **is null**". You start to realize that, for your own purposes, you really would like to see the data differently. It would be nice, in fact, if the database contained a table OUTSTANDING with one row for every contract, with the customer name, full address, date_out and date_in. Then you could simply write, instead of [8.1],

**select** *                                    [8.2]
**from** OUTSTANDING
**where** DATE_OUT + 10 **days** < **current date**

| NAME | ADDR | DATE_OUT | DATE_IN |
|------|------|----------|---------|
| Adams, A. | 123 Pine St, San Jose CA | 1986-06-11 | 1986-07-13 |

OUTSTANDING captures the join and all predicates that are constant for your purpose. Thus, in [8.2], you need only to think about the additional and variable predicates.

How can this be done? One possible way is to actually create a table OUTSTANDING and make sure that:

• Every time a CONTRACT row is added or updated, a corresponding row is also added or updated in OUTSTANDING.

• Every time an address is updated in CUSTOMER, all affected rows are also updated in OUTSTANDING.

But the approach is far from satisfactory. Not only you have to worry about making sure that all modifying programs obey that protocol, but the extra insertions or updates will degrade performance. In addition, OUTSTANDING has been tailored for you; if another user wants to see the data in still a different way, another table must be created and maintained, adding redundancy and making the problem even worse. Not to mention the extra disk space required to store these redundant tables.

To provide the desired functionality without the drawbacks that we just mentioned, SQL provides a mechanism that enables you to create virtual tables, called *views*, that can be queried as regular tables but are not stored as such.

The contents of these virtual tables change when the contents of the regular tables on which they are defined change. But this happens logically: updates are only made on regular, stored tables, and the system computes dynamically the contents of a view, when needed.

A word of clarification is needed to understand the impact on performance. For most queries, the view mechanism provides the same performance as the one provided by operations on the stored tables on which the views are defined. In this sense there is no penalty in using views. Since the view mechanism recomputes the result when it is accessed, it may be slower than using a stored table which materializes the view and which is kept up-to-date at each update. It is a matter of trade-off. Do you want to pay a price at each update to speed up the queries? The answer is probably no. In case it is yes, the burden is on the application program to manage the redundancy.

A **create view** statement enables you to define the shape and logical contents of a view and give it a name. For example, the following statement creates the view OUTSTANDING used in [8.2]:

> **create view** OUTSTANDING (NAME, ADDR,                    [8.3]
>           DATE_OUT, DATE_IN)
> **as**
> **select** NAME, ADDRESS, DATE_OUT, DATE_IN
> **from** CUSTOMER, CONTRACT
> **where** CUSTOMER.NAME = CONTRACT.CUSTOMER
>      **and** FEE **is null**

The virtual table has four columns: NAME, ADDR, DATE_OUT, and DATE_IN, containing, respectively, the NAME, ADDRESS, DATE_OUT, and DATE_IN from tables CUSTOMER and CONTRACT. It is noteworthy that, in a reasonable implementation of the view mechanism, the system does not need to materialize the contents of OUTSTANDING in any way; it is able to take the definition of the view [in 8.3], combine it with the submitted query [8.2], and obtain exactly [8.1], which is then evaluated.

To complete our example, let us use the same view for a quite different type of query. To find the number of outstanding contracts, you simply write

> **select count**(*)                                               [8.4]
> **from** OUTSTANDING

| COUNT(*) |
|---|
| 2 |

## 8.2 The general concept of view

The concept comprises two parts: the definition and the use. The definition of a view assigns a name to the view, (optionally) a name to each of its column, and a virtual content. The content is defined by an SQL **select** statement. The types of the columns are automatically derived from the **select** statement. For all intents and purposes, the view is thus a table, and it should be possible to refer to a view anywhere SQL refers to a table. As we shall see later, there are some restrictions, but just ignore them for the moment.

The syntax is defined by the following diagram:

```
CREATE VIEW vname ( ——⊤— colname —⊤— ) AS SELECT statement
                     └—◀—— , ——◀—┘
```

The select statement defines a result which has k columns. The list of column names must also contain k names, each identifying the corresponding column in the result.

## 8.3 Several uses of views

The view mechanism is useful for a variety of functions, some of which are described in the following sections.

### 8.3.1 Selecting rows and columns

Consider the following query on the table CONTRACT:

> **select** *                                       [8.5]
> **from** CONTRACT

Since the canonical order of the columns in CONTRACT is CONTRACT, CUSTOMER, TOOL, DATE_OUT, DATE_IN, and FEE, the result of the query [8.5] will contain the columns in that order. For example, one row may be

| CONTRACT | CUSTOMER | TOOL | DATE_OUT | DATE_IN | FEE |
|---|---|---|---|---|---|
| 98 | Adams, A. | 2 | 1986-05-15 | 1986-05-15 | 11.95 |

If a view is defined using

**create view** CT (TOOL, CUSTOMER, FEE, D_IN, D_OUT)    [8.6]
**as**
**select** TOOL, CUSTOMER, FEE, DATE_IN, DATE_OUT
**from** CONTRACT

then the query

**select** *    [8.7]
**from** CT

returns the columns in the order specified in the view definition:

| CT | | | | |
|---|---|---|---|---|
| TOOL | CUSTOMER | FEE | D_IN | D_OUT |
| 3 | Wilson, P. | 18.00 | 1986-05-17 | 1986-05-15 |
| 2 | Adams, A. | 11.95 | 1986-05-15 | 1986-05-15 |
| 1 | Smith, J. | 24.60 | 1986-05-25 | 1986-05-23 |
| 2 | Wilson, P. | 0.00 | 1986-06-25 | 1986-06-22 |
| 3 | Wilson, P. | ? | 1986-06-28 | 1986-06-22 |
| 1 | Adams, A. | ? | 1986-07-13 | 1986-06-11 |

Note that not only the order of the columns has changed (and some of their names), but the contract number does not appear. This is because we omitted to name the column CONTRACT in the view definition. Note also that the following two statements yield the same result:

**select** TOOL, DATE_IN, DATE_OUT    [8.8]
**from** CONTRACT

and

**select** TOOL, D_IN, D_OUT    [8.9]
**from** CT

If you are always interested in a subset of the rows of a table and if that subset can be defined by a **where** clause (which does not contain any variable), you may choose to define a view which takes the **where** clause into account so that the virtual table contains only the rows of interest. Of course, the selection of rows can be combined with the selection and reordering of the columns:

```
exec sql include sqlca
exec sql begin declare section
        declare number Fee
exec sql end declare section

exec sql declare C1 cursor for
        select FEE
        from BIG_CT
        for update of FEE

exec sql whenever not found go to The_End
exec sql open C1
do forever

        exec sql fetch C1 into :Fee
        compute the new fee
        exec sql update BIG_CT
                set FEE = :Fee
                where current of C1


        end
The_End:
exec sql commit work
```

**Figure 34. Updating a table through a view**

```
create view BIG_CT (TOOL, CUSTOMER, D_IN, D_OUT, FEE) [8.10]
as
select TOOL, CUSTOMER, DATE_IN, DATE_OUT, FEE
from CONTRACT
where FEE>15
```

BIG_CT contains only rows that correspond to contracts with a fee greater than 15.

In all preceding examples, each row in the result comes from one particular row in the stored table. In other words, there exists a one-to-one mapping between a row in the view and a row in the stored table. This is a very important property because it makes possible the update of rows through a view.

Consider the program in Figure 34 which uses the view defined in [8.10]. The cursor C1 identifies a current row in BIG_CT. To this current row in the view corresponds one and only one row in the stored table CONTRACT. Thus, there is no ambiguity as to which row of CONTRACT needs to be updated. Clearly, if the view includes only a subset of the columns of the stored table, columns that are not seen through the view cannot be updated through it.

## 8.3.2 Computed columns

Suppose that, for managing cost, you are often interested in knowing the ratio between the rental fee and the purchase price of the tool. You can define a view that extracts the relevant information from TOOL and contains a new column RATIO:

> **create view** MY_TOOL (NBR, TYPE, RATIO)                    [8.11]
> **as**
> **select** NUMBER, TYPE, RENTAL_FEE/PURCH_PRICE
> **from** TOOL

Then you can simply select RATIO from MY_TOOL, when needed, rather than respecifying it each time on the stored table TOOL. Again, each row in the view corresponds to one and only one row of the stored table, and the view can be used for updating NBR (from the view definition, the system knows that what is to be updated is actually NUMBER). An attempt to update RATIO would result in an error since that column does not exist in the database.

## 8.3.3 Joining tables

Joins can be used in a view definition. Consider a cursor declared on [8.3], where each contract is joined with one CUSTOMER row. One particular row of the result (identified by a particular position of the cursor) logically contains the information of one particular contract. In addition, it is the only row that contains information from that contract; so there is no problem at all in updating contract information through the view. But the situation is different for CUSTOMER. The information about a particular customer is repeated in many rows of the result. So, what does it mean to update the customer information in one row only? It cannot mean updating the address of a customer only for the particular contract. It cannot mean changing the address of a customer for all contracts either, because this is equivalent to updating several rows of the view with a single positioning of the cursor (which is contrary to the semantics of a cursor). As a result, SQL will generally prohibit such an update through a view. This does not constitute a weakness of implementation; it is actually imposed by the semantics of the update.

## 8.3.4 Aggregate functions, grouping

As the manager responsible for the cost policies of the rental company, you may be mostly interested in statistical information. For example, if you need to refer often to the average purchase price of a certain type of tool, you may want to define the following view:

> **create view** TOOL_AVG (TYPE, AVERAGE)    [8.12]
> **as**
> **select** TYPE, **avg**(PURCH_PRICE)
> **from** TOOL
> **group by** TYPE

Then, a simple **select** on the view TOOL_AVG will return averages without grouping, as in

> **select** AVERAGE    [8.13]
> **from** TOOL_AVG
> **where** TYPE = 'mower'

| AVERAGE |
|---------|
| 576.9333 |

When grouping is involved in the **select** of a view definition, each row in the view corresponds to a set of rows in the stored table, and no update can be done through the view.

It is interesting to note that views can be used to transform complex SQL statements into simple ones by moving the complexity once to the view definition (rather than having to deal with it each time the query is used). But a view can also be used to extend the power of **select**. For example, suppose you want to know the minimum average purchase price of tools of the same type. It is not possible to find the answer to this question with a single **select** on TOOL. However, if the view [8.12] is available, then the answer is given by

> **select min**(AVERAGE)    [8.14]
> **from** TOOL_AVG

Of course, the same result would be obtained by inserting the average into a temporary table T with a single column AVERAGE:

> **insert into** T                                                    [8.15]
>     **select avg**(PURCH_PRICE)
>     **from** TOOL
>     **group by** TYPE

and then using

> **select min**(AVERAGE)                                              [8.16]
>     **from** T

The use of a view is much simpler however, since only the view definition and the **select** are needed, while the use of a temporary table T involves creating T, inserting into T, selecting from T, and finally dropping T. Essentially, when you use a view, you let the system decide if a temporary table is needed. As mentioned earlier, some views do not need to materialize any data to answer queries on them; others, such as [8.14] may. A good system implementation will materialize a view in a temporary table only if absolutely needed; and this is done in a completely transparent way.

# 8.4 Summary

In its whole generality, the concept of view is quite easy to understand. The result of a **select** statement becomes a virtual table, and any **select** can be applied to this virtual table. For **update** through views, we have seen that there are restrictions. Essentially, the update through a view makes sense only when the row/column being updated clearly comes from a single row/column value in a stored table. While restrictions should only apply to operations that violate this condition, some systems do introduce additional restrictions to simplify the implementation.

Some restrictions may even apply to querying through a view. For example, an implementation may decide not to support views that force a full materialization of the view before it can be used in a **select**. The user should refer to the reference manual for a detailed explanation of what is supported by a specific implementation and what is not.

# 8.5 Exercises

The exercises use the database application described in Chapter 2.

**8.1.** Write the statement to create a view named ALLRECORDS, with columns containing the student name, the subject taken, the year in which the subject was taken, and the grade.

**8.2.** Two statements are needed to find the student with the highest average grade. What are they?

**8.3.** Create a view GOODSTUDENT containing a subset of the rows in STUDENT. A student belongs to GOODSTUDENT only if he or she had at least one grade above 4.5.

**8.4.** Create a view FULLCLASS, showing the subjects taken by at least 20 students in 1987.

**8.5.** Create a view EMPTYCLASS, showing the classes (number and subject) that were not taken by any student in 1987.

# Chapter 9

# Data Protection

## 9.1 Introduction

Since a database contains all important data of an individual, business, or organization, it constitutes an invaluable asset indeed. It is therefore essential that the information be always there, correct, and protected from unauthorized access.

If, for some reason, the database is destroyed, it may take a long time to reconstruct it (if at all possible) and this may affect the functioning of the enterprise which relies on it. If the data are corrupted, further updates based on invalid information may propagate errors, corrupting a larger and larger portion of the database. Finally, the database may contain information of a confidential or sensitive nature that you want to protect from any access by some or all other users.

The protection of data under any circumstances is quite a challenging problem. Fortunately, it is something that most good SQL implementations do automatically, with very little user involvement. It is this "very little" that we are going to cover here. Our motivation in doing so is, as always, to give the reader enough background to understand why certain things may happen when using SQL, and how some aspects of the system behavior may be controlled through special SQL commands.

# 9.2 Protection against user errors

The simplest way to get bad data in a database is to enter them erroneously in the first place. If the rental fee for a tool is 12.30 and you enter 13.30, the database contains an incorrect piece of information. Is it possible to have some of these errors detected automatically by the system? Suppose you could tell the system that the value in a particular column of a particular table must always fall inside a certain range. Then the system could check the condition every time such a data element is inserted or updated. However, the method lacks flexibility. For example, since tools may be relatively cheap or relatively expensive, their rental fees may vary in a large range, decreasing the efficiency of the test. The solution to such a problem is to specify much more precise conditions. Suppose that you never rent a tool for less than 2% or more than 6% of its purchase price. Then the condition

RENTAL_FEE **between** PUR_PRICE * 0.02                    [9.1]
        **and** PUR_PRICE * 0.06

provides a very efficient test. Rather than adding new features to SQL, some relational systems use a very elegant way of providing a lot of power with a minimal construct. In fact, the only construct that is added is that of a ***check view***. Suppose you define the following check view on TOOL:

**create view** V                                                    [9.2]
**as**
**select** *
**from** TOOL
**where** RENTAL_FEE **between** PURCH_PRICE * 0.02
        **and** PURCH_PRICE*0.06
**with check option**

If all rows in TOOL verify [9.1], then they will all belong to the view V as well. The check view mechanism works as follows. When a row is inserted (or modified) into a table through a check view V, the view is checked to ensure that the new row belongs to the view; if not, the insertion or update is rejected. If the view V is defined on top of other check views, these also participate in the verification process. When a check view is used for selecting rows, the check option has no effect and the check view acts as a regular view.

The syntax of a check view is identical to the syntax of a view as discussed in Chapter 8, except for the additional clause **with check option**. This means that the full power of the view mechanism is available for checking, making it possible to specify very specific conditions and decreasing the probability that erroneous values make their way into the database.

# 9.3  Referential integrity

Consider the following join between CONTRACT and TOOL:

**select** *                                                    [9.3]
**from** CONTRACT, TOOL
**where** CONTRACT.TOOL = TOOL.NUMBER

In our discussion on joins, we made it clear that all contracts appear in the result table because there is always a tool number in TOOL that matches the tool number in CONTRACT. Such matching is intrinsic to the relational model and to SQL. It is therefore important to be sure that, when a CONTRACT row is inserted in the database, the tool number that it contains does exist in TOOL. In other words, it is essential that a value referenced in one table does exist in the other table. This property is called *referential integrity*. If the insert statement happens to be embedded in a program, the programmer would probably have added some extra logic to fetch the TOOL row corresponding to the contract tool - just to be sure it exists - before even attempting to insert the row. But leaving the checking to the individual programmer is a burden and does not guarantee the overall correctness of the data. It is even more so if the statement is submitted by an interactive end user. What is needed is that the system itself be able to enforce referential integrity automatically.

In the previous section, we saw that a check view can be used to check a variety of constraints. Can it be used for checking referential integrity? Consider the following statement:

**create view** V                                              [9.4]
**as**
**select** *
**from** CONTRACT X
**where exists**
    ( **select** *
    **from** TOOL
    **where** NUMBER = X.TOOL)
**with check option**

A row inserted in the view V will be inserted in CONTRACT only if it satisfies the check view, that is, only when there exists a TOOL row with a number equal to the tool number in the CONTRACT row to be inserted. This is exactly what we wanted, at least for an insert. But the problem is much more tricky for the deletion of a tool. If tool 3 is deleted, what happens to contracts 97 and 101 which reference that tool? Should the operation be rejected? Should the TOOL column in CONTRACT rows 97 and 101 be also updated? If so, to what new values? Or should all contracts referencing tool 3 be deleted? In fact, there is no single optimal answer to these questions. It actually depends on the semantics of the application. This is why SQL, at least in some versions, introduces a more direct and more flexible mechanism to deal with referential integrity.

Basically, the mechanism introduces two concepts: the ***primary key*** and the ***foreign key***. In our example, the column TOOL.NUMBER is defined as the primary key column of table TOOL, and CONTRACT.TOOL is defined as a foreign key column in table CONTRACT referencing the primary key TOOL.NUMBER (see Figure 35). When a row is deleted from a table having a primary key, SQL supports three options regarding the action taken against the rows containing a foreign key referencing the deleted primary key:

- **Restrict**: a row with a primary key cannot be deleted if there is one or more rows which contain that key in the foreign key column. For example, a tool cannot be deleted while it is referenced by some contract.
- **Cascade**: if a row with primary key x is deleted, all rows that reference x in a foreign key column are also deleted. Since the deleted rows may themselves have a primary key that is used as a foreign key in another row, that row too will be deleted, and so on in a cascading manner. When a tool is deleted, all the contracts referencing that tool are also deleted.

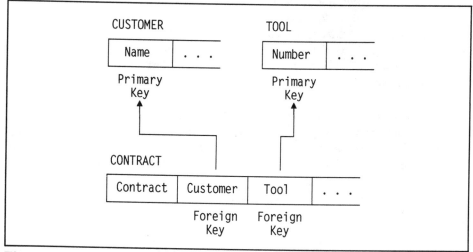

**Figure 35. An example of integrity constraints**

- **Set null**: if a foreign key value is referencing a primary key and if that primary key is being deleted, the foreign key value is updated to **null**. When a tool is deleted, the corresponding values in CONTRACT.TOOL are set to **null**.[1]

Since primary key and foreign key are properties of columns in a table, the definition of these properties appear in the **create table** statement. The following example shows how the syntax is extended.

```
create table TOOL                                              [9.5]
    (NUMBER integer not null,
    TYPE varchar(8) not null,
    PURCH_DATE date,
    PURCH_PRICE decimal(8,2),
    RENTAL_FEE decimal(8,2) not null,
primary key (NUMBER))
```

```
create table CUSTOMER                                          [9.6]
    (NAME varchar(16) not null,
    ADDRESS varchar(64),
    ZIP char(5),
primary key (NAME))
```

```
create table CONTRACT                                          [9.7]
    (CONTRACT integer not null,
    CUSTOMER varchar(16) not null,
    TOOL integer not null,
    DATE_OUT date not null,
    DATE_IN date not null,
    FEE DECIMAL(10,2),
foreign key (TOOL) references TOOL on delete restrict,
foreign key (CUSTOMER) references CUSTOMER on delete restrict)
```

The **primary key** clause in the **create table** statement specifies which column constitutes the primary key, if any. Only one primary key may be defined for a table. The **foreign key** clause designates one column (or a group of columns) as a foreign key; the column name is given in parentheses. The **references** attribute specifies the table referenced by the foreign key. Since there is only one primary key per table, the name of the primary key column

---

[1] The system generally creates and maintains automatically the indexes needed to enforce referential integrity in an efficient way.

does not need to be specified in the **references** clause.  The **references** attribute also specifies the option controlling the deletion of the primary key.

Note that a primary key is not necessarily defined as a single column.  A list of k columns can be specified.  Then, any foreign key referencing that multi-column key will itself be defined on k columns.  Assume, for a moment, that customer names are unique only inside a certain zip code area.  Then the NAME column in CUSTOMER does not constitute a primary key; but NAME and ZIP, considered together, do.  The **primary key** clause in the definition of table CUSTOMER becomes

> **primary key** (NAME, ZIP)                                         [9.8]

For the same reason, column CUSTOMER in table CONTRACT is not sufficient to identify the customer uniquely.  Thus an extra column (ZIP) is needed.  The columns CUSTOMER and ZIP considered together define the foreign key.  The definition of CONTRACT is altered as follows:

a column is added:

> ZIP **char**(5) **not null**                                         [9.9]

and **foreign key**(CUSTOMER) is replaced by

> **foreign key** (CUSTOMER, ZIP)                                      [9.10]

The clause

> **references** CUSTOMER **on delete restrict**                        [9.11]

is not altered because, here, CUSTOMER represents the table, not the column.

Both check views and referential integrity mechanisms enable the system to recognize an abnormal condition and to notify the calling program.  Sometimes, the calling program may be able to correct the condition right away.  But, more often, it will decide that the transaction cannot be completed with the current input values. This may cause a problem because some changes which have already been made in the database may be meaningful only if the transaction does all of its changes. If a transaction execution is stopped because of an abnormal condition, what should the system do with the previous changes made by the same transaction?  Let us study this problem and see how SQL solves it.

## 9.4  The notion of transaction

Consider a rental transaction: P. Wilson wants to rent a mower. An attendant is helping him, invoking the application program, via a terminal. The application program is shown in Figure 36; it assumes that a table AVAILABLE contains the set of all available tools.

Imagine now that the insert statement fails because one of the submitted values is invalid. What happens to tool 4? It is probably lost forever. It has been deleted from AVAILABLE but is not in any contract; therefore no condition will ever free the tool and return it to AVAILABLE. This situation cannot be tolerated. Intuitively, you feel that changes done by an incomplete transaction should be, in a sense, **undone**.

```
          exec sql include sqlca
          exec sql begin declare section
              declare number N

              . . .
          exec sql end declare section

          exec sql declare C1 cursor for
              select NUMBER
              from AVAILABLE
              where TYPE= 'mower'
          exec sql open C1
    (1)   exec sql fetch C1 into :N
          /* execution returns number 4 */
          exec sql close C1


    (2)   exec sql delete AVAILABLE
              where NUMBER = :N


    (3)   exec sql insert into CONTRACT
              (..., TOOL, ...)
              values (...,:N, ...)
```

**Figure 36. Upd: A program changing two tables**

## 9.4.1  Unit of work, transaction

In SQL, the sequence of statements that constitutes a logical update of the database, such as the program Upd in Figure 36, is called a *Logical unit of work* (LUW). Often, it is also called simply a *transaction* by analogy to what is generally called a transaction in the application world. In what follows, we use the term *transaction* with that meaning. A transaction transforms the database from one correct state into another correct state. When a transaction is executing, it sees the changes that it already did to the database. However, at any time, it can decide to terminate the transaction normally, committing all its changes permanently, or abnormally, undoing all of its changes. Since only the transaction knows when it completes a logical unit of work, SQL provides two statements that can be used to control the commit of changes. The first statement is

```
COMMIT WORK
```

which indicates the end of a LUW. There is no explicit statement to signal the beginning of a LUW. This is done implicitly the first time a program accesses the database or at the first SQL statement executed after a previous **commit work**. The program in Figure 36 should be terminated by adding a **commit work** statement; its general flow becomes

(1)  **exec sql fetch** ...                                    [9.12]
(2)  **delete** ...
(3)  **insert** ...
      **commit work**

The second statement is called **rollback work**, with the simple syntax

```
ROLLBACK WORK
```

The purpose of **rollback work** is to signal the end of a LUW without committing the data to the database. Consider the following sequence:

(1)  **exec sql fetch** ...                                    [9.13]
(2)  **delete** ...
(3)  **insert** ...
      *test for some conditions to be verified*
      *if verified then* **commit work**
      *else* **rollback work**

It illustrates how a LUW may choose for some logical reason to roll back all changes made to the database. When a **rollback work** is performed, all changes made by the LUW disappear from the database, and the previous values, existing at the beginning of the LUW, are restored.

The **rollback work** statement in a program is often used in conjunction with the **whenever sqlerror** statement. When SQL detects an abnormal condition, the **whenever sqlerror** statement activates the section of code identified by the label specified in the **whenever sqlerror** statement. That section of code may be able to take care of the situation; if it cannot, it will issue a **rollback work** to clean up the database. It is generally useful, at this point, to display the content of the **sqlca** data structure in order to get more precise information on the error that just occurred. Thus, the overall structure of a program looks like

```
        exec sql include sqlca
        exec sql whenever sqlerror go to It_Failed
        . . .
        /* Body of the program */
(1)         . . .
(2)         . . .
(3)         . . .
        . . .
        exec sql commit work
        return

        It_Failed:
        exec sql rollback work
        display sqlca
        end
```

# 9.5  Protection against effects of concurrency

In previous chapters, we never considered more than one user accessing and updating the database at a time. This is certainly the common case if your database resides on a small personal computer. If, however, your computer allows for any kind of multiprogramming on behalf of one or several users, then the problem of concurrent updates to the database must be addressed. As we shall see in the next section, such updates, if uncontrolled, could jeopardize the integrity of the data; and protection against such effects is absolutely required.

Let us return to the transaction for P. Wilson. While this activity is going on, another user may have access to the system at the same time. Assume that the second user is an auditor who wants to be sure that all tools are accounted for.

The audit program will look for tool 4 to be sure that it appears either in AVAILABLE or in the TOOL column of a CONTRACT row. If the audit program is executed before the Upd program, then it will find tool 4 in AVAILABLE; if it is executed after Upd, it will find tool 4 in CONTRACT. Both of these execution scenarios yield a correct result. If, however, the audit program is executed after statement (2) of Upd but before statement (3), then the program will not find any trace of tool 4. What happens is that the audit program sees an incomplete state of the database, where tool 4 has already been removed from AVAILABLE, but not yet entered in CONTRACT. Intuitively, the system should enforce that all updates by Upd be done as an atomic action, prohibiting another program to see partial updates.

Here again changes should be seen by other users only when the logical sequence of updates has been successfully completed, in other words, only when the transaction commits all its changes. In general, this will make some transactions wait for the termination of another transaction as soon as there is some conflict on accessing the same piece of information.

We discussed above the concepts of **commit work** and **rollback work**. These concepts play a double role in a multiuser system. Not only do they allow a transaction to control the commit or roll back of its own changes according to a decision taken by the program, but they also determine at which point in time all changes made by one transaction can be seen by others.

# 9.6 Locking

One obvious way to avoid any problem is to serialize all transactions. But this approach results in a very poor utilization of the resources, since it does not allow for any multiprogramming. In practice, most systems allow for concurrent access and update to the database and use a *locking* mechanism to provide the effect of such a serial execution. The mechanism is rather complex, but is practically entirely hidden from the user. In other words, you do not have to pay much attention to it. If you are the only user on the system, the problem is irrelevant. But if you do share the system with others, you may encounter situations that are worth understanding.

For this reason, we discuss some issues of locking, albeit without going into details. Another reason for doing so is that SQL systems often provide some ways to control performance by influencing how and when locks are acquired.

The implementation of locking varies from one system to another. However, the basic principles are identical, and the next section describes a fairly typical lock protocol.

## 9.6.1  A simple lock protocol

Suppose you want to update a particular row. The system first tries to acquire a lock for you on that row. Getting a lock means ensuring that nobody else can access the same row. If it succeeds, the row is yours, and the system will return it to you. To be sure that another user does not see a new value of that row before you commit all changes of your LUW, the system will hold that lock until the end of your LUW (commit time). If another LUW wants to update the same row, the system will also try to acquire a lock on the row. It will decide not to grant the lock because you already hold a lock on the same row. The other LUW is then put into wait.  When your LUW commits, your locks are released and the other LUW can resume its execution; this time, it will get the lock on which it was waiting.

If the system follows that protocol, it can be proved that running a series of LUWs L1, L2, Li,... concurrently, gives the same results as a serial execution of the LUWs in some order. In fact, the order is defined by the times at which the LUWs commit their data. In other words, the system behaves logically as if there were no concurrency: one LUW is isolated from another.

## 9.6.2  Lock modes

In the previous explanation we considered two LUWs that wanted to update the same row. In such a case the system locks the row in what is called *exclusive mode*. Two requests for exclusive locking on the same row conflict and the system will only grant one of them. Now, suppose you simply want to read the content of a row. A lock is also needed because you do not want to see uncommitted changes, and because you do not want the data that you just read to be modified by somebody else before the end of your transaction (just in case you decide to read it again).  For that reason your lock must conflict with an exclusive lock for another transaction.  But if another LUW is merely reading the same row, then there is no reason for you to wait before reading it: two reads of the same data do not conflict. Therefore, asking for an exclusive lock is too stringent; and for that reason most systems use two types of locks: the exclusive lock and the *shared* lock. An exclusive lock conflicts with any lock, while a shared lock does not conflict with another shared lock.

Figure 37 summarizes the lock protocol.

## 9.6.3  Lock granularity

The amount of concurrency is highly dependent on the size of objects that can be identified and locked. In the previous paragraph, we discussed a protocol

*What to lock:* a row in a table

*When and how to lock:*
    for reading: acquire shared lock
    for writing: acquire exclusive lock

*Conflict table:*

|  | *shared* | *exclusive* |
|---|---|---|
| *shared* | ok | conflict |
| *exclusive* | conflict | conflict |

*When to release locks:* at end of LUW.

**Figure 37. Lock protocol**

based on row locking. The row is a small unit of information (we could of course use the individual data elements in the row as unit of locking, but few, if any, systems do). What happens if your LUW touches a very large number of rows? As an example, you may read a full table in a complex **select** statement, or you may execute a set-oriented update. Then, the system will have to remember a large number of locks. There are other alternatives. An extreme one is to lock at the database level. This would lock everything for you, suspending all accesses by any other transaction. Clearly a compromise is needed.

Many systems use locks on pages. A page is a reasonably small number of rows; so there is still a pretty good amount of concurrency. In addition, if a page contains typically 40 or 50 rows, the number of locks to be managed is 40 or 50 times smaller that the number required by row locking. So this is a reasonable compromise. Some systems, independently of whether they support page-level locking or not, may also support table locking or table-group locking (the notion of groups of tables varies from implementation to implementation).

Table locking works as follows. A lock is requested on a whole table, in exclusive or shared mode. A table lock in exclusive mode conflicts with any lock on the same table or on any row in the same table (or any page containing rows for that table, if page locking is used). A table lock in shared mode conflicts only with exclusive locks on the table or any row (or page) in the table.

We have not yet shown how the locking granularity is specified. In fact, this varies from implementation to implementation and is generally considered to be outside the scope of the SQL language. In many systems the granularity is specified for a table or a group of tables, mostly at the time the table is defined. In addition, the **lock** statement is available to override the option and force a higher granularity of locks. For example, a possible syntax for locking a table explicitly is

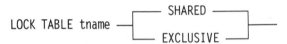

```
                    ┌────── SHARED ──────┐
LOCK TABLE tname ───┤                    ├───
                    └──── EXCLUSIVE ─────┘
```

As an example, consider a program that reads all records in TOOL and, based on some information, updates a large number of them. Then, it may pay off to lock TOOL in exclusive mode by writing

      **lock table** TOOL **exclusive**                                                  [9.14]

## 9.6.4 Practical advice

What does this mean for you, as an SQL user? In fact, most of the time you do not have to worry about locking at all; generally SQL systems make reasonable trade-off decisions and handle locking internally. But they sometimes ask you to choose one out of various options, such as lock granularity, and you should be prepared to do so. According to our discussion above, the following rules of thumb can be used:

- If a table is used as a whole, use table locking. If the lock is exclusive, be prepared to wait and/or see other transactions wait if they access the same table. If the lock is for read only, transactions that want to modify the table will wait.

- If a table is very active in the sense that many transactions update one or a few rows of the table but these rows are, in all likelihood, different, then row locking will work very well. Note that some systems are very sophisticated in their locking methods and support escalation from small granularity to high granularity, dynamically, during the execution when appropriate. These techniques are outside the scope of our general discussion.

- Since locks are kept until the end of a LUW, lock objects as late as possible. Therefore, be sure to access data at the last moment, rather than accessing everything at the beginning. And, if possible, when you know that some data are frequently accessed by many LUWs, try to access them later in the LUW. Then, locks on this data will be kept for less time and the overall concurrency will increase. For example, consider a banking transaction which updates the balance of a given account and the balance of the branch which owns the account. Since there are fewer branches than accounts, there will be much more contention on the branch record. Therefore, the transaction should be written in the following order:

> **update** ACCOUNT
> **update** BRANCH
> **commit work**

## 9.6.5 Deadlock

Consider a scenario where two transactions are being executed concurrently, and suppose the following elementary operations are started at the indicated time:

| time | LUW 1 | LUW 2 |
|------|-------|-------|
| 1 | read A | |
| 2 | | read B |
| 3 | read B | |
| 4 | update B | |
| 5 | | read A |
| 6 | | update A |

At time 4, LUW 1 initiates the update of B; it requests an exclusive lock and enters into wait state since LUW 2 already holds a lock on B. LUW 2 proceeds until it starts its update A operation; at that time, it requests an exclusive lock on A which it cannot get because A is locked by LUW 1. The situation is as follows: LUW 1 waits for a lock held by LUW 2 which waits for a lock held by LUW 1: none of the transaction is able to proceed; they are in *deadlock*.

Systems commonly use the following procedure to handle deadlocks:

- Periodically check the outstanding locks to see if a deadlock has occurred.

- When a deadlock has occurred, stop the execution of one of the transactions involved in the deadlock:

  - Undo all its changes.
  - Terminate the transaction (this includes releasing the locks that it holds).

- Return a special return code value to the caller (note that the caller is waiting for the completion of the last request).

Since locks have been released, the deadlock has been broken, and the surviving transaction(s) can continue. Checking for the code is the responsibility of the program. The **whenever sqlerror** ... facility can be very helpful in that respect.

# 9.7  Protection against failures

The potential problems discussed above are relevant to normal execution of the system. Now we turn our attention to what may happen in case of failure. (Actually, we only provide a short overview since protection is handled internally and does not require any SQL language feature.)

Failures are of two types:

- Soft failure: a processor, memory, or software error may abruptly interrupt the system while transactions are being executed. As a result, the state of the system, represented by the contents of the memory and registers, is lost.

- Hard failure: a disk gets damaged and some or all information stored on it is now unreadable.

Hard failures are very rare, but the consequences may be so serious that a good system must provide a way to reconstruct the data. However, the time needed to recover is not too critical. On the contrary, soft failures are more frequent and the recovery needs to be fast.

## 9.7.1  Recovering from soft failures

In the previous section, we defined the transaction as the unit of work. If the transaction completes normally, then all changes that it performed are permanently committed to the database. If the transaction does not complete, then none of the changes are committed. An abnormal termination may come from the fact that the program issues a **rollback work** or that the system finds an abnormal condition that forces it to roll back the transaction (such as a deadlock situation). In both cases, the program remains in control.

If there is a soft failure, the program or system stops and the execution cannot be resumed where it stopped. So another technique must be used.

## 9.7.2 Logging

First assume page locking: all changes done on a page during the time of a transaction T are done by T and by no other transaction. When the database system updates a piece of data, say a field in a row, the value is changed in the copy of the page that resides in the buffer. If it were possible to keep in the buffer all pages that are changed by a transaction until commit time, then writing all these pages at commit time would actually commit the changes. Notice the importance of "all pages... at commit time": this means as a single operation which is either done or not done; in other words the writing of all pages must be *atomic*.

This method is, at first glance, interesting - since no uncommitted data are ever stored in the database. If the transaction is rolled back, pages are simply marked as invalid in the buffer - and the old copy of a page will be read from the database the next time it is used.

There are several drawbacks with this simple method. First, it may be impossible to keep in the buffer all pages modified by the transaction (and other concurrent transactions) due to insufficient space. Second, writing all modified pages at the end of a transaction may be very time consuming. Third, the problem remains of how to write multiple pages as an atomic action. So another method is generally used, based on *logging*.

A log is a sequential file, and the system appends information to that file in a continuous way during execution. When a transaction updates some values, the old and new values are saved in the log; this does not mean that the information is necessarily written on disk; it just means that it is appended to what is already in the part of memory reserved for logging. When there is no more room in memory, the information is written in the sequential file on disk. When a LUW issues a **commit work**, the system appends a "commit" record to the log and then forces the log to disk; this operation forces to disk all logging information up to and including the commit record. It is the successful write of this commit record on disk that actually commits the transaction.

Note that, even when a transaction commits, the pages that it modified may still be in the memory buffer. At some point they will be written back onto disk; but what happens if a failure occurs before all modified pages are written back? That is where the log comes into play. The log contains all the information needed to take any page in the database and undo the changes that were made, on that page, by uncommitted transactions and redo the changes for committed ones. This process works only if the system knows which pages have been written back on disk and which ones have not. That information is also kept in the log. The details are quite involved and beyond the scope of this overview. What is important is to realize that the same logging mechanism is used for roll back (using the undo information), for soft failure (using both undo and redo information), and for hard failure, as explained in the next section.

### 9.7.3 Recovery from hard failures

Assume for a moment that you start with an empty database. Since the log contains all new values inserted in the database, it can be used to re-create any page lost as a result of a hard failure. However, the recovery time increases with the amount of updates done since the beginning. After a while, the time gets to be unacceptable. The solution to such a problem is to ensure that the contents of all modified pages are saved periodically. This forcing of actual pages from the buffers onto disk is called *checkpoint*.

Taking a checkpoint does not mean that the log written up to that point can be discarded. The reason is that some of the pages written by the checkpoint may contain uncommitted data. The log must thus be kept, since this is the only record of what has been committed or not. Fortunately, the portion of the log that is useful tends to be the youngest one, and the oldest portion can be discarded. Clever techniques are used internally to determine where the useful portion starts.

The whole process of logging and checkpointing is automatic in most systems. Only the system administrator, who is responsible for the overall functioning of the SQL system, needs to be aware of the recovery mechanism for operational reasons. He or she may have to specify how frequently checkpoints need to be taken and must make sure there is room on disk (or tape) for the log.

## 9.8  Protection against unauthorized access

The database may contain sensitive data that the owner does not want to share with all users who have access to the database. On the other hand, one of the main purposes of storing the data in an integrate database is to share information with others. Too little sharing reduces the usefulness of the database; too much sharing compromises the value of the data. Here again a flexible scheme to exercise control is needed.

Consider the table TOOL. Ms. Boss created the table. She should have access to all information stored in it. John, the attendant, needs to see the rental fee corresponding to a given tool; therefore he must certainly be authorized to select values in RENTAL_FEE. But he cannot decide on his own to change the rental fee of a tool; therefore, he should not be authorized to update any value in the RENTAL_FEE column. Likewise, he does not need to know what the purchase price of the tool is. Since the ratio rental_fee/price is a measure of profit, Ms. Boss may decide to "hide" this information from her employees; therefore, John should not be authorized to select values in PURCH_PRICE.

This short scenario illustrates the fact that access to data should be controlled, authorizing some users to perform some operations on some specified subsets of the data. In the remainder of this section we show how SQL provides such an authorization mechanism, using two powerful statements: **grant** and **revoke**.

## 9.8.1 Granting a privilege

First, we note that all systems have some way of identifying a user. Generally, the database system relies on the user identification understood by the operating system. In Chapter 3 we already referred to such a *user name* when we discussed the creation of a table. Assume "Ms. Boss" is the name of the user who created the table TOOL. Ms. Boss automatically becomes the *owner* of the table, authorized to perform any operation on it. By default, nobody else can refer to the table unless Ms. Boss grants certain privileges to others, and John in particular.

The general syntax of **grant** is

```
GRANT privilege ON object TO users
```

and is specified in more details in Figure 38. The statement grants a certain privilege on a certain object to one or more users (also called the *grantees*). Although not all SQL systems support all of the options shown in the syntax diagram, a read-only privilege and a read/write privilege on a table or view are standard. The read-only privilege is indicated either by **read** or **select**. The privileges that modify a table or an updatable view can be specified globally as **write** in some systems, while others support a more selective privilege, using **insert**, **update**, or **delete** explicitly. The **grant** command for authorities like creating a table, changing a table structure, dropping a table, and creating and dropping indexes varies too much from one system to another to be explained in this book. Refer to the description of the **grant** command for the system you are using for a more precise specification.

The set of grantees can be specified in various ways, depending upon the implementation. One way is to specify a list of user names; another is to give

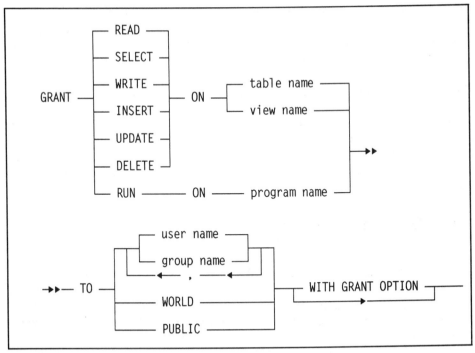

**Figure 38. Syntax of the grant statement**

the name of a group of users. Some systems use **world** or **public** in order to give authorization to all users.

The option "**with grant option**" authorizes a grantee to extend the authority to more users. If Ms. Boss issues

    **grant read on** TOOL **to** JOHN **with grant option**           [9.15]

then John may issue

    **grant read on** TOOL **to** FRANK           [9.16]

When the object is a table, the authorization is given on the whole table. The fact that privileges can be granted on views rather than tables expands drastically the power and flexibility of the function. A view can show some of the columns and hide others. If authorization is given on the view, it applies only to the columns shown in the view, and not the ones that are hidden. Similarly, a view can use a **where** clause to restrict the rows that appear in the view, hiding completely the other ones. Again, authorization on the view applies only to the subset of rows that belong to the view.

Another interesting option is the **run** privilege. As we saw in the introductory chapter, some SQL system implementations allow for compiling the program first and then executing it later. Often, the user who exploits the program may not be the same as the one who compiled it. To make this possible, the user who compiles the program - who becomes automatically the owner of the program - grants it to others with the **run** privilege. Note that the privilege to run a program will enable you to access a table even if you do not have the necessary authorization to do so; but, of course, you are only authorized to do exactly what the program does, and nothing more.

Coming back to our example, suppose that Ms. Boss decides to authorize John to use an interactive SQL program to look at rental fees when a customer asks for a quote and to use Program_A to execute the actual rental transaction. To that effect, she executes

    **create view** V1 (NUMBER, RENTAL_FEE)            [9.17]
    **as**
    **select** NUMBER, RENTAL_FEE
    **from** TOOL

    **grant read on** V1 **to** JOHN

    **grant run on** PROGRAM_A **to** JOHN

Let us expand slightly the scope of the application in order to illustrate the use of a where clause in the authorization view. Assume Ms. Boss has several buyers who buy the tools from suppliers, and she decides to store the buyer's name in an additional column BUYER in table TOOL. In addition, she develops a program that lists the TOOL information. Any buyer can run the program but should not be allowed to see the tools bought by others. How can this be controlled?

A first possibility is to write as many views as there are buyers and to grant each buyer access to one of these views. For example, for buyer 'Peter', write

**create view** PVIEW                                                      [9.18]
**as**
**select** NUMBER, PUR_PRICE
**from** TOOL
**where** BUYER = 'Peter'

**grant read on** PVIEW **to** PETER

Note that in the **where** clause 'Peter' refers to a data element stored in the table. In the second statement Peter is the user name. Although this is a viable solution, it is cumbersome when there are many buyers. There is a better alternative, which uses a specific SQL feature, known as the **user** keyword.

**User** can be used instead of a variable name or constant in any SQL statement. At execution time its value is the name of the user executing the statement (actually, it is the user identifier; we assume it is also the user's name). The alternative to [9.18] is then

**create view** PVIEW                                                      [9.19]
**as**
**select** NUMBER, PUR_PRICE
**from** TOOL
**where** BUYER = **user**

**grant read on** PVIEW **to** PETER, JOHN, JEANNE

**User** acts as a parameter. At execution time, the effect on Peter is the same in both [9.18] and [9.19].

### 9.8.2 Revoking a privilege

**Revoke** is the inverse of **grant**. Its syntax is similar to **grant**; it revokes the privileges that were granted earlier.

## 9.9 Summary

The protection of the information stored in a database is extremely important. The SQL systems use various internal mechanisms to ensure as much protection as possible without unnecessary involvement of the user or system administrator. Recovery from failure, for example, is handled internally. The user does not need to worry about it (although some intervention of the operator may be needed). In other words, there is no special SQL command dealing with recovery.

Other aspects of data protection have to do with ensuring the integrity of the data. Maintaining integrity can be thought of as making sure that certain conditions on the data are always satisfied. The system checks the conditions; but the conditions themselves are part of the semantics of the data and must be specified to the system. For doing so at a logical level, SQL provides features such as views **with check option**, referential integrity based on the definition of **primary** and **foreign** keys, and the concept of transaction controlled by **commit work** or **rollback work**.

To control the access to the data, SQL introduces a notion of authorization. Here again the user must be able to specify who is authorized to access what portion of the data. The language provides a **grant** command which, combined with the notion of view, controls authorization in a powerful and flexible way. More complex schemes to protect against unauthorized accesses are discussed in Chapter 12.

Finally, of the SQL constructs covered in this chapter, **lock** a table is special in the sense that it has an impact only on performance. It was introduced because the user alone has an idea of the overall pattern of access of the whole program. **Lock** is a way to convey that information to the system. In fact, the whole issue of locking was discussed so that the user fully understands how the system behaves in a multiuser situation. Some hints were given as how to minimize the effects of locking and maximize the throughput of the system.

# 9.10  Exercises

The exercises use the database application described in Chapter 2.

**9.1.** How can you tell the system to make sure that any grade entered in the database is between 0 and 5.

**9.2.** In Exercises 3.1 to 3.4, you were asked to write the **create table** statements for the college application. Extend these statements to capture the referential integrity conditions.

**9.3.** Assume that your SQL system uses row locking by default. For each of the following situations, would you override the default and choose table locking instead (and, if yes, on which table)?

1. There exists an index on RECORDS.STUDENT and you want to evaluate

```
select GRADE
from RECORDS
where STUDENT = 1342
```

2. There is no index and you want to evaluate

```
select avg(GRADE)
from RECORDS
```

3. There is an index on CLASSNO in CLASS and you want to evaluate

```
select *
from RECORDS, CLASS
where CLASS = CLASSNO
```

**9.4.** Assuming a database administrator created all tables used in the application, design an authorization mechanism that enables a professor to update RECORDS and a student to read his or her records only.

# Part 3. Applications

## Chapter 10

## Account Receivable

As a first case study, we consider a simple but common application in business accounting: the account receivable. We choose this particular case study because its definition is straightforward while the corresponding database design offers interesting trade-offs. In particular it provides the following opportunities:

- To discuss how information, often kept as many separate units in a manual organization, may be integrated in more global structures supporting more global operations.

- To show how the same set of data may be used in a variety of operations, each addressing data in their own way.

- To characterize different types of operations: those short transactions that involve a small amount of data and those batch operations that are generally much longer (because they repeat the same operation on many data instances).

## 10.1 Overview

We first describe the application and its data, assuming a simple manual organization.

*Customer name:* Smith, George

| Date | Description | Debit | Credit | Balance |
|------|-------------|-------|--------|---------|
| 1/4/1989 | Table | 623.00 | | 623.00 |
| 1/15/1989 | Check N. 352 | | 137.00 | 486.00 |
| 2/15/1989 | Check N. 428 | | 137.00 | 351.00 |
| 3/15/1989 | Check N. 538 | | 137.00 | 214.00 |

*Customer name:* Wilson, Mary

| Date | Description | Debit | Credit | Balance |
|------|-------------|-------|--------|---------|
| 1/6/1989 | Desk | 725.00 | | 725.00 |
| 1/31/1989 | Cash payment | | 150.00 | 575.00 |
| 2/12/1989 | File cabinet | 255.00 | | 830.00 |
| 2/28/1989 | Check N. 321 | | 280.00 | 550.00 |

**Figure 39. Journal of account receivable**

When buying some merchandise on a revolving charge account, a customer receives an invoice containing all data pertinent to the transaction, and the customer's account is debited for the amount of the sale. When the customer later reimburses a portion - or all - of the balance, the account is credited for the amount of the payment. In a manual organization, this information is recorded in a book called a *journal*.

Consider the activity on the account of George Smith, shown in Figure 39. On January 4 he bought a table for $623. He then paid three installments, one on each 15th of the month. At the end of March his balance is $214.

A customer may buy a second item before the first one is totally paid for, as did Mary Wilson. The second journal in Figure 39 indicates that Mary bought a file cabinet before she paid her debt on the purchase of the desk. Note that the name of the customer appears once at the top of the journal, like a title indicating to which customer the journal belongs. The journal for a particular customer clusters together all the information pertinent to transactions made on behalf of that customer.

Actually, one needs to keep some supplemental data for each customer such as the full name, address, and zip code. These data elements may be simply stored in a customer file (see Figure 40).

| CUSTOMER | | | |
|---|---|---|---|
| CUST_NBR | NAME | ADDRESS | ZIP |
| 123123 | Smith | 888 Main Street, Anycity - CA | 99999 |
| 223344 | Wilson | 553 Cedar Street, Othercity - MA | 21060 |

**Figure 40. The CUSTOMER table**

# 10.2 Operations

We now analyze the various operations that the data organization must support. First consider a sale transaction for customer X. If X is a known customer, then the name X already exists in the customer file and the corresponding journal also exists (otherwise the name must be added to the customer file and the journal created); the transaction then consists of inserting a row in the journal.

But other, more global operations also need to be carried out. An example of such a global operation is the preparation of a reminder for late payment. The operation involves finding the customers who have a positive balance due and whose journals do not contain any recent record of payment. For each of these customers, the program will format the information and print it. The operation for a single customer is straightforward, but it is repeated on many customers - hence the name *batch operation*.

In the following section we study the implementation of the application using a relational DBMS. The goal is to design the database in a way that provides good performance both for short transactions and longer batch operations.

# 10.3 The database design

Let us start with the easy part: the customer file. Obviously it maps directly into the CUSTOMER table of Figure 40. But storing the information contained in the individual journals is much more interesting. First, try an obvious mapping of many journals into as many tables. Thus the journal for Mary Wilson may be stored in a table WILSON containing the same columns as the journal shown in Figure 39. Although quite natural, this design has drawbacks. First, remember that the name of the table in a static SQL statement must appear explicitly in the program and cannot be dynamically specified in a program variable. This means that an application program which must be able to work on any account has to use dynamic SQL, decreasing performance sub-

| JOURNALS | | | | | |
|---|---|---|---|---|---|
| CUSTOMER | TRANS_DATE | DESCRIPTION | DEBIT | CREDIT | BALANCE |
| 123123 | 1989-01-04 | Table | 623.00 | ? | 623.00 |
| 223344 | 1989-01-06 | Desk | 725.00 | ? | 725.00 |
| 123123 | 1989-01-15 | Check N. 352 | ? | 137.00 | 486.00 |
| 223344 | 1989-01-31 | Cash | ? | 150.00 | 575.00 |
| 223344 | 1989-02-12 | File cabinet | 255.00 | ? | 830.00 |
| 123123 | 1989-02-15 | Check N. 428 | ? | 137.00 | 351.00 |
| 223344 | 1989-02-28 | Check N. 321 | ? | 280.00 | 550.00 |
| 123123 | 1989-03-15 | Check N. 538 | ? | 137.00 | 214.00 |

**Figure 41. Combination of all journals in a single table**

stantially. Second, adding a new customer implies creating a new table. The result is that many tables exist in the database, all accepting rows with the same format. Finally, if each customer journal is stored in a different table, it becomes very awkward to ask global queries such as select all accounts satisfying a certain condition (for example balance>0). The number of tables in an SQL database may increase when new applications are designed, but should not increase when new instances - such as new customers - enter the system (this generally indicates a bad design).

This analysis probably convinced you that it is better to integrate all journals into a single table, say JOURNALS. The JOURNALS table will have the columns shown in Figure 39 plus an extra column containing the identification of the customer (see Figure 41).

By selecting all rows which contain in the additional column the identifier of Wilson, we can reconstruct Wilson's journal:

```
select TRANS_DATE, DESCRIPTION, DEBIT,          [10.1]
       CREDIT, BALANCE
from JOURNALS
where CUSTOMER = 223344
order by TRANS_DATE
```

| TRANS_DATE | DESCRIPTION | DEBIT | CREDIT | BALANCE |
|---|---|---|---|---|
| 1989-01-06 | Desk | 725.00 | ? | 725.00 |
| 1989-01-31 | Cash | ? | 150.00 | 575.00 |
| 1989-02-12 | File cabinet | 255.00 | ? | 830.00 |
| 1989-02-28 | Check N. 321 | ? | 280.00 | 550.00 |

| JOURNALS | | | |
|---|---|---|---|
| CUSTOMER | TRANS_DATE | DESCRIPTION | AMOUNT |
| 123123 | 1989-01-04 | Table | 623.00 |
| 223344 | 1989-01-06 | Desk | 725.00 |
| 123123 | 1989-01-15 | Check N. 352 | -137.00 |
| 223344 | 1989-01-31 | Cash | -150.00 |
| 223344 | 1989-02-12 | File cabinet | 255.00 |
| 123123 | 1989-02-15 | Check N. 428 | -137.00 |
| 223344 | 1989-02-28 | Check N. 321 | -280.00 |
| 123123 | 1989-03-15 | Check N. 538 | -137.00 |

**Figure 42. Final form of the JOURNALS table**

Recall that the order of the rows in a table is arbitrary; since we are used to seeing the entries in a journal ordered by date, we added the **order by** clause in the SQL statement.

This may seem optimal. However, we can still simplify the design. By noting that an entry is either a debit or a credit but never both, we can use a single column (call it AMOUNT), using positive numbers for credit entries and negative numbers for debit entries. We also note that the balance is not actually an independent piece of data, but can instead be derived by computing the sum of all amounts for the same account. Generally, storing derived data explicitly in the database is not recommended; the main reason is that the derived data must be updated each time the underlying data change if the integrity of the database is to be preserved. But this is by no means an absolute rule, and trade-offs for reasons of performance must sometimes be considered. In the example, we can get rid of the BALANCE column, obtaining the lean table shown in Figure 42.

The balance of Mary Wilson can be computed by writing:

> **select sum** (AMOUNT)                                    [10.2]
> **from** JOURNALS
> **where** CUSTOMER = 223344

| SUM(AMOUNT) |
|---|
| 550.00 |

At this point we have a simple and reasonable design:

- The number of tables is independent of the database size.
- Information is not duplicated.
- Data which can be computed are not stored.

We still need to validate the design by analyzing the operations that it must support.

## 10.4  Sales transaction

Consider a sales transaction. Smith goes to the counter and buys a chair. He probably does not know his customer number; so he gives his name. The attendant uses the terminal to access a program which invokes SQL. A menu is used to identify the operation, enter the data, and invoke the appropriate SQL statement. For finding the customer information the program declares a cursor as follows:

> **exec sql declare** C **cursor for**                                            [10.3]
>     **select** CUST_NBR, ADDRESS, ZIP
>     **from** CUSTOMER
>     **where** NAME = :A

and then uses it to retrieve the desired information:

> *store the customer name in A*                                              [10.4]
> **exec sql open** C
>
> *do forever*
> **exec sql fetch** C
>     **into** :*Customer*, :*Addr*, :*Zipcode*
> *end*

After execution of the **exec sql fetch**, the program variables *Customer*, *Addr*, and *Zipcode* contain the data which can then be displayed on the screen. The result may contain more than one row if several customers have the same name (this is why we used a cursor construct rather than a **select** without cursor). Again, a menu selection can be used to choose the appropriate row. This method is quite appropriate if all selected rows fit on a single screen. If the programmer anticipates that the answer could consist of numerous rows, he should use a more selective **where** clause, such as

> **where** NAME = :*A*                                                       [10.5]
>     **and** ZIP = :*B*

| CUSTOMER | | | | | |
|---|---|---|---|---|---|
| CUST_NBR | NAME | ADDRESS | ZIP | BAL_DATE | BALANCE |
| 123123 | Smith | 888 Main . . . | 99999 | 1989-02-28 | 486.00 |
| 223344 | Wilson | 553 Cedar . . . | 21060 | 1989-02-28 | 575.00 |

**Figure 43. Final form of the CUSTOMER table**

If, instead, the name is not found in the database, the program asks for information about the new customer and issues an **insert** into CUSTOMER. Assume the customer does exist; then [10.4] returns the customer number in the program variable *:Customer*. This identifier can then be used to select all related information from the JOURNALS table.

Before renting a new tool to a customer, the program will want to check the balance. This can be done by adding the amounts for all entries pertaining to that customer. A **select** statement with aggregation will do the job:

> **select sum**(AMOUNT)                                          [10.6]
> **into** *:Amounts*
> **from** JOURNALS
> **where** CUSTOMER = *:Customer*

The program can then compare the returned balance to a certain treshold to determine if a new contract can be issued. If it can, a new entry is made in CONTRACT, and a **commit work** is issued.

You probably think that the approach lacks elegance. It is true: the computation time increases proportionally to the number of rows for that particular account. In addition, old journal entries have to be kept forever just to be able to compute the balance. A better trade-off exists: it consists of keeping in the database the value of the *Balance* at a certain date. After that date, the current balance *Current* can be computed by adding to *Balance* the journal amounts for transactions that happened after *Balance* was computed. Since the balance date and values are attributes of a customer, the right place to store them is in the CUSTOMER table. Figure 43 shows the new table. Note that accessing the balance is practically free since the CUSTOMER row needs to be accessed anyway in the transaction. The program logic becomes

```
exec sql declare C cursor for
    select CUST_NBR, ADDRESS, ZIP, BAL_DATE, BALANCE
    from CUSTOMER
    where NAME = :A
```
*store the customer name in A*
```
exec sql open C
```
*do forever*
```
    exec sql fetch C
        into :Customer, :Addr, :Zipcode,
                  :Date, :Balance
```
*end*

```
exec sql select sum(AMOUNT)
    into :Amounts
    from JOURNALS
    where CUSTOMER = :Customer
        and TRANS_DATE > BAL_DATE
```
*Current = Balance + Amounts*

# 10.5 Batch processing

Now we consider a program that performs a certain operation on many data items, one after another. The typical organization of such a program is a loop on some processing that is repeatedly executed for each data item in a batch; and the batch is defined by a **select** statement. Our particular example is the sending of reminders to customers who are late for payment.

More precisely, suppose the balance in CUSTOMER is updated every month. After a certain period, say two weeks, our program needs to send reminders to customers who satisfy both of the following conditions: the balance is positive and no payment has been made since the last balance update. Once a reminder is sent, the balance date is updated to the current date.

The query is on table CUSTOMER; the first condition is a simple predicate on BALANCE; the second condition is easily expressed as a **not exists** predicate. In the subquery, the first predicate expresses the fact that the customer's name in JOURNALS must match the customer's name from the parent query (correlation):

**select** CUST_NBR, NAME, BAL_DATE, BALANCE             [10.7]
**from** CUSTOMER C
**where** BALANCE > 0
    **and not exists**
       ( **select** *
       **from** JOURNALS J
       **where** J.CUSTOMER = C.CUST_NBR
          **and** J.TRANS_DATE > C.BAL_DATE)

| CUST_NBR | NAME | BAL_DATE | BALANCE |
|---|---|---|---|
| 223344 | Wilson | 1989-02-28 | 575.00 |

Let us now summarize the logic of the program that sends reminders (see Figure 44 for details):

**exec sql declare** C **cursor for**                           [10.8]
    **select** ...           see [10.7]
    **where** ...
**exec sql open** C
*do forever*
    **exec sql fetch** *C*
       **into** *:Customer*
    *print reminder*
    **exec sql update** CUSTOMER
       **set** BAL_DATE = **current date**
       **where** CUST_NBR = *:Customer*
    *end*
**exec sql commit work**

Although the program is logically correct and quite efficient if it runs alone and to completion, it has drawbacks if other programs execute concurrently on the same data or if a failure occurs. The program contains a single **commit work** statement, invoked once at the end of the execution. The whole program thus executes as one single unit of work, a possible source of trouble both for concurrency and for recovery.

The concurrency problem stems from the fact that locks are held until the end of the unit of work, thus prohibiting other units of work to access the same data. The remedy consists of chopping a long unit of work into many short ones, ensuring that locks are held for much shorter periods of time, thus enhancing concurrency. This technique is applicable here since the processing of one account is actually a transaction as far as the application is concerned.

```
exec sql include sqlca
exec sql begin declare section
        declare number Customer
        declare string(30) Name
        declare number Balance
        declare string(10) Date
exec sql end declare section
exec sql declare C cursor for
        select CUST_NBR, NAME, STMT_DATE, STMT_BALANCE
        from CUSTOMER C
        where not exists
            ( select *
            from JOURNALS J
            where J.CUSTOMER = C.CUST_NBR
                and J.TRANS_DATE > C.STMT_DATE)

exec sql open C

do forever
        exec sql whenever not found go to C_end
        exec sql fetch C
        into :Customer, :Name, :Date, :Balance

        print the reminder
        exec sql update CUSTOMER
            set BAL_DATE = current date
            where CUST_NBR = :Customer
        end
C_end:
exec sql whenever not found continue

exec sql close C
exec sql commit work
```

**Figure 44. A program to send reminders - Single unit of work**

Grouping the processing of all accounts in one unit of work is certainly artificial, although it has the advantage of simplifying the program and minimizing the commit overhead.

If we decide to make the unit of work as small as the processing of a single account, the program logic can be modified as follows:

```
exec sql declare C cursor for                                    [10.9]
    select CUST_NBR, NAME, BAL_DATE, BALANCE
    from CUSTOMER C
    where CUST_NBR > :Last_Customer
        and BALANCE > 0
        and not exists
            ( select *
            from JOURNALS J
            where J.CUSTOMER = C.CUST_NBR
                and J.TRANS_DATE > C.BAL_DATE)
    order by CUST_NBR
Last_Customer=0
do forever
    exec sql open C
    exec sql fetch C
        into :Customer, ...
    process Customer data
    Last_Customer = Customer
    exec sql commit work
    end
```

A word of explanation: as you see, we moved the **commit work** statement inside the do loop. However, in most SQL implementations, cursors are closed automatically when the commit is done. Therefore, we had to make sure we could reopen the cursor and position it just after the last account processed. This is done by saving the last customer number in *Last_Customer*; then, the next iteration opens the scan at the first customer number with a value greater than *Last_Customer*, and saves a new value in *Last_Customer*. The method implies the use of an **order by** clause on the **select** statement which defines the cursor.

Issuing a commit each time a single customer is processed may be going too far. After all, there is a fixed overhead for committing; there is also a fixed overhead for opening a cursor. Therefore a good trade-off may be to commit after a certain number of customers have been processed. Assuming that number to be 10, the modified logic becomes:

```
do forever                                              [10.10]
    exec sql open C
    do I = 1 to 10
            exec sql fetch C ...
            end
    exec sql commit work
    end
```

Still, this method has some performance limitations. The **select** statement is precompiled and the system optimizes for retrieving all CUSTOMER rows that satisfy the predicate > :Last_Customer. It will generally assume that this is a large portion of the CUSTOMER table. Therefore the optimizer may decide to materialize the result at open time (creating a temporary table and sorting it). This would be bad for performance since the program would use only the first 10 rows in the result before reopening the cursor and materializing a full result again. There are two techniques to avoid the problem.

• The first one consists of making sure that access paths exist so that no materialization of the result is required. If clustered indexes exist on the columns CUST_NBR of CUSTOMER, and CUSTOMER of JOURNALS, there is a good chance that the optimizer will choose a method without global materialization. Then the overhead of OPEN is acceptable.

• The second technique consists of telling SQL explicitly that the program is interested only in a few result rows, by using a more precise predicate such as

    CUST_NBR > :Last_Customer **and** CUST_NBR < :Last_Customer + 10

Assuming that customer numbers are contiguous, this predicate can replace the > :Last_Customer one in [10.9]: the result will contain 10 rows, and the loop will process 10 rows. If the customer numbers are not contiguous (because of deletions), then the logic must be changed slightly: The number of rows in the result will vary and the loop must be able to handle it. For the sake of simplicity, we ignore this programming issue.

### Remarks

• The width of the interval must be explicit in the **where** clause. Assume for example that variables Start and End contain the first and last values of the interval. You can write a predicate such as

    **between** :Start **and** :End                          [10.11]

But now, again, the optimizer, at compile time, does not know what the width of the interval is.  It will make assumptions which can be largely erroneous.

• If instead of dealing with a customer number, the program had to deal with a character string, the predicate could be

> **like** :Like_Expr                                                [10.12]

where *Like_Expr* can be set to some letters 'ABC' concatenated with '%'. Then the interval of value will be all values starting with ABC.

# 10.6 Recovery

In a program, the place where a commit is invoked also affects the recovery. When the commit is invoked only once at the end, the situation is simple: either the whole program completed and all changes are committed, or the program did not complete and the recovery system undoes all changes: nothing is committed. If the execution of the program is long, invoking the commit only at the end is not advisable since the whole program must be rerun from its beginning in case of failure. The solution is again to chop the program in smaller units of work, exactly as we did for concurrency.  Then, in case of failure, the program must be rerun starting at the account immediately following the last processed one.

In order to know where to restart we must save somewhere in the database the identifier of the first account which must be processed after the commit.  The changes and the identifier are committed together; so there is no danger that the changes be made without the identifier being updated, or vice versa.  To store the customer identifier in the database, we suggest using a special table with a single column and a single row (call the table SAVE and the column FIRST_NBR).  The program first reads the value in SAVE to know where to start:

```
exec sql declare C cursor for
    select ...
    where ...
        and CUST_NBR >= :Next_Customer
        and CUST_NBR < :Next_customer + 10
    order by CUST_NBR
exec sql select FIRST_NBR
    in :First_Customer
    from SAVE
```

```
do Next_Customer = First_Customer to 999999 by 10
    exec sql open C
    do forever
        exec sql fetch C
        process Customer data
        end
    exec sql update SAVE
        set FIRST_NBR = :Next_Customer + 10
    /*There is only a single row in SAVE */
    exec sql commit work
    end
exec sql update SAVE
    set FIRST_NBR = 1
exec sql commit work
```

Note that, after all accounts have been processed successfully, the value in SAVE is reset to 1 so that the next execution will start at the beginning.

Figure 45 shows the final version of the program.

# 10.7  Summary

The analysis of the account receivable application yielded a discussion of several techniques and trade-offs.

First, we discussed the use of a single table T versus many small tables of identical format and types, T1, T2, and so on. The table T will have the same columns and types as the individual tables Ti, plus one column which will contain some identifier, say i, of the table Ti to which the particular row would normally belong if multiple tables had been used. The one-table solution allows for global queries and is much more suitable to the use of static SQL.

Then we saw how to handle the situation in which the number of rows in the answer to a query varies widely. While it may be feasible to show a few tens of rows as a result of an interactive query, longer answers may be cumbersome and difficult to grasp. The suggestion is to first look at how many rows there are and refine the query by changing its parameters, or even the query itself if dynamic SQL is used, until a reasonable answer size is reached.

We again mentioned the trade-off of using redundant data. If a result is often requested and is relatively difficult to evaluate, it may be advantageous to store it in the database. But do not forget that every time the underlying basic data are updated, the result must be recomputed and stored again.

```
exec sql include sqlca

exec sql begin declare section
        declare number Customer
        declare number First_Customer
        declare number Next_Customer
        declare string(30) Name
        declare string(10) Date
        declare number Balance
        declare number New_Balance
exec sql end declare section

exec sql declare C cursor for
        select CUST_NBR, NAME, BAL_DATE, BALANCE
        from CUSTOMER C
        where BALANCE > 0
                and not exists
                    ( select *
                    from JOURNALS J
                    where J.CUSTOMER = C.CUST_NBR
                        and J.TRANS_DATE > C.BAL_DATE)
                and C.CUST_NBR >= :Next_Customer
                and C.CUST_NBR < :Next_Customer + 10
                order by C.CUST_NBR

exec sql select *
        into :First_Customer
        from SAVE

do Next_Customer = First_Customer to 999999 by 10

        exec sql open C

        do forever

                exec sql whenever not found go to C_end
                exec sql fetch C
                        into :Customer, :Name, :Date, :Balance
```

**Figure 45. Final version of the monthly reminder program (Part 1)**

```
            print the reminder

            exec sql update CUSTOMER
                set BAL_DATE = current date
                where CUST_NBR = :Customer
            end

C_end:

        exec sql whenever not found continue
        exec sql close C

        exec sql update SAVE
            set FIRST_NBR = :Next_Customer+10

        exec sql commit work
        end

exec sql update SAVE
    set FIRST_NBR = 1
exec sql commit work
```

**Figure 45. Final version of the monthly reminder program (Part 2)**

Finally, we dwelled on the development of batch applications. When a particular process is repeated for each row in a result set, the definition of the unit of work becomes very interesting. If the unit of work is small, the overhead of open and commit becomes large; if the unit of work is large, problems may arise for concurrency and recovery. Techniques are presented on how to control the trade-off.

# Chapter 11

# Resource Allocation

In this chapter we turn our attention to a class of applications dealing with the management of resources. There are several types of resource management problems. Some of them are pretty simple and were covered, in one form or another, in previous chapters. Others, however, are more tricky and use SQL in some very interesting ways. This chapter shows how the design of a database is influenced by the operations it must support. Several trade-offs between query performance and design rules, including the use of redundant information, are discussed.

## 11.1 Find an object in a set

Remember that, in Chapter 1, we asked the question "how to find an available mower?" Mowers are resources. Finding an available mower is equivalent to finding a free element in a set. The contents of the set is stored in the table AVAILABILITY shown in Figure 46.

In AVAILABILITY, NUMBER and TYPE have the same data type as NUMBER and TYPE in TOOL; STATUS has the value 'A' if the tool identified by the value in NUMBER is available; otherwise it has the value 'U' for used. To find a free mower, we simply write

| AVAILABILITY | | |
|---|---|---|
| NUMBER | TYPE | STATUS |
| 1 | mower | U |
| 2 | mower | A |
| 3 | saw | U |
| 4 | mower | A |
| 5 | tractor | A |

**Figure 46. The AVAILABILITY table**

**select** *                                                                    [11.1]
**from** AVAILABILITY
**where** TYPE = 'mower'
    **and** STATUS = 'A'

| NUMBER | TYPE | STATUS |
|---|---|---|
| 2 | mower | A |
| 4 | mower | A |

Consider another example: the management of seats in a theater. Again the resource is a set of objects (seats) and a table SEATS is used (Figure 47). It contains a row for each seat at each function; initially all seats are available. For the sake of explanation, we assume that there are 20 seats. At any time, a free seat for the function 15 can be found by writing

**select** NUMBER                                                              [11.2]
**from** SEATS
**where** FUNCTION = 15
    **and** STATUS = 'A'

Suppose you assign seat 13 to Smith; this implies updating both columns STATUS and CUSTOMER_NAME.

**update** SEATS                                                               [11.3]
**set** STATUS = 'U', CUSTOMER_NAME = 'SMITH'
**where** FUNCTION = 15
    **and** NUMBER = 13

In the above example, we assume that all seats are equivalent. In practice there may be several types: front, back, mezzanine, and so on. A TYPE column can

| SEATS | | | |
|---|---|---|---|
| FUNCTION | NUMBER | STATUS | CUSTOMER_NAME |
| 15 | 1 | A | ? |
| 15 | 2 | A | ? |
| 15 | 3 | U | Yvette |
| 15 | 4 | A | ? |
| 15 | 5 | A | ? |
| 15 | 6 | U | John |
| 15 | 7 | U | Maria |
| 15 | 8 | A | ? |
| 15 | 9 | A | ? |
| 15 | 10 | A | ? |
| 15 | 11 | A | ? |
| 15 | 12 | U | Peter |
| 15 | 13 | A | ? |
| 15 | 14 | A | ? |
| 15 | 15 | A | ? |
| 15 | 16 | U | Elisabeth |
| 15 | 17 | A | ? |
| 15 | 18 | A | ? |
| 15 | 19 | A | ? |
| 15 | 20 | A | ? |

**Figure 47. The SEATS table**

then be added to SEATS and more predicates added to the query to find the appropriate seat.

## 11.2 Find a sequence of objects

As you know, an SQL table does not have an implicit ordering. As a result, two consecutive rows returned by [11.2] will not necessarily correspond to two consecutive seats. Therefore, something else is needed to book several contiguous seats for a single party. There are several ways to tackle the problem. Let us assume there is a single sequence of numbered seats and that we want to book n consecutive ones.

A first method consists of simply using [11.2]. The answer is an unordered set of seats that the program will display on the screen. Actual consecutive seats can then be selected manually. Once the choice is made, the program will invoke the update function as in [11.3]. In such a method, SQL is used to help narrow the search domain; the ultimate selection is done manually. This adds flexibility for taking decisions that are subjective and very difficult to express, or just to let the customer make the last decision.

But you may want to solve the problem of finding n consecutive seats without manual intervention. What kind of construct should you use? Consider the following reasoning: you need to access the table SEATS to find a first available seat; then you need to access the table again to find an adjacent seat, and so on. Intuitively, this corresponds to an n-way join.

The following statement provides the desired result for n=3:

```
select T.NUMBER, U.NUMBER, V.NUMBER                    [11.4]
from SEATS T, SEATS U, SEATS V
where T.FUNCTION  = 15
    and U.FUNCTION  = 15
    and V.FUNCTION  = 15
    and T.STATUS = 'A'
    and U.STATUS = 'A'
    and V.STATUS = 'A'
    and U.NUMBER = T.NUMBER + 1
    and V.NUMBER = U.NUMBER + 1
```

| T.NUMBER | U.NUMBER | V.NUMBER |
|---------:|---------:|---------:|
| 8 | 9 | 10 |
| 9 | 10 | 11 |
| 13 | 14 | 15 |
| 17 | 18 | 19 |
| 18 | 19 | 20 |

Other conditions could be added, for example to obtain seats in a certain area. The query has the obvious drawback of using an n-way join for finding n seats. If we want a large number of seats, the query itself becomes very large; but, worse still, if the query is embedded in a program, it will be able to handle only the n=3 case but will not work for another value of n. In fact, every value would require another statement. Two ways are possible; either 1) these statements can all be embedded explicitly in the program or 2) dynamic SQL can be used. Both solutions have drawbacks: the first lacks elegance; the second may be less desirable for performance reasons. We now look at an alternative.

Think about the problem in the following way: find one seat which has the property that the n-1 following seats are available; this suggests the use of a subquery. In fact, the following query produces the answer for n=4 (note that the value of n appears only as a constant; in a program, this constant comes from a program variable which parameterizes the query).

**select** *                                                                    [11.5]
**from** SEATS T
**where** STATUS = 'A'
   **and** T.FUNCTION = 15
   **and** 'A' = **all**
      ( **select** STATUS
      **from** SEATS U
      **where** U.FUNCTION = 15
         **and** U.NUMBER > T.NUMBER
         **and** U.NUMBER <= T.NUMBER + 4-1)

| FUNCTION | NUMBER | STATUS | CUSTOMER_NAME |
|---|---|---|---|
| 15 | 8 | A | ? |
| 15 | 17 | A | ? |
| 15 | 18 | A | ? |
| 15 | 19 | A | ? |
| 15 | 20 | A | ? |

For each seat T, the subquery finds the status of the seats U that have a number greater than the number of seat T, but not greater than the number of T plus 3 (these seats must be available). If T corresponds to seat 8, the seats selected by the subquery are 9, 10, and 11. The ALL predicate requires that all these seats be available. Actually, only 8 and 17 should be returned. The seats 18, 19, and 20 should not be returned because they are not followed by three seats. To exclude them from the answer, a condition is added to restrict T to seats that are followed by at least three seats. The query becomes

**select** *                                                                    [11.6]
**from** SEATS T
**where** STATUS = 'A'
   **and** T.FUNCTION = 15
   **and** 'A' = **all**
      ( **select** STATUS
      **from** SEATS U
      **where** U.FUNCTION = 15
         **and** U.NUMBER > T.NUMBER
         **and** U.NUMBER <= T.NUMBER + 4-1)
   **and** T.NUMBER <= 20 - 4 + 1

Note that the table SEATS contains a row for each existing seat and each function. In practice, this does not present a problem for functions in the near future. However, if booking is allowed a long time in advance, many rows will exist - even if most of them have an 'A' status. It is therefore worth looking at an alternative way that stores information only for booked seats.

# 11.3  Storing allocated resources only

If we only keep in the database information about seats already allocated, the table SEATS does not need to contain a STATUS column. Figure 48 shows the new SEATS content: the information is equivalent to the one shown in Figure 47. An SQL query can only return things that are stored in the database. Since we decide to have rows for booked seats only, any query on SEATS will return some booked seats. So the best we can do is to select an occupied seat such that there does not exist in the database a row for any of the n following seats. This will give us n available seats as desired. Now the query is straightforward:

**select** NUMBER                                      [11.7]
**from** SEATS T
**where** T.NUMBER <= 20-4
    **and** T.FUNCTION=15
    **and not exists**
        ( **select** *
        **from** SEATS U
        **where** U.FUNCTION = T.FUNCTION
            **and** U.NUMBER > T.NUMBER
            **and** U.NUMBER <= T.NUMBER + 4)

| NUMBER |
| --- |
| 7 |
| 16 |

| SEATS | | |
| --- | --- | --- |
| FUNCTION | NUMBER | NAME |
| 15 | 3 | Yvette |
| 15 | 6 | John |
| 15 | 7 | Maria |
| 15 | 12 | Peter |
| 15 | 16 | Elisabeth |

**Figure 48. The SEATS table, booked seats only**

The query has a drawback: it will not return an available seat that precedes the first booked seat, and for the same reason it will not return any seat if no seat has yet been booked for this function, making no difference between a full house or an empty one!

Thus, we really need to address the problem of finding the first booked seat. If none exists, then we know that all seats are available. A first way to find the first booked seat is to declare a cursor as

    select *                                                    [11.8]
    from SEATS
    where FUNCTION = 15
    order by NUMBER

Then the **fetch** of the first row returns the first booked seat; there is no need to go on fetching the following ones.  The same query can be expressed in several ways; the three following examples return the useful row (and only that one).

    select *                                                    [11.9]
    from SEATS T
    where FUNCTION = 15
        and NUMBER =
            ( select min(NUMBER)
            from SEATS U
            where U.FUNCTION = T.FUNCTION)

    select *                                                    [11.10]
    from SEATS T
    where FUNCTION = 15
        and not exists
            ( select *
            from SEATS U
            where U.NUMBER < T.NUMBER
                and U.FUNCTION = T.FUNCTION)

    select *                                                    [11.11]
    from SEATS T
    where FUNCTION = 15
        and NUMBER <= all
            ( select NUMBER
            from SEATS U
            where U.FUNCTION = T.FUNCTION)

This roster of possible queries gives us a chance to discuss the question of which constructs are more likely to be efficiently processed by the SQL system. Of course, any particular system will try to choose a good strategy for its implementation. Since you do not generally know the details of the implementation - nor should you - guessing is not going to help. However, what you can do is realize that some query may in fact ask for something more complex than the strict answer you want. Consider query [11.8]. It fails to tell the system that your are interested only in the first seat. Some systems will, very naturally, select all rows and sort them before returning the first row to you. If the system chooses to use an index, the sort may not be needed; but the way a query is written should never be influenced by implementation issues. On the other hand, query [11.9] specifies precisely that you are interested in one row only. This form gives at least a chance to the system optimizer to take this fact into account in choosing an access path that is optimal for finding this single row, and not necessarily all of them. Statements [11.10] and [11.11] are equivalent to [11.9]; they only use other means of expressing the notion of minimum.

We considered the problem of finding the first seat because it is an interesting case. However, we could have solved the drawback of query [11.2] in a different and easier way. Just think about introducing in SEATS, and for each function, a dummy booked seat (for example NUMBER = 0). Then query [11.7] will return a correct answer in any case.

# 11.4  From discrete to continuous resources

Seat booking deals with discrete resources: finding a small number of units. But some resources are allocated in large numbers at a time. Let us take the example of disk space allocation on a mainframe computer. On some systems, each user is given a certain number of contiguous blocks for private use. Assume the administrator has 10 disks with 200,000 blocks on each. Slots can then be managed exactly as seats were managed in the previous section, by allocating space in large sequences of blocks. For example, if an entry in the allocation table corresponds to 1,000 blocks, asking for a 4,000-block slot is like asking for 4 consecutive blocks, exactly as 4 seats in the previous application.

But now, suppose we want a more flexible way to distribute the disk space, without imposing constraints on the size of the unit of allocation. In other words, we want to manage the disk space as an almost continuous resource. A disk slot can be as small as one block or as big as a full disk. The idea is to store in the database a row in a table for each allocated slot, independently of its length. To that effect we use the ALLOCATION table shown in

| ALLOCATION | | | |
|---|---|---|---|
| DISK | START | LENGTH | DESCRIPTION |
| DISKA | 100 | 200 | Programs |
| DISKA | 500 | 300 | System |
| DISKA | 2800 | 200 | Payroll |
| DISKA | 4900 | 100 | Database |
| DISKA | 8000 | 200 | Invoices |

**Figure 49. The ALLOCATION table**

Figure 49.  The problem consists now of finding a free slot of a given length, say 2,000 blocks, on a certain disk, DISKA for example.  Again, the database can only return information that is stored.  So our goal is to write a query that returns a slot which precedes an available slot of at least 2,000 blocks.  The following query provides the answer by selecting a slot A such that no slot B overlaps the interval of blocks between the end of A and the end of A plus 2,000 blocks.  The last test ensures that the new free slot does not fall off the end of the disk.

```
select *                                               [11.12]
from ALLOCATION A
where not exists
  ( select *
  from ALLOCATION B
  where A.DISK = B.DISK
      and B.START > A.START + A.LENGTH
      and B.START < A.START + A.LENGTH + 2000)
  and A.DISK = 'DISKA'
  and A.START + A.LENGTH + 2000 < 200000
```

| DISK | START | LENGTH | DESCRIPTION |
|---|---|---|---|
| DISKA | 500 | 300 | System |
| DISKA | 4900 | 100 | Database |
| DISKA | 8000 | 200 | Invoices |

The query returns several possible slots; the user can choose one, based on some other, maybe subjective, criterion.

Let us take a moment to evaluate the design of the table ALLOCATION, given the query [11.12].  Since the critical information - the length of available slots - is not stored in the database, it is not possible to maintain an index

| ALLOCATION | | | | |
|---|---|---|---|---|
| DISK | START | LENGTH | STATUS | DESCRIPTION |
| DISKA | 0 | 100 | A | ? |
| DISKA | 100 | 200 | U | Programs |
| DISKA | 300 | 200 | A | ? |
| DISKA | 500 | 300 | U | System |
| DISKA | 800 | 2000 | A | ? |
| DISKA | 2800 | 200 | U | Payroll |
| DISKA | 3000 | 1900 | A | ? |
| DISKA | 4900 | 100 | U | Database |
| DISKA | 5000 | 3000 | A | ? |
| DISKA | 8000 | 200 | U | Invoices |
| DISKA | 8200 | 191800 | A | ? |

**Figure 50. The ALLOCATION table (with allocated and free slots)**

on it. So query [11.12] may have to look at all rows in ALLOCATION. An alternate design is to make sure that there is a row for each allocated (used) slot, but also for any free (available) slot between two allocated ones. A STATUS column is again necessary, where the value 'A' stands for available and 'U' for used. The new ALLOCATION table is shown in Figure 50. Based on this new table, the query for finding an empty slot of 2,000 blocks becomes simply

**select** *                                                                    [11.13]
**from** ALLOCATION
**where** STATUS = 'A'
        **and** LENGTH >= 2000
        **and** DISK = 'DISKA'

| DISK | START | LENGTH | STATUS | DESCRIPTION |
|---|---|---|---|---|
| DISKA | 800 | 2000 | A | ? |
| DISKA | 5000 | 3000 | A | ? |
| DISKA | 8200 | 191800 | A | ? |

With an index on LENGTH, you can now expect a fast answer. But there is a price to pay: inserting allocation information is now more costly since more steps are involved than simply inserting a new row. As expected, the row corresponding to the available slot must be updated to reflect the start, length, and status for the new allocation. But additionally, rows have to be inserted also for the new available slots created just before and/or just after the new slot. This is a very common situation: a trade-off exists between optimizing the database design for selection or for update. Here, the update may take a little longer but the select will be much faster and our choice of the last ALLOCATION design shown in Figure 50 looks quite reasonable.

# 11.5 Summary

In this chapter we used resource management problems to illustrate various constructs of SQL, in particular the powerful **exists**.

We showed that there is a trade-off between the amount of information stored in the database and the simplicity or efficiency of the queries used to retrieve information. Sometimes, adding some redundant information may simplify queries, although updating the information may become more complex.

# Chapter 12

# Document Management

In this chapter we study the storage, retrieval, and manipulation of documents in an SQL database system. First, what do we mean by document? In all applications that we have analyzed until now, the information is represented as a collection of data elements of very limited length: numbers, short character strings, dates. These data elements are associated first in rows, then in tables, and their values as a whole are frequently used in comparison predicates. The information is said to be represented as *formatted* data. By contrast, consider a piece of text, an image, a speech. These also are data; but they are generally much longer and ***unformatted***: barring the order of the characters inside the string, they have no structure; they are never involved as a whole in a comparison.

A document, in a broad sense, is a body of information that contains both formatted and unformatted data. A book is a document; so is a memo, a letter, or an insurance policy. A document has a creator, a creation date, a type, a publisher if it is a book, a department number if it is a memo. These are formatted data. But the bulk of information in a document is composed of one or several pieces of text, drawings, images, and the like. These are unformatted. The relative amount of formatted and unformatted data involved in a particular application varies; and the types of operations performed on the database vary accordingly. In order to cover the full spectrum of interest, we borrow examples from two environments: library and office. Our emphasis is on unformatted data, mainly text, although image and audio data can be handled in a similar way.

For the library, we assume that the full text of a book is not stored electronically; what is stored is information that describes the text: title, abstract, and keywords which identify the subject of the book. The formatted data include the identification number, authors, publishing date, publisher, physical location, and loan status. The following activities must be supported:

- Search: identify the books that satisfy some given conditions about the author, the publication date, and the publisher, and/or are relevant to a particular area of interest.

- Inventory: control the mere existence of the book, its physical location, the aisle, the shelf number, the number of copies.

- Loans: is a book on the shelf? if not, when and to whom was it loaned? Issue reminders, collect fines.

Inventory and loan control deal with formatted data and do not present any difficulty. In fact, there is not much difference between books being loaned or tools being rented. So our main focus will be on searching the database for relevant books.

The office application does not deal with books, but with documents that are shorter and have a stronger information content. Therefore, the text itself is stored in the database. Among the operations to be supported, we note the following:

- Filing: when a new document enters the system, it must be registered and stored. This happens much more frequently than entering books in a library; each memo, letter, even phone call, is susceptible of becoming a document in the database. Also, every user may enter documents.

- Searching: it is important to be able to retrieve a document; this problem is similar to finding a book with some given characteristics.

- Distribution: a single document may be distributed to many people in an unsolicited way. Since the document is entirely stored in the database, sending a document to some user does not make it unavailable to others.

- Authorization: while books are generally available to the entire public, without restriction, the situation is very different with documents. Some letters, memos, and messages should be seen only by the addressees and must therefore be "hidden" from others. As a consequence, specific authorization mechanisms must be developed as part of the application.

In summary, library and office environments have many aspects in common, particularly the storage and search for text.  They also exhibits some important differences, but these mainly pertain to the area of document control.  In order to cover the subject broadly, we have identified the following list of topics to be covered in the remainder of this chapter: formatted and unformatted data, how to store long strings, how to store very long strings, data structuring, search, indexing, and document control.

# 12.1  Storing a document

## 12.1.1  Formatted data

Formatted data elements are used to specify attributes of the document.  In this section we use books as our paradigm.  Then, the formatted data elements are the title, the author, the publisher, the date of publishing, and the cost, to consider just a few.  These elementary attributes of a document must be associated with something that uniquely identifies the document. The title is not a unique identifier, since several books may have the same title. The author is not an identifier neither, since an author may have written more than one book.  The pair <title, author> is generally sufficient to identify the book unambiguously, but it is cumbersome; and matching it with a value submitted in a query is highly sensitive to the precise spelling and punctuation.  In practice, a short surrogate name is preferable.  When dealing with books, the Library of Congress Number is a good candidate.  For documents in general, a unique number is assigned when the document is initially created (for example, for a technical report) or enters the system (for example, for a memo).  Once an identification scheme has been established, the descriptive information about the document can be stored in a table DOCUMENT (see Figure 51).

You can immediately imagine some useful queries that can be expressed using the SQL facilities. You can also imagine some variants of this representation.

| DOCUMENT | | | | |
| --- | --- | --- | --- | --- |
| NO | TITLE | AUTHOR | PUBLISHER | YEAR |
| 123 | Cinderella | Perrault | ABC Pub | 1978 |
| 231 | Alice in Wonderland | Carroll | Alpha | 1966 |
| 472 | The Story of Alice in Wonderland | Smith | Beta Pub | 1984 |

**Figure 51. The DOCUMENT table**

Assume for example that a book has multiple authors. While our representation allows you to store in the AUTHOR column a single string obtained by concatenating the various names, it may be more appropriate to create a second table, AUTHOR (book, author), containing, for each book, as many entries as it has authors. Joins are then used to correlate information between DOCUMENT and AUTHOR. But you know how to do this; so let us keep our single-table design and consider some queries of particular interest.

Assume you are interested in the book "Cinderella", and you know that this is the exact title. To find the information on the book, you simply write

> **select** *  [12.1]
> **from** DOCUMENT
> **where** TITLE = 'Cinderella'

| NO | TITLE | AUTHOR | PUBLISHER | YEAR |
|----|-------|--------|-----------|------|
| 123 | Cinderella | Perrault | ABC Pub | 1978 |

Be careful, however, when you deal with text. First, the execution of [12.1] will not return a row containing "CINDERELLA": "a" is not equal to "A". A similar loss of relevant rows may happen if you look for books with a title "Cinderella "; the blank character at the end makes this title different from "Cinderella".

If you use a general query system supplied with your SQL system, you may not experience the problem. But this is simply because the package converts the strings to a canonical format (all lowercase, for example), both when strings are entered and when strings are submitted as part of a query. Similarly, it can suppress nonessential blanks or punctuation. But, when you write a program yourself, it is your responsibility to handle these types of conversion.

A similar problem occurs in strings that are made of several words. Assuming you are interested in "Alice in Wonderland", you may write

> **select** *  [12.2]
> **from** DOCUMENT
> **where** TITLE = 'Alice in Wonderland'

| NO | TITLE | AUTHOR | PUBLISHER | YEAR |
|----|-------|--------|-----------|------|
| 231 | Alice in Wonderland | Carroll | Alpha | 1966 |

Again, make sure that all words in the title appear in the string, in the right order and with the right spacing.

# 12.2  Unformatted data

In the previous section the column TITLE has a **varchar** type; the same is true for AUTHOR.  Generally, the length of a **varchar** data element is at most 256 characters; this seems enough for a title or author list, and that is why we used it.  The way queries [12.1] and [12.2] refer to TITLE is by comparison predicates.  This is typical of formatted data. But any piece of text, independently of its length, can be looked upon as an unformatted data element.  In "Alice in Wonderland" the characters are simply stored as a sequence; the database does not see any structure, does not understand word, paragraph, or punctuation.

SQL uses the **like** operation to query unformatted data:

> **select** *                                                                              [12.3]
> **from** DOCUMENT
> **where** TITLE **like** '%Alice%'
>    **and** TITLE **like** '%Wonderland%'

| NO | TITLE | AUTHOR | PUBLISHER | YEAR |
|----|-------|--------|-----------|------|
| 231 | Alice in Wonderland | Carroll | Alpha | 1966 |
| 472 | The Story of Alice in Wonderland | Smith | Beta Pub | 1984 |

Any title with these two words in any order, with any punctuation or spacing between words, will qualify. This search method is more flexible than the one used in [12.2]:  it does not force you to know precisely the whole title. But this flexibility comes with a cost.  While queries [12.1] and [12.2] may be amenable to substantial speed-ups if an index on TITLE is maintained, no index, of the type supported by SQL, will help the execution of query [12.3].  The only possible method is to read every row in DOCUMENT and apply the **like** predicates to determine whether it qualifies or not.  As we shall see in Section 12.4, you may want to implement some indexing scheme of your own to solve that problem, choosing to store redundant information in the database in order to facilitate access.

## 12.2.1  Long strings

We now consider strings that are too long to fit in a column of type **varchar**.  Storing a large object can always be accomplished by cutting the object into pieces and storing the various pieces independently. Then some auxiliary information must also be kept in the database, describing how the pieces hold together. Such a cut and paste technique may be quite appropriate for storing very large strings; but we would certainly like to avoid its complexity when dealing with strings of a few thousand characters (an abstract for example). It is for this reason that SQL supports the **long varchar** type. To store an abstract of a book, you would simply add a column ABSTRACT of type **long varchar** to the table DOCUMENT.

The **long varchar** type typically supports strings of about 32,000 characters (the actual number varies with the implementation). So, if you are sure that all instances in a particular column are shorter than this limit, the **long varchar** type is your best bet. To get a better idea of what a long string might represent, just think about regular memo pages. Each page contains 50 lines of 70 characters each, for a total of 3,500 characters. A **long varchar** string might contain about 9 such pages. If some or all of the instances of text to be stored in a column are larger than that limit, the cut and paste method remains your only alternative.

Before we analyze this technique in some details, we need to issue a warning. Some SQL systems have substantial restrictions on which operations are valid on **long varchar** strings. For example, the column cannot be involved in a join, it cannot have an index, and so on. So refer to the user manual for specific information. However, **like** is generally supported for **long varchar** strings and is, in most implementations, the only way to search the content of the string.

## 12.2.2 Storing a very long string

We have seen that **varchar** columns can be used to store small strings and **long varchar** to store strings up to a certain limit. Now, what do we do if the string exceeds that limit? If you were to use a file system in order to store such a very long string, you would cut the string into roughly equal-size records and write these records in a sequential file in their natural order. When you want to retrieve the string, you simply read the file and get the records in the same order. In a relational system, however, two things are different. First, the only ordering supported is value based (supported by the **order by** operation). Second, it is always a good idea to group in a single table all instances of the same row type. Taking these two facts into account, we come up with the design shown in Figure 52.

The DOCUMENT table remains unchanged; each row describes a document. The table CONTENTS is used to store the actual text of the document. The text is divided into blocks that fit in the column DATA of type **long varchar**.

| CONTENTS | | |
|---|---|---|
| DOCUMENT_NO | ROW_NO | DATA |
| 123 | 1 | Once upon a time, there was |
| 123 | 2 | a gentleman who lost his wife. |
| 123 | 3 | One year later, he got remarried. |
| 231 | 1 | Cinderella is the story of |
| 231 | 2 | the daughter of a gentleman |
| 231 | 3 | who remarried a terrible woman. |
| 472 | 1 | Do you know where Wonderland |
| 472 | 2 | is? It is the country that |
| 472 | 3 | you visit in your dreams. |

**Figure 52. The CONTENTS table**

The first column indicates to which document a certain row belongs, and the second column indicates the position of the block in the text (1 for first block, 2 for second block, and so on). To fetch the text for document 123, you use the following statement:

> **select** ROW_NO, DATA                                     [12.4]
> **from** CONTENTS
> **where** DOCUMENT_NO = 123
> **order by** ROW_NO

| ROW_NO | DATA |
|---|---|
| 1 | Once upon a time, there was |
| 2 | a gentleman who lost his wife. |
| 3 | One year later, he got remarried. |

The order will be the one you want. Note that, although you probably do not care about the values of ROW_NO, it must be specified in the select list because the **order by** clause requires that the column on which the sort is based be retrieved.

# 12.3 Structuring the information

In order to store very large strings, we had to cut them into more manageable pieces. It is worthwhile to ask ourselves if there is a more meaningful way of cutting a string by exploiting logical breaks in its content.

| CONTENTS1 | | | | | |
|---|---|---|---|---|---|
| DOCUMENT_NO | CHAPTER | SECTION | SUB_SECTION | ROW_NO | DATA |
| 12 | 2 | 123 | 75 | 1 | . . . |
| 12 | 2 | 123 | 75 | 2 | . . . |
| 12 | 2 | 123 | 78 | 1 | . . . |
| 12 | 2 | 123 | 78 | 2 | . . . |

**Figure 53. The CONTENTS1 table with components**

Take a technical paper, for example, composed of several sections: a summary, a body, a conclusion, a reference section. You may want to retrieve them separately. Thus, you want to preserve the individuality of these various sections by storing them in the database as different items. For bylaws, you may want to be able to retrieve a specific chapter, a section, or a subsection. Let us study this example in more detail. This time, the CONTENTS1 table may be defined as shown in Figure 53. The column DATA is of type **long varchar**. If the section is not too long, it will fit in a single DATA element, and there will be only one row in CONTENTS1 for that particular section. If it is very long, several rows will be required, as discussed in the previous section.

To retrieve the chapter 2 of document 12, you define an SQL cursor for

[12.5]

```
select SECTION, SUB_SECTION, ROW_NO, DATA
from CONTENTS1
where DOCUMENT_NO = 12
    and CHAPTER = 2
order by SECTION, SUB_SECTION, ROW_NO
```

| SECTION | SUB_SECTION | ROW_NO | DATA |
|---|---|---|---|
| 123 | 75 | 1 | . . . |
| 123 | 75 | 2 | . . . |
| 123 | 78 | 1 | . . . |
| 123 | 78 | 2 | . . . |

On the other hand, to browse only through section 123.78 of the same chapter, you define a cursor on

**select** ROW_NO, DATA                                                  [12.6]
**from** CONTENTS1
**where** DOCUMENT_NO = 12
    **and** CHAPTER = 2
    **and** SECTION = 123
    **and** SUB_SECTION = 78
**order by** ROW_NO

| ROW_NO | DATA |
|--------|------|
| 1 | . . . |
| 2 | . . . |

The technique just discussed supports a hierarchical partition of the document content into subdocuments. In order to retrieve a subdocument at a certain level x, all levels above and including x must be identified in the **where** clause. In order to retrieve a chapter, the document number and the chapter identification must be specified; in order to retrieve a section, document, chapter and section must be specified, and so on.

# 12.4  Text indexing

Earlier in this chapter, we showed how the **like** feature of SQL is used to find documents of interest by searching for particular words or strings of characters. We also mentioned that SQL indexes, which are based on the order of the values in one or more columns, are not helpful for evaluating **like** predicates. But do not be discouraged. You can use SQL in creative ways in order to implement *text indexing* schemes that are appropriate for your particular application.

Text processing specialists have always used indexing techniques which consist of creating redundant formatted data from textual unformatted data. Indexes, in general, increase substantially the performance of searches for relevant documents. We show here how SQL nicely supports the storage and manipulation of these indexes. In order to avoid confusion with the standard SQL indexes, we refer to text indexing as text *inversion*.  The name comes from the fact that the technique implements an access path from the contents of a text to its identifier, rather than from identifier to contents.

Consider again the DOCUMENT table shown in Figure 51, and let us build an inverted table on the TITLE column; we call it INVERT (see Figure 54). It contains a row for each word in each title (assuming a lowercase canonical form).  To find the books on Cinderella, you can simply select from INVERT

| INVERT | |
|---|---|
| WORD | DOCUMENT |
| alice | 231 |
| alice | 472 |
| cinderella | 123 |
| in | 231 |
| in | 472 |
| story | 472 |
| of | 472 |
| the | 472 |
| wonderland | 231 |
| wonderland | 472 |

**Figure 54. The INVERT table**

the rows that contain "cinderella" as a title word, and then join these rows
with DOCUMENT in order to find the document information:

**select** DOCUMENT.*                                        [12.7]
**from** DOCUMENT, INVERT
**where** DOCUMENT.NO = INVERT.DOCUMENT
    **and** WORD = 'cinderella'

| NO | TITLE | AUTHOR | PUBLISHER | YEAR |
|---|---|---|---|---|
| 123 | Cinderella | Perrault | ABC Pub | 1978 |

A similar search for books with "Alice" and "Wonderland" in their titles
requires an extra join, as in

**select** DOCUMENT.*                                        [12.8]
**from** DOCUMENT, INVERT A, INVERT B
**where** DOCUMENT.NO = A.DOCUMENT
    **and** DOCUMENT.NO = B.DOCUMENT
    **and** A.WORD = 'alice'
    **and** B.WORD = 'wonderland'

| NO | TITLE | AUTHOR | PUBLISHER | YEAR |
|---|---|---|---|---|
| 231 | Alice in Wonderland | Carroll | Alpha | 1966 |
| 472 | The Story of Alice in Wonderland | Smith | Beta Pub | 1984 |

There are two simple techniques to reduce the amount of space needed to implement an inverted table.

1. Common words like "the" and "in" should not be entered in the inverted table. They are present in too many entries and are useless for specifying the target of the search.
2. Words may be encoded. Instead of repeating a long word such as "wonderland" in several instances, a short encoded representation of the word can be used. The encoding is maintained in a two-column table associating the code with the word.

Taking these two techniques into account, we can replace INVERT by two tables ENCODE and CODE_INVERT (see Figure 55). Query [12.8] can then be reformulated as

> **select** DOCUMENT.*                                                    [12.9]
> **from** DOCUMENT, CODE_INVERT I1, CODE_INVERT I2,
>         ENCODE E1, ENCODE E2
> **where** DOCUMENT.NO = I1.DOCUMENT
>     **and** DOCUMENT.NO = I2.DOCUMENT
>     **and** I1.WORD = E1.CODE
>     **and** I2.WORD = E2.CODE
>     **and** E1.WORD = 'alice'
>     **and** E2.WORD = 'wonderland'

| NO | TITLE | AUTHOR | PUBLISHER | YEAR |
|-----|-------|--------|-----------|------|
| 231 | Alice in Wonderland | Carroll | Alpha | 1966 |
| 472 | The Story of Alice in Wonderland | Smith | Beta Pub | 1984 |

As we noted earlier, what we have done is to add to the database a certain amount of redundant information in terms of formatted tables, making it possible to use the full generality of SQL when searching for relevant documents. In addition, performance can now be improved substantially by making sure that the appropriate SQL indexes exist on the additional tables. In the example, the set of useful indexes includes the following:

- Index on NO in table DOCUMENT
- Index on WORD in CODE_INVERT
- Index on WORD in ENCODE

The efficiency of the encoding scheme varies with the length of the words and the number of occurrences of the same word. The best choice is a matter of trade-off between complexity and space. This is even more true if you apply

| ENCODE | |
|---|---|
| CODE | WORD |
| 1 | alice |
| 2 | cinderella |
| 3 | story |
| 4 | wonderland |

| CODE_INVERT | |
|---|---|
| WORD | DOCUMENT |
| 1 | 231 |
| 1 | 472 |
| 2 | 123 |
| 3 | 472 |
| 4 | 231 |
| 4 | 472 |

**Figure 55.  The ENCODE and CODE_INVERT tables**

the same inversion technique to the body of the document itself. Then the amount of space required by the inverted tables and SQL indexes on these tables becomes much larger. On the other hand, the evaluation of **like** predicates may become so time consuming that inversion is probably worthwhile. Another consideration is the time needed to construct inversion tables such as CODE_INVERT. Each addition of a title in the DOCUMENT table must be accompanied by several operations (search and/or insert) in ENCODE and CODE_INVERT. On the other hand, the information in these tables is practically never updated; so the overhead occurs only once at insertion time. Again, this overhead may well be acceptable, considering the performance improvements that the method provides for queries.

Let us discuss some more useful queries without using the encoding technique (look therefore at Figure 54).   All the following queries return document numbers without repetition. A join with the DOCUMENT table will return more information; we omit it here for the sake of clarity.

Let us first look for documents containing at least one word in a pair of words:

> **select distinct** DOCUMENT                                    [12.10]
> **from** INVERT
> **where** WORD = 'story'
>     **or** WORD = 'wonderland'

| DOCUMENT |
|---|
| 231 |
| 472 |

An equivalent statement is

```
select distinct DOCUMENT                              [12.11]
from INVERT
where WORD in ('story', 'wonderland')
```

If the document is to contain at least k of the specified words, one way of expressing the query is (for two words among three)

```
select DOCUMENT                                       [12.12]
from INVERT
where WORD in ('alice', 'wonderland', 'story')
group by DOCUMENT
having count(distinct WORD) >= 2
```

| DOCUMENT |
|---|
| 231 |
| 472 |

Note that we never worried about the order in which different words appear in a piece of text. This may result in irrelevant documents being selected. The same is true for the distance between two words: it is often important to specify that two words appear in the text contiguously.  Let us solve these problems by introducing a third column, POSITION, in the table INVERT. The number in that column specifies the numeral position of the word in the document. Generally, programs are used to build inverted tables; thus, computing the position does not require any extra effort.  As an example, suppose we search for documents about "modern algebra"; the query below provides the right answer:

```
select A.DOCUMENT                                     [12.13]
from INVERT A, INVERT B
where A.WORD = 'modern'
    and B.WORD = 'algebra'
    and A.DOCUMENT = B.DOCUMENT
    and A.POSITION + 1 = B.POSITION
```

Note that a text "on a modern approach to classical algebra" will not qualify.

Similarly, the following statement will find documents about either "modern algebra" or "set theory".

| LIST | |
|------|------|
| SEARCH_NO | DOCUMENT |
| 23 | 231 |
| 23 | 472 |

**Figure 56. Result of a search in the database**

**select** A.DOCUMENT                                                       [12.14]
**from** INVERT A, INVERT B
**where** (A.WORD = 'modern'
   **and** B.WORD = 'algebra')
  **or** (A.WORD = 'set'
    **and** B.WORD = 'theory')
  **and** A.DOCUMENT = B.DOCUMENT
  **and** A.POSITION + 1 = B.POSITION

As mentioned above, all these examples produce a list of document numbers. We said that, for reasons of clarity, we did not include the join. However, there is another reason for doing so.

# 12.5 Progressive refinement of a search

When retrieving documents, you do not always submit the correct request on the first try. Your search criteria may not be selective enough, and, as a result, you get a lot of uninteresting documents. One solution is to change the initial query and resubmit it. A better solution is to start from the list of documents resulting from a previous search and use it in order to refine the query. Such a technique implies that you save the result of the current search in a table (see format in Figure 56). To distinguish among the results of various queries, you assign a unique number to each query. Assume your search 23 consists of finding the documents about "Alice". The statement below inserts the document numbers in LIST.

**insert into** LIST                                                         [12.15]
  **select distinct** 23, DOCUMENT
  **from** INVERT
  **where** WORD = 'alice'

To restrict the search target, you use a join and specify additional predicates:

**select** A.DOCUMENT                                              [12.16]
**from** INVERT A, LIST B
**where** A.DOCUMENT = B.DOCUMENT
    **and** A.WORD = 'story'
    **and** B.SEARCH_NO = 23

| DOCUMENT |
|---|
| 472 |

You may also want to save the new result in the list, under query number 24. Note that the target table cannot also be the source table. Therefore, you may have to save the result, first, in an intermediate table (say TEMP_LIST) and use the following statement to insert its content into LIST:

**insert into** LIST                                              [12.17]
    **select** *
    **from** TEMP_LIST

Once you believe you nailed down your search, you get the document contents by joining the document numbers with the CONTENTS rows, as in

**select** DOCUMENT_NO, ROW_NO, DATA                              [12.18]
**from** CONTENTS A, LIST B
**where** A.DOCUMENT_NO = B.DOCUMENT
    **and** SEARCH_NO = 24
**order by** DOCUMENT_NO, ROW_NO

| DOCUMENT_NO | ROW_NO | DATA |
|---|---|---|
| 472 | 1 | Do you know where Wonderland |
| 472 | 2 | is? It is the country that |
| 472 | 3 | you visit in your dreams. |

Enough said about the storage and retrieval of documents. We now turn our attention to the control of documents: where they are located, who has access to them, and the like. As we mentioned earlier, control of books in a library is not very special. In an office environment, however, the control of documents is a different matter all together and is worth studying.

# 12.6 Document control

In an office environment, a document is a controlled resource that circulates among users of the office automation system. Documents are created and then distributed to one or several users; a document needs to be explicitly sent to somebody in order for that somebody to be able to access it. At each leg of its journey a document may or may not be modified. Changing a document does not only mean editing its content; it may also mean adding an approval notice which will trigger some action.

In a manual office system, documents are sent and received through a mail system; each user receives its input in an in-basket. An office automation system emulates similar functions: each user can insert a document in the in-basket of one or several co-workers. An important difference is that, in the automated system, a document can be entered once and then remains in one location. When it needs to be sent to somebody, a simple message which essentially says "look at the document No x" is inserted into the in-basket of the destination. When a document is to be sent to several destinations, such a message is inserted into each of their in-baskets. Let us design a table for controlling these operations.

We use a single IN_BASKET table (Figure 57) for the whole company (you are getting used to this way of grouping information; we justified it in detail in Chapter 10). A row in the table has four columns. The first row in the table indicates that document 123 has been sent by Smith to Jones on May 12. It is the sender (Smith) who inserted that row to notify Jones. Wilson also wants to notify Jones that he is sending him a document, and inserts the second row. Jones can look into his in-basket by issuing the following query:

**select** *                                                              [12.19]
**from** IN_BASKET
**where** RECEIVER = 'Jones'
**order by** TRANSFER **asc**

| SENDER | RECEIVER | TRANSFER | DOCUMENT |
|--------|----------|----------|----------|
| Smith  | Jones    | 1989-05-12 | 123 |
| Wilson | Jones    | 1989-06-17 | 456 |

The first row of the result corresponds to the document that was sent first.

Many SQL systems have a special keyword (**user**) which denotes the name of the user who is executing the query. An easy way of making use of that information is by defining a view which always constructs your in-basket:

| IN_BASKET | | | |
|---|---|---|---|
| SENDER | RECEIVER | TRANSFER | DOCUMENT |
| Smith | Jones | 1989-05-12 | 123 |
| Wilson | Jones | 1989-06-17 | 456 |
| Smith | Wilson | 1989-05-27 | 789 |

**Figure 57. The IN_BASKET table**

**create view** MY_BASKET                                [12.20]
**as**
**select** *
**from** IN_BASKET
**where** RECEIVER = **user**

The same view definition can be used by all users; each of them will see only the entries corresponding to the name in **user**. For example, Wilson will see the third row. The SQL authorization mechanism can also be exercised to make sure that anybody can only see the restricted MY_BASKET, and not the full IN_BASKET. But this may not be necessary since IN_BASKET contains only document numbers and no contents.

Protection against unauthorized access to the contents of documents is of course important. So, let us devise a scheme based on an AUTHORITY table (Figure 58). Anybody who wants to authorize somebody to see a document inserts a row in AUTHORITY, which associates a document number with an authorized user. Anybody is authorized to read the contents of documents only through a view called AUTH_DOC, defined by

**create view** AUTH_DOC                                [12.21]
**as**
**select** DOCUMENT_NO, ROW_NO, DATA
**from** CONTENTS C, AUTHORITY A
**where** USERID = **user**
          **and** A.DOCUMENT = C.DOCUMENT_NO

When an entry is made into an in-basket, a corresponding entry must be made into AUTHORITY. The first row in AUTHORITY authorizes Jones to see document 123. But entries can be made into AUTHORITY without necessarily notifying the user. The corresponding documents can be browsed through AUTH_DOC as well. Although Jones has not been notified that he

| AUTHORITY | |
|---|---|
| USERID | DOCUMENT |
| Jones | 123 |
| Jones | 456 |
| Jones | 888 |
| Wilson | 888 |

**Figure 58. The AUTHORITY table**

was sent document 888, the last row in AUTHORITY will enable him to read it.

A tricky problem is to ensure that somebody inserting entries in AUTHORITY is authorized to do so and does it only for documents that he or she controls. The rules for controlling the operation may be complex; and the best solution is to write a program that checks all necessary conditions before inserting rows. Anybody is granted SQL authorization to the program rather than the table itself.

Inserting individual authorization in AUTHORITY may be cumbersome, and a group authorization may be preferable. Assume that a table GROUP keeps information on who belongs to a certain group and that table GROUP_AUTHORITY keeps track of which documents can be accessed by all members of which group (see Figure 59). Then the information equivalent to the table AUTHORITY above can be constructed by the following view:

```
create view AUTHORITY                                    [12.22]
as
select USERID, DOCUMENT
from GROUP, GROUP_AUTHORITY
where GROUP_AUTHORITY.GROUP_NAME =
        GROUP.GROUP_NAME
    and USERID = user
```

The view AUTH_DOC defined in [12.21] is still applicable; it refers to the view AUTHORITY rather than a stored table.

| GROUP | | | GROUP_AUTHORITY | |
|---|---|---|---|---|
| USERID | GROUP_NAME | | GROUP_NAME | DOCUMENT |
| Jones | Managers | | Managers | 123 |
| Jones | New Project | | Managers | 456 |
| Wilson | New Project | | New Project | 888 |

**Figure 59. The GROUP and GROUP_AUTHORITY tables**

# 12.7 Summary

In this chapter, we have considered applications that deal not only with formatted data, but with unformatted data as well. We have shown that unformatted data can be stored in an SQL database, whatever their length. This is done sometimes as a single string and sometimes as multiple strings held together by structuring information also stored in a table.

The fact that we can integrate formatted and unformatted data means that the same query can access both. It also means that the integrity of the database is enhanced. If text had to be stored in a different database (or file) system, it would be much more difficult to ensure that deleting a document description in SQL is always accompanied by deleting the text in the other system. In fact, cross-system atomic transactions of this type are hard and rarely supported.

A very important feature of a database system for documents is its search facility. We have seen how SQL can be used to search for documents that satisfy some conditions on the formatted data related to these documents; we also saw how conditions can be expressed on unformatted data. Since both types of data are integrated in the same SQL repository, a single query can mix conditions on text and nontext data. For performance reasons it is often advisable to transform nonformatted data searches into formatted data searches. This is implemented by maintaining inverted tables. A search on the contents of a document becomes a search on the data stored in these inverted tables, making all the power of SQL available for simple or complex queries.

Finally, a short analysis of some document control functions helped illustrate how SQL can be used to implement control systems in general. Control always implies checking for conditions to hold, based on evolving data. The control data can be stored in tables; and SQL can be used to maintain that information and check for conditions while accessing it.

# Chapter 13

# An Object-oriented Application

In this chapter we investigate the use of SQL to manage clusters of intricately related data. We first discuss an example that exhibits that kind of complex data structure and compare different possible relational schemas. We then try to characterize in more general terms the properties of *object-oriented* applications and introduce some useful new techniques.

## 13.1 A graphics application

Graphics are known to be rather demanding on the organization of data. Although it sounds specialized, it serves as a paradigm for many applications. Additionally, it has the advantage that everyone understands readily the problems at hand. The application involves simply the storage of drawings made of icons connected by lines, where an icon is itself a simple drawing made of line segments. Drawings and icons are generic names. But you may prefer to think in more specific terms. If you are interested in computer-aided design for electronic boards, then an icon may be a chip and a connection, a wire. For a utility company, the icon may be a pole, a transformer, or a house, while lines may be cables. In a geographical map application, icons may be used to represent cities of various types, while lines represent roads.

But let us return to our generic drawing and look at how to organize the data in the database and how to access it. Figure 60 represents a drawing: it is built out of three icons; two of them (A and B) are copies of the same model

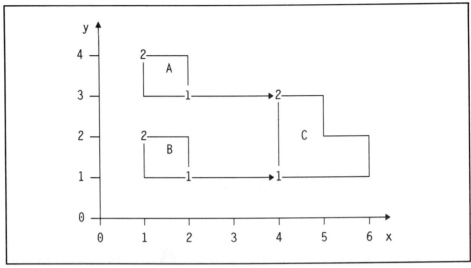

**Figure 60. Drawing with three icons and two connections**

(rectangle), the third one (C) is a copy of another model (L-shape). Each icon is associated with a pattern but also with a certain number of anchor points where connecting lines can be attached. In the example, the lower right corner anchor of icon A is connected to the upper left anchor of icon C, while the lower right corner anchor of icon B is connected to the lower left anchor of C. The database contains a catalog of icons and a set of drawings. Figure 61 shows a portion of the collection of icons.

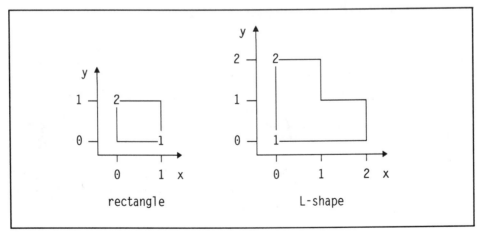

**Figure 61. Catalog of icons**

## 13.1.1 Describing icons

Let us first look at what kind of information needs to be stored in the database in order to fully describe icons. An icon seems such a simple object; nevertheless some trade-offs must be considered.

There must clearly exist a table that serves as a catalog of icons; call it ICONS (see Figure 62). It contains a row for each icon; a row contains a name (any kind of unique identifier) and information on the shape of the icon. The shape can be represented as a sequence of (x,y) pairs of coordinates; each pair identifies a point. Two consecutive points are joined by a line. For the rectangle, the shape is obtained by going from point (0,0) to (1,0), then to (1,1), then to (0,1), and then back to (0,0). For anchors, consider the two following schemas; both capture the relevant information.

•   Schema a (see Figure 62): The information is stored as a list of triples (n,x,y) - one for each anchor. The number n identifies the anchor in the icon; x and y are the coordinates of that particular anchor. In the rectangle, anchor 1 is at (1,0) and anchor 2 at (0,1).

| ICONS | | |
|---|---|---|
| ICON | SHAPE | ANCHORS |
| rectangle | 0 0 1 0 1 1 0 1 0 0 | 1 1 0 2 0 1 |
| L-shape | 0 0 2 0 2 1 1 1 1 2 0 2 0 0 | 1 0 0 2 0 2 |

**Figure 62. Representation of icons using a single table ICONS (Schema a)**

•   Schema b (see Figure 63):  Here, the information about anchors is stored in a second table named ANCHORS.  ANCHORS contains one row for each anchor.  The first column determines to which icon the anchor belongs; the second column identifies the particular anchor described by the row.  The third and fourth columns contain the coordinates of that anchor.  For example, anchor 1 of the L-shape icon is at coordinates (0,0), while anchor 2 is at (0,2).

We now analyze the trade-offs between the two approaches.  In schema a, a single SQL statement suffices to read the complete information about a given icon:

| ICONS | |
|---|---|
| ICON | SHAPE |
| rectangle | 0 0 1 0 1 1 0 1 0 0 |
| L-shape | 0 0 2 0 2 1 1 1 1 2 0 2 0 0 |

| ANCHORS | | | |
|---|---|---|---|
| ICON | NBR | X | Y |
| rectangle | 1 | 1 | 0 |
| rectangle | 2 | 0 | 1 |
| L-shape | 1 | 0 | 0 |
| L-shape | 2 | 0 | 2 |

**Figure 63. Representation of icons using two tables (Schema b)**

> **select** SHAPE, ANCHORS                         [13.1]
> **from** ICONS
> **where** ICON = 'L-shape'

| SHAPE | ANCHORS |
|---|---|
| 0 0 2 0 2 1 1 1 1 2 0 2 0 0 | 1 0 0 2 0 2 |

Since the whole information about the shape of one icon has been packed into a single character string in column SHAPE, it is the responsibility of the application program to decode the contents of the string and isolate the various vertexes and line segments. The same thing is true for ANCHORS. Similarly, it is also the responsibility of the program to pack the numerical values into a string when a new icon is inserted into the database.

Using schema b (Figure 63), the retrieval of an icon will need to touch two tables. The first reaction is to use a join. Since there are only two tables, it would work: the ICONS row would simply be replicated for each matching row in ANCHORS. It does not, however, generalize: think about a case where there is a third table; call it ANCHORS'; a join will "multiply" rows from ANCHORS with rows from ANCHORS', when you are really interested in fetching some rows in ANCHORS plus some rows in ANCHORS'. So, in order to remain general in our discussion, we prefer to use two **select** statements, one for ICONS and one for ANCHORS. Compared to schema A, the fetch is more complex. Not only do we need two **select** statements, but the one on ANCHORS needs a cursor since it will generally retrieve multiple rows. However, the application program now receives the values about anchors in a directly usable form, avoiding the need for decoding or conversion. Also, the full power of SQL is available to ask queries about the details of an icon. For example, the following SQL statement finds the icons that have at least one anchor outside the unit square:

**select distinct** ICON                                    [13.2]
**from** ANCHORS
**where** X > 1
    **or** Y > 1.

| ICON |
|---|
| L-shape |

Moreover, the indexing power of SQL becomes automatically available. If there is an index on X or Y, SQL may well choose to use it, avoiding the time-consuming scan of all rows in the table. In schema a, again, since SQL does not understand the internal data structure of ANCHORS, no index can be used.

The difference between the two schemas can be characterized as follows: in the first schema the information is stored in an *unformatted* way, while it is stored in a *formatted* way in schema b. The formatted representation may be less efficient when the information is created or retrieved. On the other hand, it allows for the full power of SQL to be used for querying the data. The unformatted representation optimizes the creation and retrieval of the information but delegates a substantial amount of the work to the application program. Note that both schemas use an unformatted representation for the shape. A consequence of that choice is that SQL cannot be used to "recognize" the individual vertexes of the shape. This is quite reasonable since the only operation on the shape will probably be to retrieve it all together in order to display it.

In schema b, two tables are used to represent an icon. But these tables are interconnected by a matching value on the icon name. Therefore the value in ANCHORS.ICON must always exist in ICONS.ICON. To ensure that property automatically, the SQL referential integrity mechanism, explained in Chapter 9, can be applied. Column ICON in ICONS should be defined as a primary key, column ICON in ANCHORS, as a foreign key referring to ICONS.ICON.

It is interesting to note that an icon is a quite simple object; nevertheless the decision on how to organize its data in the database is not trivial: the trade-offs must be analyzed and the optimal choice finally depends upon the way the multiple applications are going to use the information. Later in this chapter we use schema b again.

| DRAWING | | |
|---------|------|--------|
| NAME | DATE | AUTHOR |
| D1 | 1988-03-22 | J. Smith |

Figure 64. The DRAWING table

## 13.1.2 Describing a drawing

We now turn our attention to the storage of data describing more complex objects such as drawings. Refer to Figure 60.

A drawing has attributes such as name, date of creation, author, and so on. Therefore, the database design will certainly include a table, call it DRAWING (see Figure 64), containing a row for each drawing.

A drawing contains instances of icons (including their anchors) and connections between them. Again, the information about which icons are used and how they are connected could be stored in an unformatted way: then the whole structure describing the object would be packed in a single string and stored in a fourth column of DRAWING. The application program would then be responsible for decoding the data; additionally, SQL could not be used to query it.

We assume here that the facility of asking questions such as "which drawing uses a certain icon?" or "which are the drawings that use more than five distinct icons?" is important. Then the unformatted approach ceases to be the right choice, and a formatted representation is chosen instead. Such a representation uses a table INSTANCES (see Figure 65) containing, for each drawing, as many rows as there are instances of icons in it. All rows belonging to the same drawing have the same drawing name in the first column. The second column contains the unique name of the instance. Together with the drawing name, it uniquely identifies a row in INSTANCES. The third column specifies the model of the icon, and the third and fourth columns specify the placement of the icon in the drawing (actually the coordinates of the lower left corner of the icon). For simplicity, we assume in the example that icons cannot be enlarged or reduced.

To keep track of the connections we again choose a formatted representation and define a table CONNECTIONS (see Figure 65). For each drawing, the table CONNECTIONS contains as many rows as there are connections in the drawing. The first column contains the name of the drawing to indicate to

| INSTANCES | | | | |
|---|---|---|---|---|
| DRAWING | INST | MODEL | X | Y |
| D1 | A | rectangle | 1 | 3 |
| D1 | B | rectangle | 1 | 1 |
| D1 | C | L-shape | 4 | 1 |

| CONNECTIONS | | | | |
|---|---|---|---|---|
| DRAWING | INSTANCE_1 | ANCHOR_1 | INSTANCE_2 | ANCHOR_2 |
| D1 | A | 1 | C | 2 |
| D1 | B | 1 | C | 1 |

**Figure 65. The INSTANCES and CONNECTIONS tables**

which drawing a particular row belongs. The next pair of columns identifies the "from" anchor; the next pair identifies the "to" anchor. Each pair designates an anchor; the first column in the pair specifies the name of the instance in the drawing; the second one specifies which anchor in the icon instance is used for that connection.

# 13.2 The notion of object

Based on the above discussion, we now attempt to characterize what makes object-oriented applications so different from, say a classical data management application. Consider the tool rental company again. A tool is an entity; it has a "life" of its own; it is represented as a single row in a table. The same is true for a customer. Although a contract is always related via some matching values to both a tool and a customer, it is also meaningful to refer to a contract or to fetch such a contract as an entity.

In the graphics application, the real-world entity is a drawing. It does not mean much to fetch an anchor without fetching the icon to which it belongs; similarly, fetching a drawing implies fetching instances, and probably icons, and connections. In other words, a real-world object is represented in the database by a collection of rows belonging to various tables, and one must be able to retrieve such a collection from the database in an efficient way. In addition, these rows are often linked together in many intricate relationships; here again it must be easy to establish and exploit such relationships. Finally, it is symptomatic of many object-oriented applications that an object is built out of simpler objects, as drawings are built out of icons. Very often one object refers several times to the same object at a lower level.

In the next section we discuss some general techniques that are useful when dealing with data that exhibit these characteristics.

# 13.3  Techniques for managing object data

### 13.3.1  Use of identifiers

Consider the tables ICONS and ANCHORS. A row in ICONS is uniquely identified by the icon name stored in column ICON. These icon names are used in the table ANCHORS to identify the icon to which a particular anchor belongs. This kind of parent-children relationship is very common:  the icon row is a parent; it "owns" as dependents, as children, a certain number of (child) rows in ANCHORS.  Since the name of an icon is of variable size and may be long, using it repeatedly in another relation (as in ANCHORS) may be awkward. Very often it is preferable to substitute for such a long name a short unique identifier.

The question arises of how to allocate such a unique identifier to a row in a table T.

One way is to use a time stamp mechanism. A time stamp is a monotonically increasing value provided generally by the operating system. It is often based on the machine clock. In order to be unique it is generally quite long.

Another way consists of associating with the table T a relation T' which has a single row and a single column: the only data element in T' is the last identifier allocated to a row in T. The next identifier is acquired by reading the value in T' and adding 1 to it. The result is then stored back into T' to prepare for the next request.  The technique may need to be modified slightly to support concurrent users, because contention on modifying T' may become intolerable if several users try to acquire identifiers for the same table T at the same time.  A possible modification is to add 100 rather than 1 to the contents of T' and, by so doing, return 100 identifiers instead of 1. This clearly decreases contention.  Some of these 100 identifiers may not actually be used; but this is not a serious drawback since the only effect is to waste some numbers from a very large range.

When the schema becomes more complex, there are more relationships between tables, and the use of identifiers becomes even more important.  For the sake of explanation, let us complicate the application slightly, assuming that we want to keep in a table COMMENTS an arbitrary number of comments about a connection. COMMENTS must have at least two columns: one to identify a connection and one to contain the comment. But in the schema shown in Figure 65 the only way to uniquely identify a connection is by spec-

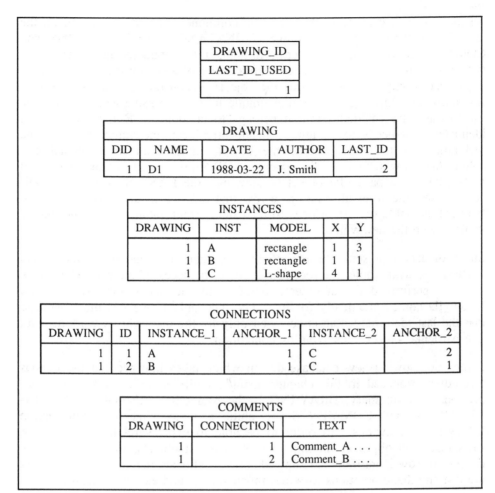

| DRAWING_ID |
| --- |
| LAST_ID_USED |
| 1 |

| DRAWING | | | | |
| --- | --- | --- | --- | --- |
| DID | NAME | DATE | AUTHOR | LAST_ID |
| 1 | D1 | 1988-03-22 | J. Smith | 2 |

| INSTANCES | | | | |
| --- | --- | --- | --- | --- |
| DRAWING | INST | MODEL | X | Y |
| 1 | A | rectangle | 1 | 3 |
| 1 | B | rectangle | 1 | 1 |
| 1 | C | L-shape | 4 | 1 |

| CONNECTIONS | | | | | |
| --- | --- | --- | --- | --- | --- |
| DRAWING | ID | INSTANCE_1 | ANCHOR_1 | INSTANCE_2 | ANCHOR_2 |
| 1 | 1 | A | 1 | C | 2 |
| 1 | 2 | B | 1 | C | 1 |

| COMMENTS | | |
| --- | --- | --- |
| DRAWING | CONNECTION | TEXT |
| 1 | 1 | Comment_A . . . |
| 1 | 2 | Comment_B . . . |

**Figure 66. Representation of a drawing using identifiers**

ifying all of the five values in a CONNECTIONS row:  for example, (D1, A, 1, C, 2) uniquely identifies the first connection. This is very cumbersome; clearly, associating a unique name or identifier to such a row and then using this identifier in the COMMENTS table to establish the relationship is a much better alternative. Look at tables CONNECTIONS and COMMENTS in Figure 66 for an illustration.

The question now is how to create unique identifiers for connections.  The method used above to find a unique identifier for a new drawing can be applied.  Remember that such an identifier had to be unique in the whole DRAWING table. Here we suggest a more efficient two-step method.  First, we make sure that all rows that describe components of an object contain the identifier of the object. For example, all INSTANCES, CONNECTIONS, and COMMENTS rows used to describe drawing D1 contain the identifier of D1 (which is 1 in our example). Then the identifier of any row that belongs to an object needs only be unique inside the object. Recall how a value stored in T' was used for allocating an identifier unique in T. The same technique can be used to allocate an identifier that belongs to an object. But, since such an identifier only needs to be unique inside an object, the value in T' can be maintained in the root row of the object, rather than in a special one column/one row table. In the example, DRAWING will contain a column LAST_ID; for a particular object (a drawing), the LAST_ID value will indicate the last identifier allocated to a row that belongs to that object. To find the next available one, it suffices to read the current value, add 1, and update the row with the new value.

Since objects represent clusters of records that are generally fetched and manipulated as a whole, the root row needs to be accessed anyway when work is to be performed on an object; therefore the access to the extra column LAST_ID comes practically for free. The mechanism also has the advantage that the last identifier value is accessed only by the user who is working with that particular object, thus avoiding contention.

Figure 66 shows a new database design which takes into account the various techniques proposed in this chapter, using identifiers for drawings and connections. In summary, DRAWING is the root table. INSTANCES, CONNECTIONS, and COMMENTS are children tables that hold information belonging to drawings. In order to be able to express relationships among rows inside an object or among rows of different objects, we introduced the concept of row identifiers and showed how to allocate them. These identifiers are just shorthand notations for keys, much shorter and easier to manipulate.

## 13.3.2  Fetching an object

In object-oriented applications one often needs to fetch all information about an object. Suppose for example that you want to display the object D1 on a screen. The normal method to get the information is to write a program similar to the one shown in Figure 67. We need to discuss the program somewhat, as it illustrates two important trade-offs.

*First trade-off*: This has to do with the fact that, often, an object refers to another object several times. For example, the rectangle icon is used twice in the drawing D1. The program shown in Figure 67 ignores that fact and fetches the ICON row and the corresponding ANCHORS rows as often as the icon appears in the drawing. Such a situation is quite common. It stems from the

```
exec sql include sqlca
exec sql begin declare section
        declare number Drawing_id, V_c, V_c1, V_c2
        declare number V_x, V_y, V_ax, V_ay
        declare string V_model, V_shape, V_text, V_i, V_i1, V_i2
exec sql end declare section
exec sql select DID
        into :Drawing_id
        from DRAWING
        where NAME = 'D1'
/* now select all instances */
exec sql declare C1 cursor for
        select INST, MODEL, X, Y
        from INSTANCES
        where DRAWING = :Drawing_id
exec sql open C1
exec sql whenever not found go to End_c1
do forever
        exec sql fetch C1
                into :V_i, :V_model, :V_x, :V_y
        /* save V_i, V_x, V_y for future reference */
        /* now select information about icons */
        exec sql select SHAPE
                into :V_shape
                from ICONS
                where ICON = :V_model
        /* display shape at coordinates (V_x, V_y) */
        /* now select anchors */
        exec sql declare C2 cursor for
                select X, Y
                from ANCHORS
                where ICON = :V_model
        exec sql open C2
        exec sql whenever not found go to End_c2
        do forever
                exec sql fetch C2
                        into :V_ax, :V_ay
                /* display dot for anchor, save V_ax and V_ay */
```

Figure 67. Program to read a drawing (Part 1)

```
                    end /* of C2 */
        exec sql whenever not found continue
        exec sql close C2
End_c2:
        end /* of loop on C1 */
End_c1:
exec sql close C1
/* at this point, icons and anchors are displayed; get connections */
exec sql declare C3 cursor for
        select ID, INSTANCE_1, ANCHOR_1, INSTANCE_2,
            ANCHOR_2
        from CONNECTIONS
        where DRAWING = :Drawing_id
exec sql open C3
exec sql whenever not found go to End_c3
do forever
        exec sql fetch C3
            into :V_c, :V_i1, :V_c1, :V_i2, :V_c2
        /* display connection using saved V_i, V_x, V_y, V_ax, V_ay */
        /* read comments associated with connection if any */
        exec sql declare C4 cursor for
            select TEXT
            from COMMENTS
            where DRAWING = :Drawing_id
                and CONNECTION = :V_c
        exec sql open C4
        exec sql whenever not found go to End_c4
        do forever
            exec sql fetch C4
            into :V_text
            /* print comment */
            end /* of C4 */
End_c4:
        exec sql whenever not found continue
        exec sql close C4
        end /* of C3 */
End_c3:
exec sql close C3
```

**Figure 67. Program to read a drawing (Part 2)**

fact that complex objects are generally built in a hierarchical way, using several instances of simpler objects that are themselves built of instances of still simpler objects, and so on.

Esthetically, the program is quite nice: when data are needed, they are fetched from the database, whether it is the first time or not. But, practically, this way of doing things may be very inefficient. It is generally much better to maintain, in the application space, a buffer in which commonly used objects can be kept in an appropriate internal representation. Consider the display of D1. One can count the number of rows that will be fetched: 1 for DRAWING, 3 for INSTANCES, 2 for CONNECTIONS, 3 for the first rectangle icon (1 for ICONS, 2 for ANCHORS), 3 for the second rectangle, and 3 for the L-shaped icon. The 3 fetches for the second rectangle are unnecessary if recently fetched items are kept in a buffer. The total number of fetches can thus be brought down from 15 to 12. But this is a simple example. In practice, objects comprise many more rows, the duplication factor may be much higher, too, and the saving much greater.

*Second trade-off*: This has to do with the order in which rows constituting an object are fetched. The program shown above actually traverses the data in the hierarchical order. You first obtain the DRAWING row, then the information about each instances, then, for each instance, the information about each anchor. It is thus easy, if you want to keep these rows in the buffer, to translate the hierarchical information into pointers that can be stored in the buffer, together with the data. For connections, the problem is different. Since they are linked to two parent rows (the origin of the connection and its target), the hierarchical way of fetching related rows does not apply. In fact, the program will read all CONNECTIONS rows belonging to drawing 1, from the database. It will then look in the buffer for the coordinates of the instances and anchors. Between CONNECTIONS and COMMENTS, the relationship is again hierarchical; and the hierarchical method applies again.

The hierarchical method is attractive, but it does not mean that it should be blindly used as soon as relationships are hierarchical. In fact, it comes with a cost. Essentially, for each parent (for example, connection) you execute an SQL statement to find all of its children (comments). The number of SQL statements that are thus executed in the program increases with the number of rows in the drawing. An alternate solution consists of selecting all instances, all anchors, all connections, and all comments belonging to a drawing, storing them in the buffer, and then reconstituting the parent-children relationships by executing an application program that looks into the structural columns in order to re-create the structural pointers in the buffer. In this case, the number of SQL statements used in the program is much smaller. Although each of the statement returns more rows, the method is much more efficient when dealing with large objects.

The fact that the object identifier is stored in all rows that belong to the object makes such retrieval easy. Figure 68 shows only the cursor definitions for all selections, without the logic. For each cursor, the program would issue an **open**, **fetch** loop, and **close** in order to fetch all relevant rows:

• Cursor C1: to fetch the instances, knowing the drawing identifier.

• Cursor C2: to fetch the ICONS information for all icons used in the drawing. The **distinct** attribute ensures that any icon is fetched only once.

• Cursor C3: to fetch the anchors of all icons fetched above.

• Cursor C4: to fetch the connections in the drawing. A join is used to fetch the comments at the same time.

Clearly, the program will have to allocate space for each data element returned; but this is normal programming.

Once all information is in the buffer, an application program can traverse the data and insert pointers to build the structure which is the most appropriate for the application. Often the application does a substantial amount of computation on the data (think about a simulation of an electronic circuit or finding an optimal path in a road map), and building such a structure is more than worth-while.

# 13.4 Summary

This chapter discussed the use of SQL in *object-oriented* applications. Such applications are characterized by the fact that they deal with objects that are represented in the database by collections of rows belonging to various tables. We contrasted two representations. The unformatted representation provides for a simpler manipulation of the data describing an object but leaves much of the interpretation to the application program. The formatted representation makes the insertion and retrieval somewhat more complicated, but there is a high payoff in that SQL can then be used to manipulate and query the data.

We covered several important issues: the allocation of identifiers, the notion of an object buffer to avoid repeated retrieval of the same information, and the trade-off in fetching methods.

It is quite possible that, as a user, you will never encounter such object-oriented applications. After all, other applications discussed in this book do not

```
exec sql declare C1 cursor for
    select INST, MODEL, X, Y
    from INSTANCES
    where DRAWING = :Drawid

exec sql declare C2 cursor for
    select distinct I.*
    from ICONS I, INSTANCES D
    where I.ICON = D.MODEL
        and D.DRAWING = :Drawid

exec sql declare C3 cursor for
    select *
    from ANCHORS
    where ICON in
        ( select MODEL
        from INSTANCES
        where DRAWING = :Drawid)

exec sql declare C4 cursor for
    select *
    from CONNECTIONS X, COMMENTS Y
    where X.DRAWING = :Drawid
        and Y.DRAWING = :Drawid
        and X.ID = Y.CONNECTION
```

**Figure 68. A faster program to fetch a drawing**

make use of the techniques described in this chapter. However, some of these
techniques may be useful individually in other situations. And the more applications you see, the larger your initial inventory of methods becomes and the
easier your design task will be.

# Chapter 14

# Graph Problems

In this chapter, we address a class of problems requiring a specific SQL **select** statement to be repeatedly executed in order to obtain the desired answer.

Consider the hierarchical graph in Figure 69. The information can be stored in SQL as a table GRAPH with two columns, FROM_V and TO_V, as shown in Figure 70. If X is immediately above Y in the hierarchy, a row <X, Y> exists in GRAPH. We also refer to X as the *parent* of Y and to Y as the *child* of X; we also use *ascendant* or *descendant* with their obvious meaning.

Although the problem is couched here in general terms, it is easy to think about applications that deal precisely with such a structure. Consider a management hierarchy. GRAPH represents the manager relationship from one employee (FROM_V) to another (TO_V). A is the general manager of the company; B, J, and H report directly to A, while K, E, and C report to B, and so on.

As we shall see in this chapter, GRAPH comes in very handy to answer typical queries on data structured in such a way. This does not mean, however, that GRAPH is necessarily the best way of storing the information. Consider a management hierarchy where employees belong to a department that is managed by a manager (who is also an employee). Thus two tables are used:

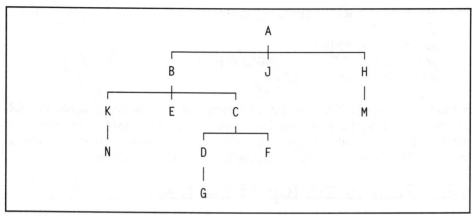

**Figure 69. A hierarchical structure**

EMPLOYEE (EMP#, DEPT#, . . .)
DEPARTMENT (DEPT#, MGR#, . . .)

We assume that the general manager belongs to a department that has no manager, and that a manager does not belong to the department that he or she manages, but rather to the department managed by his or her manager. For example, K, E, and C form a department under B; B does not belong to that department but rather to the department composed of B, J, and H. If you prefer to "see" the information in the form of a GRAPH table, you can define a view, as in

| GRAPH | |
|--------|------|
| FROM_V | TO_V |
| A | B |
| A | J |
| A | H |
| B | K |
| B | E |
| B | C |
| K | N |
| C | D |
| C | F |
| D | G |
| H | M |

**Figure 70. The GRAPH table**

```
create view GRAPH (FROM_V, TO_V)                          [14.1]
as
select MGR#, EMP#
from DEPARTMENT D, EMPLOYEE E
where D.DEPT# = E.DEPT#
```

Whatever the application context in which GRAPH is being used, the following two types of queries are important: 1) given a node in the tree, find the path to the top, and 2) given a node, find all nodes (or only leaf nodes) under it. We discuss both of these problems in the next sections.

# 14.1 Path to the top of the tree

Finding the node that is directly above a given node does not present any problem. If you are interested in finding the hierarchical parent of C, you simply write

```
select FROM_V                                             [14.2]
from GRAPH
where TO_V = 'C'
```

| FROM_V |
|--------|
| B      |

But is it possible to find the complete path above C in a single SQL statement? Consider the statement below:

```
select G1.FROM_V, G2.FROM_V                               [14.3]
from GRAPH G1, GRAPH G2
where G1.TO_V = 'C'
    and G1.FROM_V = G2.TO_V
```

What does it provide? When G1.TO_V = 'C', G1.FROM_V is equal to 'B', G2.TO_V is equal to 'B', and G2.FROM_V is equal to 'A'.

The answer is exactly what we wanted:

| G1.FROM_V | G2.FROM_V |
|-----------|-----------|
| B         | A         |

But we actually cheated somewhat because we relied on the knowledge that there are only two hierarchical levels above 'C'. If we were to use the same query for D, it would return 'C' in G1.FROM_V and 'B' in G2.FROM_V; but the complete answer should contain 'A' as well. The reason why 'A' is missing is that we actually need an extra join to handle three levels instead of two. On the other hand, query [14.3], applied to B instead of C would return an empty result: when G1.FROM_V equals 'A', there is no matching value for G2 since A has no parent in the hierarchy.

Clearly, we have not solved the problem in its generality. Intuitively, one feels that what is needed is a loop on statement [14.2]. When 'C' is specified in the **where** clause, the statement returns 'B'; the statement is then re-executed for 'B' instead of 'C' and returns 'A'. In most SQL systems, such an iterative process can only be implemented by writing a program as shown in Figure 71. Initially, the variable *Node* is set to the initial node; at any further iteration, the variable is filled with the value obtained as a result of the previous iteration. When *Node* contains 'A', the **select** statement fails and the **whenever** clause terminates the loop. Since at each level, there is only one parent for a node, there is no need for defining a cursor.

# 14.2 Finding all nodes under a node

In the previous paragraph, we navigated from a node to the top of the tree. We now consider the reverse problem: starting from a given node, walk the tree downward, collecting information on every node encountered.

The statement below finds the immediate children of node C:

> **select** TO_V                                   [14.4]
> **from** GRAPH
> **where** FROM_V = 'C'

| TO_V |
|------|
| D |
| F |

Note that, contrary to [14.2], statement [14.4] produces in general more than one row.

To find all the descendants of a node, one could try to apply the join technique used in [14.3], and write

```
    exec sql include sqlca
    exec sql begin declare section
        declare string Node
        declare string Parent
    exec sql end declare section

    read initial node

    exec sql whenever not found go to The_End

    do forever
        exec sql select FROM_V
            into :Parent
            from GRAPH
            where TO_V = :Node
        print (' The parent of ', Node, ' is ', Parent)
        Node = Parent
        end
    The_End: exit
```

Figure 71. Program to find the chain from a node to the top

```
select G1.TO_V, G2.TO_V                                    [14.5]
from GRAPH G1, GRAPH G2
where G1.FROM_V = 'C'
    and G1.TO_V = G2.FROM_V
```

| TO_V | TO_V |
|------|------|
| D    | G    |

The answer is correct but incomplete; both D and G are descendants of C. But so is F which is missing. The reason is that F has no child and therefore is eliminated during the evaluation of the join. Actually, statement [14.5] would yield the correct answer only if all leaf nodes were at the same "distance" from C.

Our conclusion is the same as in the previous section: the only solution consists of writing a program. However, the problem is slightly more complicated because going down the tree returns several nodes at each level. Many programming languages support a facility, called **recursion**, that solves the

```
initialize X to the initial node
call A(X)

A: procedure (X) recursive
        open the set S of all nodes under X
        while S returns a value
                fetch S into Y
                print Y
                call A(Y)
                end

        end
```

**Figure 72. Tree walking: recursive program**

problem in an elegant way. Essentially, recursion allows for a program to invoke itself, as shown, (at a very high level) in Figure 72. Referring to the graph of Figure 69, and if X is initialized to the value 'C', the execution of the program unfolds as shown in Figure 73.

```
Call A('C')
|       Fetch → 'D'
|       Call A('D')
|       |       Fetch → 'G'
|       |       Call A('G')
|       |       |       Fetch → no more
|       |       |       Return
|       |       Fetch → no more
|       |       Return
|       Fetch → 'F'
|       Call A('F')
|       |       Fetch → no more
|       |       Return
|       Fetch → no more
|       Return
```

**Figure 73. Tree Walking: recursive program execution**

At first, one may think that it should be possible to implement such a recursive algorithm in an SQL program, using a cursor to select all employees under a node X. But when the cursor is open and positioned on a certain node, another occurrence of the same cursor (for the same **select** statement) needs to be opened. Since multiple occurrences of the same cursor are generally not supported in current SQL implementations, we have to look for another solution.

The alternative to recursion is iteration, which is precisely what the program in Figure 71 uses. The problem was simpler, however, because the **select** statement always returned a single value; and a single value is easy to save in a variable to be used as input for the next iteration. Here we may be able to use a similar technique, but the result of the **select** is a set, and saving a set in memory is much more difficult because its size is unknown a priori. The solution is to save the set in a temporary table in the database. We can then imagine a method that works as follows: initialize a set S1 with the initial node and a set S2 as empty. For each node in S1, select the child nodes, print them, and insert them in S2. The next iteration inverts the roles of S1 and S2: empty S1 and for each node in S2, select the child nodes, print them, and insert them in S1. The process terminates when no child node is found.

The drawback with such a procedure is that it executes a **select** statement for each node in the tree. This can easily be improved by using a join to retrieve, in a single **select**, the child nodes of all nodes that are in a set. The program in Figure 74 uses precisely this technique; we now discuss it line by line.

- Statement (1) declares a cursor C1 to select all child nodes of the nodes in S1.
- Statement (2) empties S1.
- Statement (3) stores the initial node in S1 in order to start the iterative process.
- Statement (4) ensures that table S2 is empty before starting to insert into it.
- Statement (6) fetches the next node. A variable *Count* (not to be confused with the aggregate function **count**) is used to detect when the set of child nodes is empty; if *Count* is zero when tested in statement (11), the program terminates.
- Statements (5) and (7) trigger a branch to label *End2* when there is no more row for cursor C1. Note that statements (2) and (4) can also trigger a **not found** condition when they try to delete rows from an empty table. The default **continue**, which is active from the first line of the program to Statement (5), is appropriate.
- Statement (8) inserts the found child nodes in S2.

```
          exec sql include sqlca
          exec sql begin declare section
              declare string Node
              declare string Id
          exec sql end declare section
          declare number Flag init(0)
          declare number Count
(1)       exec sql declare C1 cursor for
              select GRAPH.TO_V
              from S1, GRAPH
              where S1.NODE = GRAPH.FROM_V
(1')      exec sql declare C2 cursor for
              select GRAPH.TO_V
              from S2, GRAPH
              where S2.NODE = GRAPH.FROM_V
          read the name of the initial node in Node
(2)       exec sql delete from S1
(3)       exec sql insert into S1 values (:Node)
          do forever
              count = 0
              if flag = 0 then do
(4)               exec sql delete from S2
                  exec sql open C1
                  do forever
(5)                   exec sql whenever not found go to End2
(6)                   exec sql fetch C1
                          into :Id
(7)                   exec sql whenever not found continue
                      print ('Node:',Id)
(8)                   exec sql insert into S2 values (:Id)
                      Count = Count + 1
                      end
                  end
              else do
(4')              exec sql delete from S1
                  exec sql open C2
                  do forever
(5')                  exec sql whenever not found go to End2
```

**Figure 74. Program to print all nodes under a node (Part 1)**

```
(6')                     exec sql fetch C2
                              into :Id
(7')                     exec sql whenever not found continue
                         print ('Node:',Id)
(8')                     exec sql insert into S1 values(:Id)
                         Count = Count + 1
                         end
                    end
           End2:
(9)             exec sql whenever not found continue
                if Flag = 0 then do
(10)                 exec sql close C1
                     Flag = 1
                     end
                else do
(10')                exec sql close C2
                     Flag = 0
                     end
(11)            if Count = 0 then leave
                end
```

**Figure 74. Program to print all nodes under a node (Part 2)**

• Statements (4'), (5'), and so on, repeat the process, this time starting with
  S2 instead of S1.  Flag is a binary switch which controls the flip-flop
  between S1 and S2.

Note that the **fetch** operation is executed once for every node in the answer.
There is really no way to avoid this, since the program must receive control in
order to print the node or do whatever is needed.  In some cases, you may
want to keep the answer set in a temporary table in the database itself. Clearly,
you could use exactly the same program, simply replacing the print statement
by an **insert**.  However, this may not be optimal any more; this time the
program does not necessarily need to get control for each node in the answer
if SQL can do the insert directly.  Our goal is thus to modify the program in
Figure 74 so that no statement is executed for each node in the result.

Our reasoning goes as follows.  We need to accumulate all answer nodes in a
single table determined a priori, say S1.  This means that we will have to copy
the result obtained in S2 back into S1. But, since only the result of a particular
iteration is needed as input to the following one, we need to mark in S1 the

```
           exec sql include sqlca
           exec sql begin declare section
               declare string Node
               declare number Level
               declare number Count
           exec sql end declare section
           exec sql delete from S1
(1)        exec sql declare C1 cursor for
               select GRAPH.TO_V
               from S1, GRAPH
               where S1.NODE = GRAPH.FROM_V
           read the name of the initial node in Node
           Level = 0
(2)        exec sql insert into S1
               values (:Node, :Level)


           do forever
(3)            exec sql delete from S2
(4)            exec sql insert into S2 (NODE, LEVEL)
                   select GRAPH.TO_V, LEVEL
                   from S1, GRAPH
                   where S1.NODE = GRAPH.FROM_V
                       and LEVEL = :Level
(5)            exec sql select count(*)
                   into :Count
                   from S2
               if Count = 0 then exit the do forever loop
(6)            exec sql insert into S1 (NODE, LEVEL)
                   select NODE, LEVEL + 1
                   from S2
               Level = Level + 1
(7)            /* loop back */
               end
```

**Figure 75. Program to build a list of all descendants of a node**

rows that correspond to the last iteration. This can be done by tagging every node added to S1 with a level number; an extra column LEVEL is added to that effect. The level number is initialized to zero and increased by one at each iteration. An iteration selects from S1 only the nodes that comes from the result of the previous iteration. The program is shown in Figure 75.

Note that table S2 has also a column LEVEL; this is needed in order to circumvent a restriction of SQL (which exists in some implementations) that forbids host variables in the **select** list: LEVEL needs to exist in S2 so that it can be used in (6).

## 14.3 Leaves of the tree

The previous section considered the question of finding all nodes under a given node. Now we consider the problem of finding only those nodes that are leaves of the tree (that have no children). How should the above programs be modified?

In the program shown in Figure 74, we do not know in (6) if the current node has children or not; therefore nodes with children cannot be skipped easily. In fact, it is not easy to change the program in order to solve the problem at hand. On the contrary, the program in Figure 75 is much more appropriate, even if it does construct a temporary table of nodes (if you really need to print them, you simply scan the list). What we need is to delete from S1 all nodes that are not leaves, once the content of S1 has been used to construct S2. But how do we know which rows correspond to nonleaf nodes?. One way is to keep in an extra column, called PARENT, for each node in S2 the parent from which it comes. Then a **delete from** S1 statement can be used to delete all nodes that appear in that column. Statement (4) is extended as follows:

<pre>
    exec sql insert into S2 (NODE, LEVEL, PARENT)          [14.6]
        select GRAPH.TO_V, LEVEL, GRAPH.FROM_V
        from S1, GRAPH
        where S1.NODE = GRAPH.FROM_V
            and LEVEL = :Level
</pre>

And the following statement can be added before comment (7) to delete, at each level, the nodes that have produced child nodes - the nodes that appear in S2.PARENT.

<pre>
    exec sql delete from S1                                [14.7]
        where S1.NODE in
            ( select PARENT
            from S2 )
</pre>

## 14.4 Acyclic graphs (bill of material)

The previous sections deal with hierarchical graphs: a node has never more than one parent node. Now we look at a first generalization, where a node

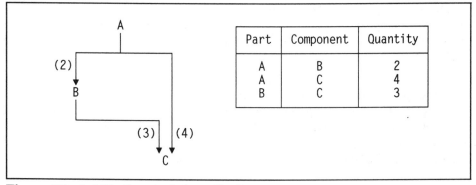

| Part | Component | Quantity |
|------|-----------|----------|
| A | B | 2 |
| A | C | 4 |
| B | C | 3 |

**Figure 76. A bill of material application**

may have more than one parent. Suppose that the graph in Figure 69 contains an extra arc between F and G. Then the table contains a row <F, G>. How does this affect the problems and techniques discussed above?

The problem of finding all descendants of a given node is not changed by the fact that a node can have multiple parents, and the program in Figure 74 is applicable. Be careful, however, that some nodes may be duplicated in the answer, since the algorithm will reach some nodes several times, coming down from different parents. Duplicates may be eliminated by reading the result with a **select distinct**.

And what about the problem of finding the path from a node to the top of the tree? Actually, there can now be several top nodes. Finding all paths going from one node to the top nodes is symmetric to find all descendant nodes of a node in the hierarchical case, and the same programs can be used by simply reversing the roles of FROM_V and TO_V.

A very typical application of the acyclic graph case is the ***bill of material***. Refer to Figure 76. The graph shows that a part A is built out of 2 B parts and 4 C parts. Part B itself is made out of 3 C parts. It is clearly an acyclic graph. Finding all basic parts that are needed to build part A is a "find all leaves" problem; finding all parts that contain a given part is a "find the nodes up" problem.

# 14.5 Cyclic graphs (network problems)

We now consider another generalization where an arc in the graph can go from a node to its parent or one of its ascendant nodes; in other words, the graph contains cycles. For example, such a cycle exists if an arc <G, C> is added to the graph in Figure 69. If we apply the programs above, unchanged, to the new graph, their execution will never end since a parent already processed will reappear as a child at a subsequent level, producing again the same children, and so on, indefinitely. Somehow, such a loop must be detected and broken.

Suppose you want to find again all nodes under a certain node without entering in an infinite loop. The program will be very similar to Figure 75. The only difference is that the result contained in S2, after each iteration, must be pruned of any node that is already in S1. Thus, the only change to the program is adding the statement below before statement (5):

```
exec sql delete                                    [14.8]
    from S2
    where exists
        ( select *
        from S1
        where S1.NODE = S2.NODE)
```

To show how the program works, suppose you want to know all nodes under C. The program execution will unfold as follows:

> *S1 is set to 'C' (initialization)*
> *First iteration:*
> > *S2 contains: 'D' , 'F'*
> > *Delete from S2 the nodes that are already in S1 (none)*
> > *Add 'D','F' to S1, with level = 1*
> 
> *Second iteration:*
> > *S2 contains: 'G'*
> > *Delete from S2 the nodes that are already in S1 (none)*
> > *Add 'G' to S1, with level = 2*
> 
> *Third iteration:*
> > *S2 contains 'C'*
> > *Delete from S2 the nodes that are already in S1 ('C')*
> > *Count is now 0 - end of program.*

In practice, cyclic graphs are found in applications that deal with networks of any kind. Consider a road map. Clearly the network has cycles. The same is true of communication networks, utility maps, and other connectivity problems.

# 14.6 Towards more support in SQL

We handled all graph problems above with the normal **select** block of SQL. In all cases we had to write specific programs. Each of these programs ended up by implementing a loop where the result of one **select** is used as input to another **select**, and this for a number of times which is generally not known a priori, but depends on the data itself. To avoid the need for programs, there is a trend towards introducing some explicit support in SQL for that type of operation. A variety of implementations and proposals exists. Here, we picked one of the proposals to illustrate the concepts.

Consider again the problem studied in Section 14.2: given GRAPH, find all nodes directly or indirectly under 'C'. An obvious way of finding the answer uses the following steps:

- First, find the set of nodes that are directly under 'C'. Assume that the set is stored in a table S with a single column, NODE.

- Then, find the nodes directly under the nodes in S by joining S with GRAPH, as in

> **select** GRAPH.TO_V                                [14.9]
> **from** S, GRAPH
> **where** S.NODE = GRAPH.FROM_V

- Add this result set to S.

- Repeat the last two steps until no new node is added to S.

The proposed syntax supports the specification of the iterative process in a single statement:

> **select** TO_V                                         [14.10]
> **from** GRAPH
> **where** FROM_V = 'C'
> **recursive union**
> S(NODE)
> **select** GRAPH.TO_V
> **from** S, GRAPH
> **where** S.NODE = GRAPH.FROM_V

**Recursive union** indicates the type of statement, while S(NODE) assigns an arbitrary name to the working table. In addition, the statement includes two

**select** statements: the first initializes S with the nodes directly under 'C'; the second is repeated as many times as needed.

The fact that the syntax refers to a table S does not mean that the implementation will actually compute the result by using such a table; it is only a syntactical element, which may or may not have a physical counterpart during the execution of the query. Also, S is not known outside the statement itself.

# 14.7 Summary

In this chapter, we covered the use of SQL for retrieving data with graph semantics. As an example of such semantics, we mentioned the manager-employee relationship, which can be represented as a hierarchical graph, or tree. This is a simple but useful case. Genealogical information is another example exhibiting the same structure.

Our first generalization introduced acyclic graphs instead of trees. This structure is even more important. The management of assemblies and components in a manufacturing application generally requires acyclic graph structures. This is because instances of the same subassembly can be used in various different subassemblies of a higher level.

The generalization to a general graph is important for a variety of applications dealing with networks: roads, airline routes, computer-aided software management systems. In the latter case, the information about which programs call which other programs forms a graph. If programs are recursive, then a program can invoke itself or a program at a higher level, and the full generality of cyclic graphs is needed.

The application programs that deal with graph structures are generally more complex, invoking nontrivial algorithms to process the information. Although these algorithms are clearly outside the scope of this book, it was important to show how the basic information could be retrieved from the database.

For all cases presented, the techniques are similar. They use SQL to find as much information as possible in a single statement and store intermediate results as temporary tables in the database so that they can be used as input for the next iteration. We did not, by any means, cover all graph-oriented problems, but we did give enough examples to help the user designing specific solutions to specific problems. Finally, we showed an example of an extension to the **select** block which permits some graph problems to be solved as a single query, without the need for a specialized program.

# Chapter 15

# Developing a User Interface

We now shift gears in the study of SQL. Part 2 introduced the reader to the most important features of the SQL language, one by one, in a logical order. In Part 3, each chapter analyzes a particular application and discusses how SQL can best be used to meet the specific data management requirements. The applications are chosen so that each of them brings forth some new issues.

In this last chapter, we return to our now well-known rental company. Imagine you are in charge of developing a program supporting interactive queries on the database. Queries come in various flavors.

- Some queries do not change: the same ones are executed day after day, with different values of parameters.

- Others, often called *ad hoc*, are submitted or constructed on the spot to retrieve information in a completely unpredictable way.

- Finally, some of them are in between: the basic query is the same but there are minor differences in the conditions that the data must meet or in the type and the amount of information to be displayed in the answer.

You will recall that Chapter 1 introduced two modes of invoking SQL: the *static* and *dynamic* modes. In static SQL, the whole statement is known at program compilation time; in dynamic SQL, it is not. In the latter case, more work has to be postponed until execution time. Once that point was made, we put aside the distinction, since the syntax is identical in both cases. This does not imply, however, that the choice between the static and dynamic options is always evident. Discussing this choice is one of the objectives of this chapter. Another related objective is to show some techniques that are useful in providing a user-friendly interface to the database.

The first task in designing the application is to identify the queries that need to be supported. After analysis, assume you come up with the following menu:

```
                          MAIN MENU

       Q1. Display all information about a contract

       Q2. Display information about a customer

       Q3. Display the cost of various tools

       Q4. Ad hoc query

       Q5. Display specific information about a contract
```

For the purposes of this chapter, the list of interesting queries does not need to be exhaustive; only a few were chosen to illustrate some important issues:

- Q1 illustrates the use of static SQL for a parameterized query.

- Q2 is similar, but deals with parameter values that are only partially known.

- Q3 shows how temporary tables can be helpful in handling a variable number of parameters in a query (an alternative is to use dynamic SQL).

- Q4 stands for any ad hoc query that requires the full power of dynamic SQL.

- Q5 illustrates a way of handling a select list that changes from one query invocation to another (it is a slightly simplified case of dynamic SQL).

# 15.1 Static SQL for parameterized queries

Q1 is clearly an example of a query that is repeatedly executed. The body of the query itself is invariant; what distinguishes one invocation from another is the contract number which acts as a parameter. The optimal way of supporting Q1 is to embed the query in a program and use a variable to specify the value of the parameter. Figure 77 displays such a program. It prompts the user to enter the contract number in the appropriate variable before executing

```
display menu

/* menu for Q1 is: */
/* Enter Contract Number: ____ */

read X    /* read contract number */

exec sql select CU.NAME, CU.ADDRESS, CU.ZIP,
           CO.DATE_OUT, CO.DATE_IN, T.TYPE
     into :Vn, :Va, :Vz, :Vo, :Vi, :Vt
     from CONTRACT CO, CUSTOMER CU, TOOL T
     where CU.NAME = CO.CUSTOMER
        and CO.TOOL = T.NUMBER
        and CO.CONTRACT = :X

display Vn, Va, Vz, Vo, Vi, Vt
```

**Figure 77. Program to display all information about a contract**

the **select**. Note that the **select** statement contains a join; this is indispensable since the complete information to be returned comes from three tables.

It is worth noticing that the end user interacts only with very simple menus and does not need to know the syntax of SQL. Also, since Q1 does not change (except for the value of the parameter), static SQL is used. No query compilation occurs at execution time; this has a positive effect on performance.

# 15.2  The use of wild characters

In Q1, the input parameter is a number. You have to know the number exactly. Therefore, a **where** clause with a strict equality, such as

    where CONTRACT = 101                                    [15.1]

is quite acceptable.  But this may not be true for character strings.  Suppose you want to retrieve information on a customer, called Wilson or Wilsen (you are not quite sure of the spelling). Then you need a more complex **where** clause such as

    where NAME = 'Wilson, P.' or NAME = 'Wilsen, P.'        [15.2]

```
/* menu for Q2: */
/* Enter Customer name (with wild characters) */
/* Example : 'Wils_n' */

read X    /* read customer name */

exec sql declare C1 cursor for
        select NAME, ADDRESS, ZIP
        from CUSTOMER
        where NAME like :X

exec sql open C1
exec sql whenever not found go to End_C1

do forever
        exec sql fetch C1
            into :Vn, :Va, :Vz
        /* display the result */
        display 'Customer Information: ' , Vn , Va , Vz
        end
End_C1:
exec sql close C1
 . . .
```

**Figure 78. Program to display information about a customer**

It looks like a simple variation, but it does affect the program quite a lot. Now the **where** clause depends on the number of possible spellings. Since the query changes, static SQL is not applicable anymore. But, since using dynamic SQL has a negative impact on performance, it is worthwhile to look at an alternative. One such alternative is to use wild characters. The **where** clause

$$\text{where CUSTOMER.NAME like 'Wils\_n, P.'} \qquad [15.3]$$

uses a wild character which matches any character. Clearly 'Wilson' and 'Wilsen' satisfy the condition. If such a **where** clause is used, the problem becomes the same as Q1 again: the statement does not change, and static SQL can be used, as shown in Figure 78. However, since the condition is less precise, more than one row may now qualify, and a cursor is needed. All qualifying rows are returned and displayed, leaving the final choice up to the user.

# 15.3 Supporting a set of parameters

The input to Q3 (display the cost of various tools) is a series of tool numbers for which prices are requested. First, assume that a couple of tool numbers are entered at each invocation. Then, if the tool numbers are read into X1 and X2, the statement

**exec sql declare** C **cursor for**                         [15.4]
    **select** RENTAL_FEE
    **from** TOOL
    **where** NUMBER **in** (*:X1, :X2*)

will do the job.

Now, if three tool numbers are specified instead of two, the corresponding statement becomes

**exec sql declare** C **cursor for**                         [15.5]
    **select** RENTAL_FEE
    **from** TOOL
    **where** NUMBER **in** (*:X1, :X2, :X3*)

In both cases, static SQL can be used. However, it is hardly a solution to the problem, since a different statement is needed for each possible number of tools specified in the query. Let us consider a much more flexible approach.

First, assume that you have access to your own table, called SET, with a single column ITEM. Such a table may have been created by executing

**create table** SET                                          [15.6]
    (ITEM **integer**)

under your own user identification. If the program is also compiled under your user identification, then, when it refers to SET, it is your SET that is going to be used. If the program is compiled only once by the person responsible but is later executed under your name, it will have to dynamically refer to your own SET when executed.

The program in Figure 79 uses SET to hold the multiple input values. By doing so, the predicate

    **in** (*:X1, :X2, :X3)*                                    [15.7]

```
        /* handling Q3 */

        exec sql delete from SET

        do for each input value
            read X   /* read tool number in X */
(1)         exec sql insert into SET
                values (:X)
            end

(2)     exec sql declare C cursor for
            select RENTAL_FEE
            from TOOL
            where NUMBER in
                ( select ITEM
                from SET )

        . . .
```

**Figure 79. Program illustrating the use of a set in the where clause**

which varies with the number of input parameters, is replaced by

**in** ( **select** ITEM **from** SET)                                           [15.8]

which accommodates any number of them.

This method imposes no limit on the size of the user-provided list of tool numbers. What we did is to devise a static SQL solution for a problem that, at first glance, seemed to involve different SQL statements for different executions. In order to compare thoroughly the static and dynamic approaches, let us write the program using dynamic SQL (see Figure 80).

In Section 1.4.5, we showed how **execute immediate** can be used to execute a statement dynamically; it actually implies the production of an execution structure followed by its execution. When a cursor is involved, the generation of the structure is initially requested by a **prepare** statement; then, **open** refers to the result of that **prepare** (named X1 in the example). The **fetch** statement identifies the program variables into which the result values are returned. Since we know that each result row consists of a single value, we only need to

```
exec sql include sqlca
exec sql begin declare section
        declare string S
        declare number V
exec sql end declare section

build statement in S

exec sql prepare X1 from :S
exec sql declare C1 cursor for X1
exec sql open C1
do until no more row
        exec sql fetch C1 into :V
        end


    . . .
```

**Figure 80. Using a dynamic statement for a cursor**

specify one program variable in the **fetch** statement. In our example, the SQL **select** statement itself can be computed by the following piece of code:

*define the strings Quote (containing a single ')*

```
/* initialize S to: */
S = 'select rental_fee from tool where number in'
Separator='('

do for each input value
     read X    /* read data */
     X = Quote || X || Quote      /* enclose it in quotes */
     S = S || Separator || X
     Separator = ','
     end
S = S || ')'  /* close parenthesis */
```

Notice that the operator || is used to indicate a string concatenation. Assume that the user enters, at the terminal,

1
3
. . .
end of input.

Then you can trace the program to convince yourself that, after execution, the
character string *S* contains the statement below:

**select** RENTAL_FEE **from** TOOL **where** NUMBER **in** (1, 3, ...)   [15.9]

## 15.3.1  Static versus dynamic SQL

Although the dynamic approach entails an overhead for doing the **prepare** of
the statement at each invocation, the performance of each individual **fetch** is
exactly the same as if it were static.  Generally speaking, static queries are
faster; but dynamic queries also have an advantage.  Since the values of variables that appear in the **where** clause are known when the statement is opti-
mized (in fact, they are constants in the statement), the optimizer may be able
to take more judicious decisions.  Consider for example the very simple static
statement

    **select** *                                                         [15.10]
    **from** TOOL
    **where** RENTAL_FEE > *:V*

At program compilation time, the optimizer does not know what the value of
the program variable *V* will be at execution. It cannot do better, therefore, than
guessing that, say, 50% of the rows satisfy the query.  But, actually, if *V* has
the value 1, then all rows will qualify; if it has the value 1000, then no row
qualifies. The best strategy may change depending upon the anticipated
number of rows that satisfy the condition.  But the system does not have
enough information, at compilation time, to take a judicious decision. In the
dynamic case, the value is known when the statement is prepared at execution
time, and the optimizer may use it to decide on the best strategy.

A similar situation occurs with the **like** predicate.  At compilation time,
nothing is known about the form of the variable used to specify the filter.
Thus, the optimizer will opt for a method which scans all rows.  On the other
hand, in the dynamic case, the optimizer knows the filter.  If, for example, the
filter is of the form

    **like** 'xxx%'

```
        /* step 1: create SET */

        exec sql begin declare section
            declare string S
            declare number V
        exec sql end declare section

        S = 'create table set (item integer)'

(1)     exec sql execute immediate :S

        /* step 2: populate the set */

        S = 'insert into set values(?)'

(2)     exec sql prepare X1 from :S
        do until last value is entered
            read V    /* read value from terminal */
(3)         exec sql execute X1 using :V
            end

        /* at this point SET is fully built */
        /* use it ... */
        /* when the query evaluation is completed: */
        S = 'drop table set'
        exec sql execute immediate :S
```

**Figure 81. Dynamic creation of working tables**

the optimizer would be able to recognize that the predicate is equivalent to **between** 'xxx' **and** 'xxy' and to choose a better access path. (A remark: we are just speculating on what is possible; it does not mean that all optimizers are that smart.)

## 15.3.2 Creating temporary tables

Consider again the program in Figure 79. It assumes that you have exclusive access to your own SET table. In more complex situations, you may need several such temporary tables, possibly with more than one column; and you may not always have these tables available. To solve that problem, the program itself can choose to create the needed tables dynamically. We now discuss this approach.

The program in Figure 81 stores the **create** statement in string $S$. Since the statement does not require a cursor, the invocation is straightforward: the **execute immediate** operation in (1) takes care of both preparation and execution in a single command.

The program also shows in (2) how a statement can refer to a program variable dynamically. The ? in $S$ indicates that the statement refers to one parameter. Since the contents of $S$ will be analyzed only at execution time, it does not do any good to specify the name of a variable. The ? is only a place holder. This is how it works:

- Statement (2): the string $S$ is prepared into X1. This dynamic handling of the **insert** is required since the set in which rows are inserted is not known at program compilation time (the creator name depends on the user running the program).

- Statement (3): the **execute** statement refers to the result of the preparation (X1) and specifies actual variables corresponding to the place holders (the variable must have a type compatible with the result of the query). Note that X1 is not a variable (it has no declaration); it is simply a name used to correlate the **prepare** and the **execute** statements.

### Four remarks

- Several place holders can appear in the same statement. Then the **execute** command needs to specify an equal number of program variables. The order of the variables specified in the **execute** statement matches the order of the place holders.

- The technique, as presented, works only because the programmer knew the number of place holders in $S$ and therefore knew how many variables needed to be specified in the **execute** statement. The following section dealing with Q4 will address the situation when this does not hold.

- The same place holder notation can be used in the **where** clause of a **select** statement. Then the actual variable is specified in the OPEN command and must be initialized before OPEN is executed.

- Place holders can be indicated using a variable name syntax, such as *:V*. Note that it is only a syntactic difference which makes it easier to see what the correspondence is between the various place holders and the variables that correspond to them.   For example, you could have written in Figure 81,

(1)     $S$ = 'insert into set values(:V)'
. . .
(3)     **exec sql execute** X1 **using** :V

# 15.4  Ad hoc statement

The purpose of the Q4 option in the menu (ad hoc query) is to enable the user to specify any kind of SQL operation to be executed on the database. This feature plays an important role in practice. First, as an application designer, you identified all queries that are important enough to appear explicitly in a menu.  Now you want to provide the flexibility to execute any SQL statement without having to develop a specific program for each of them.  After all, this is one of the most important characteristics of SQL, that the language can also be used at the end user level. Think about nonanticipated queries, creating an index, and checking a statement before embedding it in an application program; all of these are interesting ad hoc cases.

The easiest way to support Q4 is to use the interactive SQL program generally supplied with the system. However, for completeness, we chose to discuss how such a program can be written.  This may be useful to some users who may want to develop their own interactive program using a non SQL syntax (may be a two-dimensional pictorial syntax).  Then, the program will have to construct an SQL statement rather than reading it as an explicit character string.

Depending upon what type of ad hoc statement is entered, the method varies slightly. The program will therefore need to recognize these types and proceed accordingly.

Consider the program in Figure 82. Three sections are immediately apparent. One section deals with selecting multiple rows, another section with repeated insertions, while the last one handles all other cases.

## 15.4.1  Selection of multiple rows

When section 1 starts executing, the statement $S$ contains the **select** statement, with or without place holders for parameters or return variables. You then expect a sequence of commands similar to those shown in Figure 80 and Figure 81.  There is, however, a major difference. In these previous examples, the format of an answer row was known at compilation time. In the ad hoc case, this is not true.  It means that we have to build the list of variables

```
exec sql include sqlca
exec sql begin declare section
        declare string S
exec sql end declare section
allocate sqlda

read (or construct) the ad hoc statement in S

/* look at first word to determine the type of statement */
if type is select do
/* section 1 */
        exec sql prepare X1 from :S
        exec sql declare C1 cursor for X1
        exec sql describe X1 into sqlda
        allocate variables
        exec sql open C1
        do until no more row
                exec sql fetch C1 using sqlda
                display result
                end
        end

else if type is insert do
/* section 2 */
        exec sql prepare X2 from :S
        allocate sqlda
        if known, store types of variables and pointers in sqlda
        otherwise describe must be invoked before this can be done

        do until end of input
                exec sql insert using sqlda
                end
        end

else do
/* section 3 */
        execute immediate :S
        end
```

**Figure 82. Program to handle ad hoc statements**

**sqlda**:
>     *Max_nbr_cols*
>     *Nbr_cols*
>     *Column_info (Max_nbr_cols)*
>         *Type*
>         *Length*
>         *Var_addr*
>         *Null_flag*
>         *Cntl_addr*

**Figure 83. A typical SQLDA data structure**

appearing in the **fetch** dynamically. A combination of two SQL features makes such a dynamic construct possible: a data structure called **sqlda** (for SQL *dynamic area*) and a command called **describe**.

The actual format of an **sqlda** structure varies from system to system; but the basic information contained in the structure is the same (see Figure 83). Essentially, the structure contains, in some encoded way, the description of the shape of the result rows. The fields in the structure are the following:

- *Max_nbr_cols*:   indicates the maximum number of columns that can be handled by this **sqlda**. It essentially specifies the size of the *Column_info* array which follows.

- *Nbr_cols*: indicates the actual number of entries that are used in the array.

- The *Column_info* array:   each structure in the array corresponds to one column. An entry specifies the data type (*Type*), the maximum length for a variable string (*Length*), the address of the variable set aside in the program to contain the value of the corresponding column (*Var_addr*), a flag which is 1 if the value can be **null** (*Null_flag*), and the address of an indicator variable (*Cntl_addr*).

Assume that, in some way, the **sqlda** contains all the information, duly filled-in.   It is precisely that information that the **exec sql fetch** statement needs to be able to return the values with their right types in the right variables. The syntax of the **fetch** is extended by allowing the address of an **sqlda** structure to be specified instead of an explicit list of variables. The syntax is simply

```
EXEC SQL FETCH cursor_name USING addr_of_SQLDA
```

```
do I=1 to Nbr_cols
        /* for each column, allocate buffer and fill entry in sqlda */
        if Type(I) = number or float then do
                Type(I) = actual type for number
                        /* You can choose the actual type of the allocated
                                variable, but it must be compatible
                                with the one returned by describe.
                                SQL will do the necessary conversion */
                Varp = allocate(number)  /* allocate slot for actual type */
                Var_addr(I) = Varp /* store its address in sqlda */
                end
        else if Type(I) = character then do
                Type(I) = actual type for string
                Varp = allocate(string)
                Var_addr(I) = Varp
                end
        else error; /* deallocate everything and exit */

        /* If null values are possible, prepare an indicator variable */
        if Null_flag(I) = 1 then do;
                Cntlvarp = allocate(small integer);
                Cntl_addr(I) = Cntlvarp;
                end
        end
```

**Figure 84. A program to create the appropriate variables**

The question that remains is how to fill in the **sqlda**. This is where **describe** comes in. Once the statement in the string $S$ has been prepared into X1, **describe** can be invoked on the same X1 to fill in the specified **sqlda** structure. It is then the responsibility of the program to allocate memory slots for all variables and to store the addresses of these memory slots in **sqlda** (see Figure 84).

## 15.4.2 Multiple execution of the same statement

We are now looking at an ad hoc statement (an **insert** in the example) that is executed repeatedly with different values of parameters submitted in program variables. The shape of the rows involved in the statement (**insert, delete,** or **update**) is not known at compilation time; so the statement has to be prepared once. Afterward, the result of the prepare is executed repeatedly. The second section in Figure 82 shows the pseudocode. Here, also, an **sqlda** structure is used to tell the system which variables in the program contain the submitted or returned values.

### 15.4.3 Other cases

All other SQL commands are handled as shown in the third section of the program. **Execute immediate** is used as discussed earlier in this chapter.

# 15.5  Ad hoc query for a known environment

Q5 (display specific information about a contract), like Q1, allows the user to retrieve information about a contract. But here we assume that the interactive program prompts the user to specify which columns need to be displayed.

One way of handling Q5 is to use exactly the same technique as the one used for Q1, making sure that all columns, rather than five specific ones, are included in the select list. The execution of the **select** will return the values of all columns to the program. It is then the responsibility of the program to display only those that have been requested.

The method has the advantage of relying only on static SQL; but it also has its drawback. The drawback is that there is an overhead for returning the unnecessary columns. If these columns are in rows that need to be accessed anyway, the problem is not too severe. But in our example, the full query is a join between three tables, CONTRACT, CUSTOMER, and TOOL. If information from TOOL is not requested, why join CONTRACT with TOOL? If no value is requested from either CUSTOMER or TOOL, why perform any join at all?

Actually, you may prefer to use dynamic SQL. Building the statement is slightly more complicated than what we have seen until now. The reason is that you do not know how many joins you will need in order to find all the information requested. Therefore, not only the select list will vary from one invocation to another, but the **from** clause and the **where** clause will vary as well.

The general flow of the program is the same as in Figure 80. Two things have to be changed, however:  1) the line *"Build statement in S"* needs to be replaced with the actual code that builds the statement, and 2) the **fetch** statement has to be expanded to support as many variables as needed to receive the results of the **fetch**. It is important to recognize that, although much of the query varies, it is not fully ad hoc because we still know all the tables that may be involved, and we can assume therefore that we also know all column types; we rely on that knowledge.

*use menu to enter names of columns to be retrieved*

*Customer_flag = 0  /\* assume table customer is not involved \*/*
*Tool_flag = 0  /\* assume table tool is not involved \*/*
*Ncol = 0*

*/\* build **select** list \*/*

*Select_list = 'select'*
*do for each Column_name*
       *if it belongs to* CUSTOMER *then Customer_flag = 1*
       *if it belongs to* TOOL *then Tool_flag = 1*
       *allocate room for a variable (to be used in **fetch**)*
       *Ncol = Ncol + 1  /\* to compute the number of columns \*/*
       *Select_list = Select_list ‖ Column_name ‖ ','*
       *end*
*Suppress last comma in Select_list*

*/\* build **from** clause \*/*

*From_clause = 'from contract'*
*if Customer_flag = 1 then*
      *From-clause = From_clause ‖ ',' ‖ 'customer'*
*if Tool_flag = 1 then*
      *From_clause = From_clause ‖ ',' ‖ 'tool'*

*/\* build **where** clause \*/*

*Where_clause = 'where contract.contract = ? '  /\* contract number \*/*
*if Customer_flag = 1 then*
      *Where_clause = Where_clause ‖*
          *'and contract.customer = customer.customer '*
*if tool_flag = 1 then*
      *Where_clause = Where_clause ‖*
          *'and contract.tool = tool.number'*
*S = Select_list ‖ From_clause ‖ Where_clause*

**Figure 85. Building dynamically a select statement**

The pseudo-code to build the statement is given in Figure 85; it is self-explanatory.

To adjust the **fetch** statement, we can use **sqlda** and **describe** as we did in the previous section.   However, since here we know exactly which tables, and therefore which columns and types, are involved in the query, it is possible to build the **sqlda** dynamically, based on this knowledge, rather than invoking **describe**.

# 15.6 Summary

A large majority of users will use SQL in one of two ways:

*   For the development of application programs that are executed over and over again, the context and logic of the application are known and fixed. Except for the use of parameters, the SQL statements that appear in these programs do not vary from one execution to another.   Then, static SQL is clearly the best approach.

*   For browsing through the database in an unpredictable way, the interactive query program which is delivered with the system itself provides all the facilities that are needed. In fact, such a program has generally been designed very carefully and offers all kinds of nice, user-friendly features, as well as reporting facilities.   Internally, these interactive query programs use dynamic SQL, but this is irrelevant as far as the user is concerned.

It is true, however, that some more sophisticated applications may force the user to develop programs that need the facilities of dynamic SQL. This may happen because the same application deals with static as well as ad hoc queries together, or because the interface does not exteriorize the SQL language. A typical environment is when menu or graphical entry is used, rather than explicit SQL, to specify the query.   This is why we showed how special features such as **describe** and **sqlda** are used to that effect.

As exemplified by Q5, dynamic SQL can be used without **describe** if the knowledge normally retrieved by **describe** is known, due to the very limited context of the application.

We also showed how some queries, although they seem to involve a variable number of input parameters, can be slightly altered to become static.   Some trade-offs in performance need to be considered.

# *Appendix*

# Solution of Exercises

**2.1.** The statement defines the structure of the table STUDENT as it appears in Figure 14.

**2.2.** The statement adds one row to the table PREREQ.

**2.3.**

| CLASS | GRADE |
|-------|-------|
| 123   | 3.9   |
| 130   | 4.5   |
| 201   | ?     |

**2.4.**

| COUNT(*) |
|----------|
| 4        |

**2.5.** No.

**2.6.** Find the classes which do not have any prerequisite.

**2.7.**

| NAME    | SUBJECT                  |
|---------|--------------------------|
| John    | Advanced Programming     |
| Claudia | Introduction to Database |
| Louis   | Advanced Programming     |

**2.8.**

| CLASS | NAME |
|---|---|
| 148 | Claudia |
| 201 | John |
| 201 | Louis |

**3.1.   create table** STUDENT (
  STUDENTNO **integer notnull,**
  NAME **varchar**(100) **notnull,**
  FIRSTYEAR **smallint notnull)**

The type **smallint** was chosen to minimize the disk space required by the database.  In some implementations, the data type **varchar** can be replaced by a null terminated character string type, as in the C language.

**3.2.   create table** CLASS (
  CLASSNO **smallint notnull,**
  SUBJECT **varchar**(32) **notnull)**

In some implementations, the data type **varchar** can be replaced by a null terminated character string type, as in the C language.

**3.3.   create table** RECORDS (
  STUDENT **integer notnull,**
  CLASS **smallint notnull,**
  YEAR **smallint notnull,**
  GRADE **decimal**(3,1))

The type of STUDENT must be compatible with the type of STUDENTNO in STUDENT; CLASS must have the same data type as CLASSNO in CLASS, and YEAR as FIRSTYEAR in STUDENT.  The data type **decimal** is not supported by all SQL implementations; **number** or **float** types can be used instead.

**3.4.   create table** PREREQ (
  CLASS **smallint notnull,**
  REQUIRED **smallint notnull,**
  MINGRADE DECIMAL(3,1) **notnull)**

CLASS and REQUIRED must be of the same type as CLASSNO in CLASS.  MINGRADE must have the type of GRADE in RECORDS.

**3.5.** exec sql include sqlca

exec sql begin declare section
    *declare number Student*
    *declare string Name*
    *declare number Year*
exec sql end declare section

*read student number in Student*
*read student name in Name*
*read student first enrollment year in Year*

exec sql insert
    into STUDENT ( NAME, STUDENTNO, FIRSTYEAR)
    values (*:Name, :Student, :Year*)


**3.6.** exec sql include sqlca

exec sql begin declare section
    *declare number Student*
    *declare number Year*
    *declare number Class*
    *declare number Grade*
    *declare small integer GradeCtl*
exec sql end declare section

*read student number in Student*
*read class number in Class*
*read year of enrollment in Year*
*read grade in Grade*
    */\* The user enters -1 if the grade is unknown \*/*
*If Grade = -1 then GradeCtl = -1*
    *else GradeCtl = 0*

exec sql insert
    into RECORDS ( STUDENT, CLASS, YEAR, GRADE)
    values (*:Student, :Class, :Year, :Grade:GradeCtl*)


**4.1.** select NAME
from STUDENT

| NAME |
|------|
| Alice |
| John |
| Claudia |
| Louis |

**4.2.**  **select** STUDENT, GRADE*20
    **from** RECORDS

| STUDENT | GRADE*20 |
|---------|----------|
| 1467 | 76.0 |
| 1467 | 70.0 |
| 1467 | 90.0 |
| 1342 | 78.0 |
| 1342 | 90.0 |
| 1342 | ? |
| 4742 | 46.0 |
| 4742 | 90.0 |
| 4742 | ? |
| 6842 | 74.0 |
| 6842 | 84.0 |
| 6842 | ? |

**4.3.**  **select distinct** CLASS
    **from** PREREQ

| CLASS |
|-------|
| 148 |
| 201 |
| 220 |

**4.4.**  **select distinct** STUDENT
    **from** RECORDS
    **where** GRADE < 4.0

| STUDENT |
|---------|
| 1342 |
| 1467 |
| 4742 |
| 6842 |

**4.5.**  **select** *
    **from** CLASS
    **where** SUBJECT **like** 'Introduction%'

| CLASSNO | SUBJECT |
|---|---|
| 123 | Introduction to Programming |
| 148 | Introduction to Database |

**select** *
**from** CLASS
**where** SUBJECT **like** '%Programming%'

| CLASSNO | SUBJECT |
|---|---|
| 123 | Introduction to Programming |
| 130 | Programming in Pascal |
| 201 | Advanced Programming |

**4.6.**  **select** CLASS, GRADE
**from** RECORDS
**where** STUDENT = 1342
         **and** CLASS **in** (123,130)

| CLASS | GRADE |
|---|---|
| 123 | 3.9 |
| 130 | 4.5 |

**4.7.**  **exec sql include sqlca**
**exec sql begin declare section**
         *declare string Name*
         *declare number StudentNo*
         *declare number Grade*
**exec sql end declare section**

**exec sql declare** C1 **cursor for**
         **select** GRADE
         **from** RECORDS
         **where** STUDENT = *:StudentNo*

**exec sql select** STUDENTNO
         **into** *:StudentNo*
         **from** STUDENT
         **where** NAME = *:Name*

**exec sql whenever not found go to** *TheEnd*

**exec sql open** C1

*do forever*
      **exec sql fetch** C1 **into** *:Grade*
      *display Grade*
      *end*
*TheEnd:*
**exec sql whenever not found continue**
**exec sql close** C1

4.8.  **select avg(GRADE), count(*)**
      **from** RECORDS
      **where** STUDENT = 4742

| AVG(GRADE) | COUNT(*) |
|---|---|
| 3.4 | 3 |

**select avg(GRADE), count(*)**
**from** RECORDS
**where** STUDENT = 4742
      **and** GRADE **is not null**

| AVG(GRADE) | COUNT(*) |
|---|---|
| 3.4 | 2 |

4.9.  **select** STUDENT, 20 * **avg(GRADE)**
      **from** RECORDS
      **group by** STUDENT
      **order by** 2 **desc**

| STUDENT | 20*AVG(GRADE) |
|---|---|
| 1342 | 84.00 |
| 6842 | 79.00 |
| 1467 | 78.66 |
| 4742 | 68.00 |

4.10. **select distinct** STUDENT
      **from** RECORDS
      **group by** STUDENT, YEAR
      **having count(*)** > 1

```
┌─────────────┐
│  STUDENT    │
├─────────────┤
│     4742    │
│     6842    │
└─────────────┘
```

**5.1.**  **select** NAME, SUBJECT, YEAR, GRADE
   **from** STUDENT, RECORDS, CLASS
   **where** STUDENTNO = STUDENT
        **and** CLASSNO = CLASS
   **order by** NAME

| NAME | SUBJECT | YEAR | GRADE |
|------|---------|------|-------|
| Alice | Introduction to Programming | 1982 | 3.8 |
| Alice | Introduction to Database | 1983 | 3.5 |
| Alice | Advanced Database | 1986 | 4.5 |
| Claudia | Programming in Pascal | 1986 | 4.5 |
| Claudia | Introduction to Programming | 1986 | 2.3 |
| Claudia | Introduction to Database | 1987 | ? |
| John | Introduction to Programming | 1985 | 3.9 |
| John | Advanced Programming | 1987 | ? |
| John | Programming in Pascal | 1986 | 4.5 |
| Louis | Programming in Pascal | 1985 | 4.2 |
| Louis | Introduction to Programming | 1985 | 3.7 |
| Louis | Advanced Programming | 1987 | ? |

**5.2.**  **select distinct** SUBJECT
   **from** CLASS, RECORDS
   **where** CLASSNO = CLASS
        **and** YEAR = 1987

| SUBJECT |
|---------|
| Advanced Programming |
| Introduction to Database |

**select** SUBJECT
**from** CLASS C
**where not exists**
      ( **select** *
      **from** RECORDS
      **where** CLASS = C.CLASSNO
          **and** YEAR = 1987)

| SUBJECT |
| --- |
| Introduction to Programming<br>Programming in Pascal<br>Advanced Database |

**5.3.**

| SUBJECT |
| --- |
| Advanced Database<br>Advanced Programming<br>Introduction to Database<br>Introduction to Programming<br>Programming in Pascal |

**5.4.**  **select** C1.SUBJECT, C2.SUBJECT, MINGRADE
**from** PREREQ, CLASS C1, CLASS C2
**where** C1.CLASSNO = CLASS
        **and** C2.CLASSNO = REQUIRED

| C1.SUBJECT | C2.SUBJECT | MINGRADE |
| --- | --- | --- |
| Introduction to Database | Introduction to Programming | 2.0 |
| Advanced Programming | Programming in Pascal | 4.0 |
| Advanced Programming | Introduction to Programming | 3.5 |
| Advanced Database | Introduction to Database | 3.0 |

**5.5.**  **select distinct** SUBJECT
**from** CLASS, PREREQ
**where** CLASSNO = CLASS

| SUBJECT |
| --- |
| Advanced Database<br>Advanced Programming<br>Introduction to Database |

**select** SUBJECT
**from** CLASS
**where** CLASSNO **in**
        ( **select** CLASS
        **from** PREREQ)

```
select SUBJECT
from CLASS C
where exists
        ( select CLASS
        from PREREQ
        where CLASS = C.CLASSNO)


select SUBJECT
from CLASS
where CLASSNO = any
        ( select CLASS
        from PREREQ)
```

5.6.    
```
select NAME, avg(GRADE)
from RECORDS, STUDENT
where STUDENT = STUDENTNO
group by NAME
order by NAME
```

| NAME | AVG(GRADE) |
|------|-----------|
| Alice | 3.93 |
| Claudia | 3.40 |
| John | 4.20 |
| Louis | 3.95 |

5.7.    
```
        select SUBJECT, count(*)
        from CLASS, RECORDS
        where CLASSNO = CLASS
                and YEAR = 1987
        group by SUBJECT
union
        select SUBJECT, 0
        from CLASS C
        where not exists
                ( select *
                from RECORDS
                where CLASS = C.CLASSNO
                        and YEAR = 1987)
```

| SUBJECT | COUNT(*) |
|---------|----------|
| Advanced Programming | 2 |
| Introduction to Database | 1 |
| Advanced Database | 0 |
| Introduction to Programming | 0 |
| Programming in Pascal | 0 |

**5.8.**  **select** NAME
  **from** STUDENT, RECORDS, PREREQ P1
  **where** STUDENTNO = STUDENT
     **and** RECORDS.CLASS = P1.REQUIRED
     **and** GRADE > P1.MINGRADE
     **and** P1.CLASS = 201
  **group by** NAME
  **having count(*)** =
     ( **select count(*)**
     **from** PREREQ P2
     **where** P2.CLASS = 201)

| NAME |
|------|
| John |
| Louis |

  **select** DISTINCT NAME
  **from** STUDENT, RECORDS, PREREQ
  **where** STUDENT = STUDENTNO
     **and** RECORDS.CLASS = REQUIRED
     **and** PREREQ.CLASS = 201
     **and** GRADE < MINGRADE

| NAME |
|------|
| Claudia |

  **select** NAME
  **from** STUDENT S
  **where exists**
    ( **select** *
    **from** PREREQ P
    **where** PREREQ.CLASS = 201
       **and not exists**

```
( select *
from RECORDS
where RECORDS.CLASS = P.REQUIRED
    and STUDENT = S.STUDENTNO ) )
```

| NAME |
|------|
| Alice |

5.9.
```
select NAME
from STUDENT, RECORDS
where STUDENTNO = STUDENT
    and GRADE =
        ( select min (GRADE)
        from RECORDS )
```

or

```
select NAME
from STUDENT, RECORDS
where STUDENTNO = STUDENT
    and GRADE <= all
        ( select GRADE
        from RECORDS )
```

| NAME |
|------|
| Claudia |

5.10.
```
select NAME, SUBJECT
from STUDENT, RECORDS, CLASS C
where STUDENTNO = STUDENT
    and CLASS = CLASSNO
    and GRADE =
        ( select min(GRADE)
        from RECORDS
        where CLASS = C.CLASSNO)
```

or

```
select NAME, SUBJECT
from STUDENT, RECORDS, CLASS C
where STUDENTNO = STUDENT
      and CLASS = CLASSNO
      and GRADE <= all
          ( select GRADE
          from RECORDS
          where CLASS = C.CLASSNO)
```

| NAME | SUBJECT |
|------|---------|
| Claudia | Introduction to Programming |
| Louis | Programming in Pascal |
| Alice | Introduction to Database |
| Alice | Advanced Database |

**5.11.**
```
select NAME, SUBJECT
from STUDENT S, RECORDS, CLASS
where STUDENTNO = STUDENT
      and CLASSNO = CLASS
      and YEAR =
          ( select min(YEAR)
          from RECORDS
          where STUDENT = S.STUDENTNO)
```

| NAME | SUBJECT |
|------|---------|
| John | Introduction to Programming |
| Alice | Introduction to Programming |
| Claudia | Programming in Pascal |
| Claudia | Introduction to Programming |
| Louis | Programming in Pascal |
| Louis | Introduction to Programming |

**6.1.**
```
exec sql include sqlca
exec sql begin declare section
    declare number Class
    declare number Grade
    declare string Name
exec sql end declare section
```

```
exec sql declare C1 cursor for
   select NAME, CLASS
   from RECORDS, STUDENT
   where STUDENT = STUDENTNO
       and GRADE is null
   for update of GRADE
exec sql whenever not found go to The_End

exec sql open C1
do forever
   exec sql fetch C1 into :Name, :Class
   Print Name, Class
   Read Grade
   exec sql update RECORDS
       set GRADE = :Grade
       where current of C1
   end
The_End:
exec sql close C1
exec sql commit work
```

**6.2.**
```
create table ARCHIVE (
       STUDENT integer not null,
       CLASS smallint not null,
       YEAR smallint not null,
       GRADE decimal(3,1))

insert into ARCHIVE (STUDENT, CLASS, YEAR, GRADE)
       select STUDENT, CLASS, YEAR,GRADE
       from RECORDS
       where YEAR <= 1983

delete from RECORDS where YEAR <= 1983
```

**6.3.** For changing STUDENT:

```
delete from STUDENT
where not exists
       ( select *
       from RECORDS
       where STUDENTNO = STUDENT
           and GRADE is null)
```

For changing RECORDS, you probably thought of writing

**delete from** RECORDS R1
**where not exists**
    ( **select** *
    **from** RECORDS R2
    **where** R1.STUDENT = R2.STUDENT
        **and** R2.GRADE **is null**)

But in a **delete**, the subquery cannot refer to the table from where the rows are deleted. Two solutions can be used to circumvent the problem:

1. The list of students can be stored in an intermediate table, (TEMP) which has only one column (STUDENT) similar to the STUDENT column in RECORDS. The table TEMP (initially empty) is first populated with a list of student numbers:

   **insert into** TEMP
   **select** DISTINCT STUDENT
   **from** RECORDS R1
   **where not exists**
       ( **select** *
       **from** RECORDS R2
       **where** R1.STUDENT = R2.STUDENT
           **and** R2.GRADE **is null**)

   Table TEMP can then be used in an **in** clause:

   **delete from** RECORDS
   **where** STUDENTNO **in**
       ( **select** *
       **from** TEMP)

2. Since the rows in STUDENT have already been deleted, one can use the absence of records in STUDENT to decide which rows of RECORDS must be deleted:

   **delete from** RECORDS
   **where not exists**
       ( **select** *
       **from** STUDENT
       **where** STUDENTNO = STUDENT)

**6.4.**    **alter table** STUDENT
            **add** AVERAGE **decimal**(3,2)

The column must be updated by a program:

**exec sql include sqlca**
**exec sql begin declare section**
        *declare number Avg*
        *declare number StudentNo*
**exec sql end declare section**
**exec sql declare** C1 **cursor for**
        **select** STUDENTNO
        **from** STUDENT
        **for update of** AVERAGE

**exec sql open** C1
**exec sql whenever not found go to** *The_End*
*do forever*
        **exec sql fetch** C1
                **into** *:StudentNo*
        **exec sql select avg**(GRADE)
                **into** *:Avg*
                **from** RECORDS
                **where** STUDENT = *:StudentNo*
        **exec sql update** STUDENT
                **set** AVERAGE = *:Avg*
                **where current of** C1
        *end*
*The_End:*
**exec sql commit work**

Another solution consists of declaring a cursor for

**select** STUDENT, **avg**(GRADE)
**from** RECORDS
**group by** STUDENT

and using

**exec sql update** STUDENT
**set** AVERAGE = *:Avg*
**where** STUDENTNO = *:StudentNo*

where the variables *Avg* and *StudentNo* are filled by each **fetch** on the cursor.

**7.1.**  Each page contains:     $pr = 4,000 \times .80/25$
$$= 128 \text{ rows}$$

The number of pages used for each table is:

STUDENT:     $np = 20,000/128$
$$= 157 \text{ pages}$$
CLASS:     $np = 500/128$
$$= 5 \text{ pages}$$
RECORDS:     $np = 100,000/128$
$$= 782 \text{ pages}$$
PREREQ:     $np = 500/128$
$$= 5 \text{ pages}$$

**7.2.**  Scanning RECORDS is 5 times longer.

**7.3.**  1.  Without index, all rows must be touched: 100,000 rows.
2.  With index, only those rows corresponding to 1985 will be touched: 20,000 rows.
3.  Without index, each data page is read once: 782 pages to be read.
4.  An index on YEAR contains entries of 8 bytes (4 bytes for the key and 4 bytes for the row id).  Thus, with an occupancy of 80%, 400 entries fit in a single page.  The number of leaf pages is 250.  Since only 1/5 of the entries are of interest, the number of I/O operations for index pages is $250/5 = 50$.  Since the index is clustered, data pages are read once yielding $782/5 = 157$ data pages.  The total number of IO's with a clustered index is $50 + 157 = 207$.
5.  If the index is not clustered, each access to a row will require reading a data page.  Thus the number of data pages to be read is 20,000, and the total number of IO's is 20,050.

Note that, in the computation of the number of index pages, we assumed that all entries were 8 byte long.  Some implementations use what is called *front compression*, avoiding storing the same key several times if a key is repeated.  This may decrease the number of index pages needed, but the impact on the overall number of IO's is minimal because, in this particular example, the keys are small.

**7.4.** 1. Without index, all rows must be scanned: 100,000 rows.
2. With index, only those rows of one student will be scanned: 5 rows.
3. Without index, each data page is read once: 782 pages.
4. We can assume that the 5 entries of the given student are on the same index page. If the index is clustered, we can also assume that the 5 rows are on the same data page. The total number of IO's with a clustered index is $1 + 1 = 2$.
5. If the index is not clustered, each access to a row will read a new data page. Thus, the number of data pages to be read is 5. The total number of IO's is 6.

**7.5.** Without index, all rows must be scanned: 100,000 rows; 782 data pages have to be read. With index, all the necessary information can be found directly in the index and no row needs to be fetched. Whether the index is clustered or not, 1/5 of the index pages is read; the answer is 50.

**7.6.** To find the student number, knowing the name "John", table STUDENT must be scanned completely (the system does not know that there is only one "John"; therefore, it needs to touch all rows till the end): 20,000 rows.

For finding the rows in RECORDS for the particular student number: 100,000 rows.

Total: 120,000 rows

**7.7.** **create unique index** INDS
**on** STUDENT (NAME)

**create index** INDR
**on** RECORDS (STUDENT)

The number of rows touched internally is: 1 in STUDENT + 5 in RECORDS (on average).

**7.8. STUDENT:**

• There should be a **unique** index on column STUDENTNO, useful to find the name of a student, given his/her student number.

**create unique index** STUDENT1
**on** STUDENT(STUDENTNO)

This index is also used to enforce the uniqueness of student numbers. It has a high selectivity (1/20,000).

- There should be a regular index on column NAME, to be able to find quickly the number of a student whose name is known.

**create index** STUDENT2
**on** STUDENT(NAME)

- A nonclustered index on FIRSTYEAR is not interesting since it has a very low selectivity (1/5). A clustered index may be interesting if one is often interested in the records for a given year. However, we assume here that it is not worth the extra space and updating overhead.

## CLASS:

- A **unique** index on CLASSNO is needed:

**create unique index** CLASS1
**on** CLASS(CLASSNO)

It enforces the uniqueness of CLASSNO and has a high selectivity (1/500).

- An index can also be created on the subject (it would have good selectivity), but the use of the full subject name in a query is not very likely.

## RECORDS:

- A regular index on column STUDENT is useful to access all records for a given student:

**create index** RECORDS1
**on** RECORDS(STUDENT)

This index has a high selectivity (5/100,000).

- One might be tempted to create an index on (STUDENT, CLASS). But its selectivity is not much better than the selectivity of the index on STUDENT. It is certainly not worth the extra space and overhead.

- The same reasoning can be made for an index on (STUDENT, YEAR).

- As for CLASS, a nonclustered index may not be selective enough, since each class appears 100,000/500=200 times.

- An index on (CLASS, YEAR), on the other hand, is very selective (8 students per class per year). Assuming that "find the grades of the students for a particular class and year" is a frequent query, the index could be worthwhile:

**create index** RECORDS2
**on** RECORDS(CLASS, YEAR)

**8.1.** **create view** ALLRECORDS ( NAME, SUBJECT, YEAR, GRADE)
**as**
**select** NAME, SUBJECT, YEAR, GRADE
**from** STUDENT, RECORDS, CLASS
**where** STUDENTNO = STUDENT
      **and** CLASSNO = CLASS

**8.2.** First create the view TEMP:

**create view** TEMP (STUDENT, AVG_GRADE)
**as**
**select** STUDENT, **avg**(GRADE)
**from** RECORDS
**group by** STUDENT

Then use the query:

**select** *
**from** TEMP
**where** AVG_GRADE =
    ( **select max**(AVG_GRADE)
    **from** TEMP)

**8.3.** **create view** GOODSTUDENT (STUDENTNO, NAME, FIRSTYEAR)
**as**
**select distinct** STUDENTNO, NAME, FIRSTYEAR
**from** STUDENT, RECORDS
**where** STUDENT = STUDENTNO
      **and** GRADE > 4.5

Another solution consists of writing:

**create view** GOODSTUDENT (STUDENTNO, NAME, FIRSTYEAR)
**as**
**select** STUDENTNO, NAME, FIRSTYEAR
**from** STUDENT S
**where exists**
    ( **select** *
    **from** RECORDS
    **where** STUDENT = S.STUDENTNO
        **and** GRADE > 4.5)

This formulation avoids the use of **distinct** which is not always supported in the **create view** statement.

**8.4.**   **create view** FULLCLASS (SUBJECT)
     **as**
     **select** SUBJECT
     **from** CLASS
     **where** CLASSNO **in**
        ( **select** CLASS
        **from** RECORDS
        **where** YEAR = 1987
        **group by** CLASS
        **having count(*)** > 20 )

**8.5.**   **create view** EMPTYCLASS (CLASSNO, SUBJECT)
     **as**
     **select** CLASSNO, SUBJECT
     **from** CLASS
     **where** CLASSNO **not in**
        ( **select** CLASS
        **from** RECORDS
        **where** YEAR = 1987 )

Instead of **not in, not exists,** or **<> any** can also be used.

**9.1.**   The update should be authorized only through a view **with check option**. The following statement defines that view:

```
create view V
as
select *
from RECORDS
where GRADE between 0 and 5
with check option
```

9.2.
```
create table STUDENT (
    STUDENTNO integer not null,
    NAME varchar(100) not null,
    FIRSTYEAR smallint not null,
    primary key (STUDENTNO))
```

```
create table CLASS (
    CLASSNO smallint not null,
    SUBJECT varchar(32) not null,
    primary key (CLASSNO))
```

```
create table RECORDS (
    STUDENT integer not null,
    CLASS smallint not null,
    YEAR smallint not null,
    GRADE DECIMAL(3,1))
    foreign key (STUDENT) references STUDENT
        on delete restrict,
    foreign key (CLASS) references CLASS
        on delete restrict)
```

```
create table PREREQ (
    CLASS smallint not null,
    REQUIRED smallint not null,
    MINGRADE decimal(3,1) not null)
    foreign key (CLASS) references CLASS
        on delete cascade,
    foreign key (REQUIRED) references CLASS
        on delete restrict)
```

A student cannot be deleted if it appears in a RECORDS row; therefore the **references** clause in RECORDS (for student) is restricted. The same is true for CLASS in RECORDS. When a class is dropped, its prerequisite classes are of no interest. Therefore, when a CLASS row is deleted, the corresponding PREREQ rows can be deleted automatically (**cascade** option). On the other hand, if a class A is a prerequisite for a class B, class A should not be allowed to be deleted (**restrict** option).

**9.3.**   • No table lock should be acquired. The index on column STUDENT in table RECORDS is an excellent access path for the query at hand. It will provide the identifiers of the few RECORDS rows that are needed. Very few rows will be touched, and a table lock is not appropriate.

   • A table lock on table RECORDS should be acquired since all rows in the table will be accessed in order to compute the average.

   • Table locks should be acquired on both tables since all rows will be touched in both tables.

**9.4.**   The database administrator gives authority to update any data in RECORDS to all professors. This can be done by executing the following statement once for every professor:

**grant update on** RECORDS **to** Professor_Name.

In order to allow a student to see his or her RECORDS rows, the database administrator grants **select** (or **read**) authority to **public** on the view below. Note that we added to table STUDENT a new column, USERID, which contains the name under which the student is known to the system.

**create view** V
**as**
**select** RECORDS.*
**from** RECORDS, STUDENT
**where** STUDENT = STUDENTNO
        **and** USERID = **user**

Given this view, the **grant** statement is:

**grant select on** V **to public**

# Index